D0374998

Post-Suburbia

Post-Suburbia

Government and Politics in the Edge Cities

Jon C. Teaford

The Johns Hopkins University Press
Baltimore & London

© 1997 The Johns Hopkins University Press
All rights reserved. Published 1997
Printed in the United States of America on acid-free paper
06   05   04   03   02   01   00   99   98   97   5   4   3   2   1

The Johns Hopkins University Press
2715 North Charles Street
Baltimore, Maryland 21218–4319
The Johns Hopkins Press Ltd., London

Library of Congress Cataloging-in-Publication Data will be found
at the end of this book.
A catalog record for this book is available from the British Library.

ISBN 0-8018-5450-4

Contents

1 *New Government for a New Metropolis* 1

2 *The Age of the Suburban Haven* 9

3 *The Emerging Post-Suburban Pattern, 1945–1960* . . . 44

4 *Maintaining the Balance of Power* 85

5 *Post-Suburban Imperialists* 126

6 *Recognition and Rebellion* 161

7 *The Pragmatic Compromise* 206

   Notes 211
   Bibliographic Essay 241
   Index 243

New Government for a New Metropolis

By the 1980s and early 1990s a number of commentators were discovering a new phenomenon along the fringe of metropolitan America. Writing in the *Atlantic* in 1986, Christopher Leinberger and Charles Lockwood described the emergence of interdependent "business, retail, housing, and entertainment focal points" scattered about the "low-density cityscape" of the metropolitan periphery.[1] A year later, historian Robert Fishman wrote of the transformation of suburbia into a new form of settlement that possessed "all the economic and technological dynamism . . . associate[d] with the city." According to Fishman, "this phenomenon, as remarkable as it is unique, is not suburbanization but a *new city*."[2] Then in 1991 journalist Joel Garreau introduced this concept to a broader readership in his *Edge City: Life on the New Frontier.* "Americans are creating the biggest change in a hundred years in how we build cities," Garreau proclaimed. Like the prophets that had come before him, he wrote of "multiple urban cores" along the metropolitan fringe as the "new hearths of . . . civilization."[3] In this book and in numerous articles on the subject, Garreau told Americans that the traditional notion of the city was an anachronism.[4] Metropolitan America no longer conformed to the wheel metaphor with the hub in the central city and the suburbs on the rim. In fact, the former rim was now composed of a series of business hubs, which failed to rotate around the traditional core. According to all of these observers, "suburb" had become a misnomer. Economically and socially, the periphery was no longer a subordinate dependent of the center and thus no longer a candidate for the prefix *sub*.

Leinberger and Lockwood referred to these new outlying centers as *urban villages,* Fishman called them *technoburbs,* Garreau opted for *edge cities,* and still others have applied the label *post-suburban metropolis.* The phenomenon so defied tradition that no one could agree what to call it. To some it made metropolitan America almost incomprehensible. "Cities have become impossible to describe," wrote one observer in 1992. "Their centers are not as central as they used to be, their edges are ambiguous, they have no beginnings and apparently no end."[5] The periphery was not peripheral in this new illogical world, and the center was not central. As the twentieth century closed, it seemed as if Americans were going to have to discard past intellectual preconceptions about the metropolis and fashion a new vision. Just as in the post-Copernican world notions of the solar system had to change, so in the post-Garreau era Americans had to struggle to reconceptualize the city. The metropolitan fringe no longer orbited around the urban core. Consequently, a new model of the metropolis was necessary.

To any halfway conscious American, the revelations of Leinberger, Lockwood, Fishman, and Garreau should long have been apparent. By the late 1970s and early 1980s glass office towers and glitzy hotels were already sprouting at freeway interchanges, and traffic was converging on outlying office and research parks as well as the giant malls that had dominated American retailing for a decade. Anyone driving along the freeways circling major metropolitan areas could see the vast changes. The driver was as likely to face traffic gridlock at an interchange along the periphery as on a downtown street. And anyone who shopped was aware of the contrast between shuttered downtown department stores and jammed outlying emporiums. Though the minds of Americans were still programmed to think in terms of hub and rim, their eyes told them traditional concepts were obsolete. The metropolitan world had been transformed, and formerly suburban areas were now centers of commerce and industry as well as residence and recreation. In fact, the edge had an economic life of its own, which challenged that of the older central cities and in some cases seemed to supersede it.

This, then, was the new city that was the home, workplace, and playground for tens of millions of Americans. And by the 1990s it appeared to be the wave of the future. This is where construction was taking place, where employment was expanding. In the minds of Garreau, Fishman, and their fellow prognosticators, this was the America of the twenty-first century. Like it or not, this seemed to represent the direction in which America was headed.

In the growing number of books and articles about this cutting-edge world, relatively little, however, was written about its governmental institutions. Like the edge cities themselves, these institutions had emerged during recent decades, creating a pattern of government that confounded and confused many observers of the metropolitan fringe. Just as the pattern of post-suburban life defied traditional concepts, so did its governmental institutions. Political scientists had long deplored the fragmentation of suburbia into a multitude of separate municipalities, townships, and special districts. Accounts of suburban government and politics used such terms as *crazy quilt* and such damning phrases as *overlapping jurisdiction* and *wasteful duplication*. The governmental institutions of the metropolitan fringe were political perversions, violating textbook formulas of good government. As the metropolitan periphery developed into the post-suburban metropolis, the nature of its government became even more obscure and even less comprehensible. Whereas suburban government was familiar, though seemingly disorganized, the post-suburban polity was an alien being. To Americans raised on the distinction that municipalities provided police and fire protection and water and sewage services whereas counties and townships were units of rural government, the governments of post-suburban areas were a mystery. Counties exercised powers traditionally associated with municipalities, municipalities contracted for services rather than producing them, townships often seemed no different from municipalities, and a multitude of special districts, both big and small, were responsible for everything from killing mosquitoes to maintaining cemeteries. If one wanted a traffic light at the corner, whom did one petition? Who was in charge? These questions have troubled many metropolitan residents, and students of urban America have not offered adequate answers as to the origins or meaning of the government of post-suburban America.

This book will chart the emergence of the post-suburban polity and attempt to explain why and how it developed. It will discuss the adaptation of traditional units of government to the ideals and demands of the changing world along the metropolitan fringe. And it will describe the resulting pattern of rule, a pattern unlike any recommended in the traditional textbooks but well suited to the predilections of post-suburban America.

Specifically, this study will focus on six counties that were among the pioneers of the post-suburban world. They are Suffolk and Nassau Counties in New York; Oakland County, Michigan; DuPage County, Illinois; Saint Louis County, Missouri; and Orange County, California. Each of these counties has developed into a center of commerce as well as residence, and in some cases overshadow the nearby central city. They are home to millions of Americans, but they remain largely ignored. A researcher will find scores of references to the city of Oakland, California, but few citations for Oakland County, Michigan, even though it is three times more populous. To anyone living outside New York, one has to explain where Nassau County is, but every alert American knows the location of Boston, a city less than half as large. The six counties are relatively anonymous giants, which have developed seemingly without anyone paying much attention.

Each of the counties is representative of the post-suburban phenomenon. Located to the east of New York City on Long Island, Nassau and Suffolk Counties together constituted one of the first suburban regions to be designated a separate metropolitan area by the federal census bureau. During the post-World War II era, the aircraft industry provided tens of thousands of jobs in the two counties, lessening the economic dependence of Nassau and Suffolk on New York City. With the growth of other industries and the development of office parks, the typical Long Islander no longer commuted to Manhattan but worked in his or her own county. Not only were the two counties in the forefront of post-suburban economic development, they were forerunners in reforming the structure of government along the metropolitan periphery. Even before World War II, Nassau County experimented with a new structure of government which was to influence reform efforts in suburban and post-suburban areas throughout the United States.

During the 1970s and 1980s Oakland County, Michigan, north of Detroit, was the emerging business center of southeastern Michigan and the generator of what little economic vitality existed in that troubled region. Within Oakland, the cities of Southfield and Troy became centers of office employment with a full complement of high rises and corporate campuses testifying to their economic success. Moreover, by 1990 the population of Oakland had surpassed that of Detroit, and its fortunes had clearly eclipsed those of the Motor City. Yet along the county's many lakes and nestled among its hills were some of the most costly residences in the Midwest, and the county's good life remained a much sought after goal for upwardly mobile Michiganders. With an inventory of office space surpassing that of Detroit, plus some of the poshest residential communities in the nation, Oakland County was an archetypical post-suburban metropolis.

By the early 1990s DuPage County, Illinois, west of Chicago, was on everyone's list of edge cities. With high-tech research parks, a thirty-one-story skyscraper, the corporate headquarters of McDonald's, and mile after mile of high-priced residential subdivisions, it was the epitome of Garreau's vision of the future. It included some older commuter suburbs such as Elmhurst and Glen Ellyn, but it was also the site of Naperville, one of the Midwest's few boomtowns of the late twentieth century. During the 1970s and 1980s, the county proved a rare bright spot in the economic gloom of Illinois.

To the south, Saint Louis County, Missouri, was an early example of the phenomenon Garreau and Fishman identified. The county arcs around, but does not include, the city of Saint Louis, Missouri's Constitution of 1875 having authorized the permanent separation of the two governmental units. The county seat of Clayton was among the first suburban centers of office employment, rivaling the downtown of the adjacent city of Saint Louis as early as the 1960s.

In later decades, population and commerce moved westward through the county, enhancing its position in the regional economy. By the 1980s the county had more than twice the population of the central city of Saint Louis.

Finally, in the minds of many late-twentieth-century observers, Orange County, California, was the quintessential post-suburban metropolis, a land of traffic-clogged freeways, giant shopping malls, expansive office and industrial parks, and thousands of homes in what realtors call the executive price range. Located south of Los Angeles along the Pacific coast, by 1990 it had a population of more than 2.4 million. Among its largest cities were Anaheim, famed as the home of Disneyland, and the giant planned community of Irvine.

Each of these six counties was in the first wave of post-suburban development. During the mid-twentieth century they became the home of millions of middle-class residents attracted to traditional suburban bedroom communities. But in the late twentieth century the counties faced the reality that they were no longer quiet retreats from urban madness. They were themselves urban, though a new kind of urban. They were the first areas to experience this new reality, and thus they faced the extraordinary challenge of coping with it. By the close of the century, these pioneers were facing competition from newer, fresher post-suburban areas. Nassau County was clearly aging, the urban frontier of northeastern Illinois was moving into Kane County to the west of DuPage, Saint Charles County was beginning to outshine adjacent Saint Louis County, and the "inland empire" of San Bernardino and Riverside Counties was the scene of more vital economic growth than the older Orange County areas. But the six counties discussed in this book were the pathfinders; they first confronted the dilemmas of the new world of edge cities and they molded the post-suburban polity.

Each did not respond in the same way, however. Their histories and governmental institutions differ. Yet they share certain identifiable patterns. Facing similar problems, they arrived at similar solutions. Each of these areas contributed to a common governmental foundation for the future.

Basic to the emerging post-suburban polity is the tension between suburban ideals and post-suburban realities. Residents of Nassau, Oakland, and Orange Counties rebelled against what they perceived as urban. They had escaped from the city to find a better life in the suburbs, and they clung to their suburban ideal even while high rises rose at freeway interchanges a few miles from their backyards. Economically these areas may have become post-suburban, but intellectually and emotionally they were solidly suburban. Residents valued the small, the intimate, and the homogeneous—characteristics that they associated with village life and were alien to the overpowering, indifferent, and diverse big city. They sought to preserve the green open space and clear waters of the rural past and longed nostalgically for the fields and forests that had first drawn them from the city. The people of post-suburban America remained resolutely anti-urban even as their world became increasingly urbanized.

Yet at the same time they recognized the merits of the changes transforming their counties. Eager for lower tax rates, they could not help but welcome tax-paying businesses. As long as a tax-rich office tower was not visible from their patios and the employees did not jam their streets, then such development might well prove a boon. Few in DuPage or Saint Louis County yearned for a skyscraper next door, but many dreamed of a high rise easing their tax bills. Moreover, the giant malls offered the convenience of nearby shopping. The advantages of having Marshall Field's or Macy's only a few miles away were incontestable. And the more places of employment along the metropolitan fringe, the shorter the commute to work. Sylvan suburbia remained the ideal, but the merits of deviating from that ideal were readily apparent.

Consequently, life in the post-suburban metropolis was a delicate balance. The suburban ideal had to be preserved while the useful urban realities were tolerated. If the area seemed to be tipping too far toward the urban side, residents would raise cries of outrage against rapacious developers who supposedly wanted to transform Suffolk County into Manhattan and Oakland County into Detroit. But development that imposed no burden and remained at arm's length elicited applause.

The emerging post-suburban polity reflected this tenuous balance. Throughout the late twentieth century, residents of the post-suburban metropolis continued to prefer the small unit of government. Despite attacks on the governmental fragmentation of the metropolitan fringe, the myriad municipalities survived and were even joined by some newly incorporated cities and villages. Voters generally did not eschew what they perceived as grass-roots local government, and the rhetoric of post-suburbia continued to laud the supposed voluntarism and governmental intimacy of the existing municipalities. Parochialism remained part of the political creed of the post-suburban metropolis. Big government was a bogy raised repeatedly in political campaigns. It was the antithesis of the suburban ideal and anathema to the values of the village.

Yet while mouthing the glories of village life, residents of the post-suburban metropolis recognized the need for some overarching authority and supported the creation and strengthening of some unifying institutions. To some degree county government assumed a coordinating function and represented the post-suburban metropolis in its dealings with the outside world. Traditionally a unit of rural government charged with maintaining the courts, repairing country roads, and operating the local jail, county government was to expand its role markedly in the post-suburban areas of the late twentieth century. Especially during the 1970s and 1980s some politicians sought to make the county into a regional supergovernment and the principal policymaker along the metropolitan fringe. They met with only limited success, but at the close of the century the county had deviated significantly from its long-standing hayseed image. In 1990 the governments of Nassau, Suffolk, Oakland, DuPage, Saint Louis, and Orange Counties bore little resemblance to county rule in 1920 or 1930. The county was the unit that helped suburbanites move into the post-suburban era without too seriously compromising their traditional ideals.

Yet if the county became too dictatorial or centralized too much authority in the county seat, then revolt was probable. For the balance between local and central had to be maintained. Just as post-suburbanites could tolerate high rises if they did not seriously threaten the suburban way of life, residents could accept growing county authority if it did not compromise the much-vaunted values of village rule. Commercial development was a practical necessity in order to relieve the local tax burden and to provide jobs and shopping, and enhanced county authority was equally necessary in the densely populated post-suburban regions. But if commercial development or government centralization went too far, then the electorate would raise its voice in loud protest. Excessive commerce and excessive government centralization were both urban characteristics unwelcome along the anti-urban fringe.

The county, however, was not the only institution that attempted to draw together the fragmented post-suburban metropolis. In some localities, municipalities formed leagues, which developed into important players in the politics of America's edge cities. Through these leagues of municipalities, the city and village governments of DuPage or Saint Louis County could join together to act on policy issues affecting them all. Together the disparate municipalities could speak with a united voice and exert considerable influence on county and state governments. Moreover, at the league meetings, mayors forged alliances and thrashed out mutual problems. Ultimately, the goal of the leagues was the protection and preservation of the member municipalities. Thus municipalities worked together to ensure that they could work apart.

Metropolitan special districts likewise guaranteed some coordination with regard to certain functions of government as did the multitude of intermunicipal agreements binding the fragments of the post-suburban metropolis. A series of treaties defined the territorial spheres of influence of conflicting municipalities, thereby lessening the likelihood of annexation wars. Scores of contracts guaranteed mutual assistance by police and fire departments. Through these means, governments sought to cope with the demands of densely populated post-suburbia while perpetuating the village values of a semirural America.

The history of the post-suburban polity is, then, a story of an increasingly delicate balance of power. Post-suburban leaders attempted to preserve the traditional values of suburban life and government. Yet at the same time they sought to fashion a government that could deal with urbanized centers of business. The result was a complex, and not always successful, governmental system tuned to respond to the often conflicting demands of the suburban and the post-suburban. Traditional American city government had evolved in the nineteenth century to foster urbanization and to provide the public services and facilities necessary to enhance the development of a great metropolis. Mayors boosted urban growth, and the goal of both the public and private sectors was the creation of a city bigger than any of its rivals. Post-suburban government, in contrast, evolved as a mechanism to maintain a suburban way of life and to cope with post-suburban problems. The goal was not the creation of a big city. Instead, the goal was the perpetuation of small-scale village life and the creation of a big tax base. Throughout the mid- and late twentieth century, residents from Suffolk to Orange struggled to adapt their governmental institutions to this new imperative. In the process they fashioned organs of local government for the world of the future.

2

The Age of the Suburban Haven

"Nestled among the estates of rolling hills, beautiful trees and natural beauty unmarred by city invasion, there is afforded every home owner the restful and healthful license of a country atmosphere." With these words from a 1928 advertisement, one Oakland County developer expressed the suburban dream of the 1920s and 1930s. Suburbia was a haven, a retreat, where one could escape the evils and annoyances of the city and find rest and health nestled among the beauties of nature and the estates of the wealthy. A Saint Louis County promoter promised prospective homeowners they would "awake with the song of birds, and feel the warmth of a clear sun shining through pure air." A 1930 brochure for DuPage County's Clarendon Hills described it as "nature's masterpiece" and sought to attract buyers with the slogan, "Out of the smoke zone into the ozone." A Nassau County developer emphasized not clear air but socially desirable neighbors. "The people that you want for neighbors are here," promised the backer of Great Neck Gardens. These ideal neighbors were people who could "appreciate" and "afford to enjoy" the beauty of the supposedly ideal suburban subdivision.[1]

In one advertisement after another the message was the same. Suburbia was a residential environment where nature and the best people mingled to the benefit of anyone fortunate enough to purchase a homesite. It was advertised as an upscale reincarnation of the village of the past with its spreading elms, good neighbors, and socially homogeneous community life. Oakland's Birmingham was "a village of homes where children thrive." Nearby Bloomfield Downs was reminiscent of "the quaint little villages—the ivy-covered walls, the beautiful green of the trees and hedges—the quiet dignity of the landscape" of rural England. Suffolk County's Lloyd Neck Estates was designed to "attract a very desirable class of people, who [would] make good neighbors."[2] The suburbs of the 1920s and 1930s were not intended to be extensions of the city, identical to urban neighborhoods except farther from the center. What developers were selling, and urban refugees were buying, was an alternative vision of life that specifically rejected the city and embraced the village.

Yet amid the sylvan prose were reminders that America's suburban havens were not actually quaint country villages. They were integral parts of expanding metropolises and they would not attract any residents unless they offered urban conveniences and transportation links to the urban core. While extolling the similarities of Bloomfield Downs to the English countryside, the developer of that subdivision also noted that its "proximity to the world's greatest highway permit[ted] city convenience." The "parklike surroundings" of homes in Nassau's Mineola were highly touted but so was the fact that they were only forty minutes by commuter railroad from Manhattan's Pennsylvania Station.[3] No advertisement failed to note the relatively short distance to downtown. Moreover, realtors promised city improvements: the water, sewerage, and paved streets that city dwellers regarded as necessary to civilized living. In other words, the ideal suburban haven was not a wilderness retreat far from urban crowds and without plumbing or other modern conveniences. Instead, it was a tree-shaded village on the commuter rail line, or the main highway, with all the advantages that few truly rural villages could boast.

The ideal suburban haven was, then, a mixture of escapism and reality. It combined flowers, fresh air, and neighborliness with transportation links to the big city. What suburbanites wanted was the village of the past with the conveniences of the present. Moreover, the perfect village had to be within forty-five minutes of the soot and skyscrapers of the metropolitan center.

During the 1920s and 1930s emerging governmental institutions reflected this mix of the practical and the ideal. Through their municipal and county governments, suburbanites sought to realize the ideal of the suburban village yet enjoy the best public services possible. Thus they created scores of new municipalities armed with zoning powers to protect and preserve the social homogeneity and low density of their villages. The village governments were guardians of the suburban ideal embodied in the real estate advertisements. They were small-scale governments aimed at keeping the big city and its way of life at bay. The neocolonial village halls built in one community after another announced to visitors and residents alike that these suburban municipalities intended to protect the values of a supposedly simpler and purer past. City halls in the great metropolitan centers were stone-sheathed and monumental with massive facades proclaiming the material success and magnitude of the metropolis. The village halls were designed to be quaint and charming, advertising to all the ideals of suburbia.

Yet at the same time suburbanites were increasingly recognizing the need for a broader overarching authority to supplement the village. To handle the problems of the increasingly populous periphery, suburbanites began to adapt traditional units, especially county governments, to the new reality. Just as the assurances of convenient transportation to the metropolitan core testified to the fact that the suburban havens were not country crossroads of the past or quaint retreats in the English Cotswolds, so the emerging demands for greater coordination and cooperation proved that disparate village governments, each dedicated to protecting its little share of the suburban turf, were not sufficient for the fast-growing fringe. During the 1920s and 1930s, then, outlying residents already were struggling to reconcile the small-scale village ideal with the reality of a densely populated metropolis. They were to initiate reforms in county rule in an effort to create a government suitable for the new world they were fashioning in suburbia.

THE SUBURBAN POLITY

During the first two decades of the twentieth century, Suffolk, Nassau, Oakland, DuPage, Saint Louis, and Orange Counties remained largely rural. Yet these fringe areas were already experiencing the first wave of contact with urban dwellers as both the very wealthy and vacationers of more modest means sought a summer retreat in the country. In the late nineteenth century the beaches and breathing space of Nassau and Suffolk Counties lured thousands of New York City residents, and the army of summer visitors increased in the early twentieth century. America's most wealthy citizens fashioned opulent estates from the meadows and woodlands of Long Island, and by 1920 more than six hundred of these manorial domains sprawled along the north shore of the island. Appropriately labeled the Gold Coast, this plutocratic landscape was dotted with 50- to 100-room mansions where the nation's most notable millionaires played croquet games for $2,000 stakes, hosted Easter egg hunts with a one thousand dollar bill in each egg, and entertained 1,200 guests at lavish balls.[4] Polo, golf, fox hunting, and yachting were among the pastimes that made Long Island a symbol of sporting pleasure.

Oakland County offered a less ostentatious life style, but it too was attracting pleasure-seeking plutocrats. As early as 1906 the *Detroit News* observed that "within the past two seasons" a summer colony had grown up in Oakland County "which [bid] fair, ere long, to rival the pretentiousness" of the older resorts of wealthy Detroiters. As if to fulfill his newspaper's prophecy, two years later *News* publisher George Booth built his country manor in Oakland's Bloomfield Hills area, solidifying that district's reputation as a magnet for the

TABLE 1.   Population, 1920–1940

| County | 1920 | 1930 | 1940 | Density per Square Mile | |
				1930	1940
Suffolk	110,246	161,055	197,355	175	214
Nassau	126,120	303,053	406,748	1,106	1,356
Oakland	90,050	211,251	254,068	238	290
DuPage	42,120	91,998	103,480	267	313
Saint Louis	100,737	211,593	274,230	435	552
Orange	61,375	118,674	130,760	149	167

Sources: Bureau of the Census, Census of 1920, 1930, and 1940 (Washington, D.C.: U.S. Government Printing Office, 1921, 1931, 1942).

wealthy and powerful. Well-heeled Chicagoans had established country estates in DuPage County's Elmhurst and Hinsdale during the late nineteenth century, and by the 1890s nearby Glen Ellyn was a popular health resort for weary city folk. In 1893 affluent Chicago sportsmen founded the Chicago Golf Club, the first eighteen-hole golf course in the United States, on the south side of the Du-Page county seat of Wheaton, and during the early twentieth century Colonel Robert McCormick, owner of the *Chicago Tribune,* and Joy Morton of Morton Salt maintained sprawling estates in the county. Meanwhile, in 1914 Saint Louis County's Ladue became the site of the exclusive St. Louis Country Club, and in nearby Huntleigh Village Adolphus Busch of brewing fame was among the founders of a fox hunting club.[5] By 1920 the outlying districts had already established themselves as playgrounds for the affluent and had become associated in the popular mind with leisure, carefully manicured natural beauty, and life at the top of the social heap.

During the 1920s, however, full-scale suburbanization transformed these fringe areas. Members of the middle class joined the wealthy along the metropolitan outskirts, and three-bedroom homes on quarter-acre lots encroached on hunt clubs and polo fields. As seen in table 1, thousands of newcomers migrated outward, causing the populations of Nassau, Oakland, DuPage, and Saint Louis Counties to more than double during the decade. Each of these was the fastest growing county in its respective state. Farther from the urban core, Orange and Suffolk Counties grew substantially but less dramatically. Already by 1930 the population density of Nassau County, hugging the New York City limits, was more than eleven hundred persons per square mile. The southeast corner of Oakland County, closest to the city of Detroit, likewise was heavily developed by 1930, with almost two thousand inhabitants per square mile. Around the commuter rail lines in eastern DuPage County, suburban development was also well advanced, and the easternmost area of Saint Louis County, nearest the city of Saint Louis, was built up by the close of the 1920s. The rate of population growth slowed during the depression-ridden 1930s as fewer Americans could afford to purchase suburban homes. But the rate of increase still considerably outpaced that of the nation as a whole and of the nation's central cities.

One did not have to look at the census figures to realize that suburbia was booming during the 1920s. The signs of growth were everywhere and the rhetoric of real estate brokers and subdividers was decidedly upbeat. In 1925 promoters of Babylon in Suffolk County were boasting that real estate prices in that community had soared 300 percent during the past three or four years. In 1926 a leading broker observed happily, "I am looking forward to the biggest year in real estate that Long Island has ever known." To the west, in Oakland County, a local newspaper referred to real estate activity in Birmingham as "phenomenal." Meanwhile, the newspaper in nearby Berkley labeled its hometown "the fastest growing town in the world!" And the population of Ferndale, in the southeastern corner of Oakland County, grew more than 500 percent between 1920 and the end of 1924. Reflecting the booming conditions in DuPage County, the number of real estate agencies in Glen Ellyn rose from three in 1920 to twenty in 1928. The success of local developer Arthur T. McIntosh certainly inspired some DuPage Countians to seek a career in real estate. Between 1920 and 1924 his subdivision in Westmont attracted eighteen hundred purchasers, and by 1935 he had recorded a total of seventy-three subdivision plats spread across three of the county's townships.[6]

The influx of newcomers not only made some people rich, it also changed the social complexion of the suburbanizing counties. An increasing number of middle- and upper-middle class commuters invaded the domain of plutocratic estate owners along the metropolitan fringe. This was most evident along the south shore of Long Island in Nassau and Suffolk Counties. As early as 1928 the *New York Times* wrote of the "large country estates" in this area as "pretty well decimated." One manor after another was sold to developers and subdivided into lots. According to one newspaper account, the president of the American Brass and Copper Company was forced to part with his "300-acre estate, with palatial home and outbuildings, trout lake and winding stream" after the "influx of population surrounded him . . . ; too many all-year small homes adjoined him; [and] the din of traffic annoyed him." Along the north shore of Long Island population growth was less dramatic and millionaires were more successful at keeping the surging masses at bay. But even there some estates were falling into the hands of developers. For example, in 1925 multi-millionaire newspaper and magazine publisher Frank Munsey died, leaving his estate to the Metropolitan Museum of Art. The museum proceeded to subdivide the property, creating the upper-middle-class community of Munsey Park. By 1940, 1,456 people lived on the 0.6-square-mile tract.[7] In Munsey Park and elsewhere the well-to-do were realizing their suburban dream on 6,000- to 8,000-square-foot lots where the nation's wealthiest citizens had formerly tracked foxes and grazed polo ponies.

Yet in some of the future post-suburban counties, the signs of suburbanization were less pronounced. During the 1920s and 1930s Orange County remained a region of citrus groves and oil derricks. Los Angeles residents on a weekend jaunt might dock their yachts at Newport Beach or set up their easels at the art colony of Laguna Beach, but the daily commute to the city was not a part of Orange County life. Similarly, Suffolk County was still best known for its beaches and duck farms. Except for its westernmost reaches, it was a weekend destination rather than a place of permanent residence for Manhattan office workers.

Moreover, indigenous industry provided thousands of jobs and an independent economic base for most of the outlying counties. Naperville in DuPage County was the home of Kroehler Manufacturing Company, the nation's largest maker of upholstered furniture, and nearby Villa Park was the American headquarters for the manufacture of the popular chocolate drink Ovaltine.[8] In the 1920s Pontiac, the county seat of Oakland County, boomed as a center of automobile manufacturing, producing hundreds of thousands of appropriately named Pontiacs. Meanwhile, in Suffolk County Patchogue was a manufacturing hub, having acquired some fame for its lace mills.

Suburbanization was the wave of the future, however, and all of the outlying counties, except for Orange, were already acquiring a suburban identity. Moreover, the suburban ideal of home and garden nestled in a quiet village was becoming a more significant factor in the life and politics of the fringe areas. Thousands of city dwellers were moving to the periphery to find the atmosphere of a rural English village or to establish themselves as lords and ladies of mini-manors in imitation of their plutocratic social betters. This was the dream real estate developers sold, and it proved a highly popular commodity. The newcomers to Nassau, Oakland, and DuPage did not want to recreate the urban world they had left behind. Instead, they were devotees of the suburban vision, and it was this vision that would mold the future of these outlying counties.

To better realize this vision, the migrants to the periphery opted for a suburban form of government. They did not dream of creating big-city government with impersonal bureaucracies or irresponsible partisan political machines

TABLE 2.   Number of Municipalities, 1920–1940

County	1920	1930	1940
Suffolk	12	26	27
Nassau	20	47	65
Oakland	14	24	24
DuPage	13	18	18
Saint Louis	15	20	41
Orange	9	13	13

Sources: Bureau of the Census, Census of 1920, 1930, and 1940 (Washington, D.C.: U.S. Government Printing Office, 1921, 1931, 1942).

such as they had known in New York, Chicago, or Saint Louis. Instead, they founded scores of small municipalities that were the governmental antithesis of the nation's urban giants. They sought to fashion an idealized village form of government, a small-scale, nonpartisan polity characterized by volunteerism, cooperation, and consensus. Essential elements of the suburban ideal were neighborliness and homogeneity. The village governments of suburbia were expected to nurture these traits. Disinterested civic service to one's neighbors was the goal of the ideal village official in the new suburban world of the 1920s and 1930s.

As the suburban population soared, the number of small, supposedly neighborly municipalities likewise rose. As seen in table 2, the number of municipalities increased especially sharply in rapidly suburbanizing Nassau County, but in the other counties as well new village governments were forming to realize the governmental goals of suburbanites. By 1940 Nassau County could boast sixty-five municipalities, the number having more than tripled in the previous two decades. In both Suffolk and Saint Louis Counties the number of municipalities more than doubled during the twenty years prior to World War II. Except in Saint Louis County, most of the increase had occurred during the booming 1920s when suburban populations were skyrocketing. In all of the counties, however, the trend was toward governmental fragmentation, and any new wave of massive migration seemed to promise the creation of scores of additional governmental units.

Though some of the new municipalities were created to provide necessary public services, a more common motive for incorporation was to protect and preserve the small-scale, homogeneous community life style of the villages. Suburbanites did not opt for incorporation as a means of fashioning the public infrastructure for a future great city. They chose municipal status to protect the existing suburban environment and to ensure a way of life different from that of a city. Municipal incorporation was, then, a wall designed to preserve and protect and not an avenue to facilitate change and urbanization.

This was evident in the scores of municipalities that sprouted up in Nassau County. Many of those in the northern half of the county were estate communities that incorporated so that the local lords of the manor would have the legal authority to keep out unwanted persons or influences that might disrupt their aristocratic seclusion. As early as 1911 one estate owner incorporated his domain as the village of Saddle Rock in order to avoid the higher taxes necessary to fund public improvements for new residents in surrounding areas. As a separate municipality Saddle Rock could escape paying for suburban sewers and streets in nearby areas, and the manor could remain an enclave of meadows and woods in a suburbanizing world.[9] In 1920 Saddle Rock was home to only seventy-one residents; in 1930 the figure rose to seventy-four; and ten years later it dropped to sixty-nine. Throughout these decades, the village remained a low-density, steady-state domain, successfully keeping the forces of change at bay.

Elsewhere on Long Island wealthy residents likewise were attempting to suspend change through incorporation. Disturbed by the growing number of weekend picnickers flocking to Lake Success, in 1926 estate- and homeowners in the area incorporated, thereby acquiring the authority to regulate the property around the lake and the roads leading to it. Moreover, they sought to protect the village's estates through the adoption of zoning ordinances. Like Saddle Rock, Lake Success was a municipality dedicated to slowing development and perpetuating a semirural environment. According to a survey of Long Island published in the early 1940s, the municipalities of Centre Island, Cove Island, Head of the Harbor, Matinecock, North Hills, Old Brookville, and Old Westbury were also restricted estate communities.[10] Incorporated in 1929, North Hills, for example, adopted a zoning ordinance that established a minimum residential lot size of two acres. By 1940 fewer than three hundred persons lived in the almost three square miles of North Hills.[11]

Nearby upper-middle-class communities as well turned to incorporation to protect themselves from taxes and incompatible land uses. Fearful of unregulated development that could lower property values, residents of Munsey Park were just as eager to adopt zoning ordinances to protect their half-acre plots as the estate owners of Lake Success or Centre Island were to preserve their one-hundred-acre manors. Moreover, in 1929 the creation of the Manhasset Sewer District encompassing Munsey Park and its neighbors threatened to raise the taxes of local homeowners. Incorporated areas, however, were not subject to the exactions of such special districts, so Munsey Parkers opted for incorporation.

Nearby Plandome Heights was similarly threatened by the high taxes of the sewer district. Plans to build garden apartments on property adjacent to the community further mobilized Plandome Heights residents dedicated to the suburban life style of the single-family dwelling. As in the case of Munsey Park, voters concluded that incorporation and zoning would answer the problems of their community. Meanwhile, sewer taxes and zoning also brought homeowners in Plandome Manor to the polls to cast their ballots for independent municipal existence.[12] By the early 1930s, the Manhasset area of northern Nassau County was, then, splintered into an array of upper-middle-class mini-municipalities, each having resorted to incorporation as a defense against the raids of tax collectors and the insensitivity of profit-hungry real estate developers.

In the suburbanizing areas of Oakland, DuPage, and Saint Louis Counties incorporation also was, in many instances, a defensive measure to preserve small-scale, homogeneous communities compatible with the village ideal. In 1926 Oakland County's Huntington Woods incorporated in part to avoid annexation to, and taxation by, the adjacent municipalities of Royal Oak and Ferndale. Planned as a community of single-family residences, Huntington Woods soon employed its municipal powers to keep out commercial development and multiple-family structures. The enforcement of single-family zoning, in fact, was to become the predominant theme in the history of the community. In 1924 DuPage County's Clarendon Hills, likewise, opted to preserve its separate identity and ward off annexation to Hinsdale by incorporating as a village.[13]

In Saint Louis County, defensive incorporation was commonplace. Missouri municipalities could annex unincorporated territory without the approval of the voters in the area to be annexed. Opponents of annexation in areas about to be absorbed had only one recourse and that was to incorporate as a separate municipality, for one municipality could not absorb another incorporated community unless the voters in each municipality approved the merger. In other words, voters in unincorporated tracts had no voice in annexation decisions, but voters in incorporated areas could veto the aggressions of their municipal neighbors. Thus annexation threats repeatedly resulted in incorporation.

When the Saint Louis County municipality of Clayton sought to extend its boundaries westward and swallow the estate community of Ladue, that elite area incorporated. Ladue made good use of its municipal powers, creating a well-protected, low-density haven for the wealthy. In 1938 its zoning commission explained: "One of the major objectives of our proposed zoning ordinance is to protect and continue the spacious residential character now found within [Ladue]." The zoning commissioners proudly proclaimed, "Ours is one of the few communities in St. Louis County that are unspoiled by uses generally objectionable to desirable residential sections." No apartment buildings disturbed the suburban character of the community and commercial structures occupied only 7.8 acres of Ladue's 4,533 acres.[14]

Municipal status, however, not only protected the wealthy in Ladue. Less affluent residents throughout Saint Louis County resorted to incorporation to keep their bit of suburban turf from being annexed. Especially in the late 1930s in the northeastern section of the county, one subdivision after another became a separate municipal corporation. In 1937 five new municipalities appeared, and in 1938 there were three additional incorporations, followed by four the next year. Half-timbered cottages with three bedrooms and one-and-a-half baths clustered on small lots in middle-class Pasadena Park, but in the 1930s that community's residents, like their counterparts in more affluent Ladue, rejected remote government, opting for the supposed intimacy of grass-roots rule.

Not all of the suburban municipalities remained tightly knit villages running only a few blocks in each direction. By 1940 nine of Nassau County's municipalities had more than 10,000 inhabitants, yet even in these communities residents attempted to preserve the village image. Even though the New York State Conference of Mayors had concluded that the village form of government was inappropriate for communities of 7,500 or more, eight of these nine Nassau municipalities retained their village charters and refused to become cities under New York state law.[15] With over 20,000 inhabitants, both Hempstead and Freeport clung to village governments, and residents proudly spoke of the advantages of village life. Hard-pressed by economic depression during the early 1930s, a number of villages in Michigan's Oakland County did accept city status in order to escape paying township taxes.[16] But in New York, where the economic advantages to change were less pronounced, villages, no matter their size, remained villages. The term *city* had a negative connotation in suburbia, where the village was the ideal. Hempstead and Freeport were larger than 40 percent of the cities in New York, but they continued to accept village status and embrace the image of intimacy and homogeneity it implied.

The proliferating villages of suburbia not only rejected the legal structure of the city but eschewed the political practices associated with the nation's largest municipalities. Almost invariably, village elections in suburbia did not involve national political parties, with neither the Republicans nor the Democrats offering a slate of candidates. Such party politics smacked of the city with its legendary political machines and bosses. Suburbanites were dedicated to sparing their ideal villages this corrupting influence. Moreover, party leaders generally agreed to stay out of village politics. For example, in 1929 G. Wilbur Doughty, leader of Nassau County's dominant Republican party, publicly declared that his party had "no interest in village elections" and had "always followed a hands-off policy in village affairs."[17] Local parties did exist, but they usually presented themselves as good-government organizations dedicated to finding the best person for public office regardless of his or her national party affiliation. They adopted party labels that advertised their high-minded devotion to the village's welfare. Thus in one community after another, such groups as the "Citizens Party," the "Village Party," the "Independent Party," and the "Taxpayers Party" vied for office. Suburbanites accepted the benefits of banding together and sponsoring slates of candidates under a single party label, but at the village level these labels were intended to proclaim the slate's local civic devotion rather than their loyalty to the Republican or Democratic organization.

Occasionally Democrats and Republicans did openly vie for office in suburban villages, but this deviation from the ideal stirred cries of foul. For example, during the mid 1930s in Nassau County's Hempstead the Democratic party broke the prevailing rule and incurred the indignant wrath of a number of residents. For over two decades neither the Republicans nor the Democrats had offered slates in Hempstead village elections, and throughout the 1920s and early 1930s the Citizens' Party had dominated local elections, defeating such challengers as the People's Nominator ticket and the Municipal Nominators.[18] In some tranquil years, only a single slate appeared on the ballot. Following Franklin Roosevelt's smashing national victory in 1932, however, local Democrats felt it was time to take advantage of the political momentum and capture some local positions. Long excluded from any offices at the township or county level by the dominant Republicans, the Democrats decided to begin at the bottom and build a village power base. In 1933, 1934, and 1935, the Democrats offered candidates in the Hempstead village elections, allying themselves with the local Taxpayers Economy Party. Then in 1936 the Republicans responded with their own village slate, presenting Hempstead with the first openly Republican-versus-Democrat battle in a quarter century.

During each election campaign of the mid 1930s critics protested this corruption of the village political process. In 1934 the Citizens' Committee platform responded to the injection of partisanship by declaring, "We believe now, as we have always, that a more economical and efficient administration of our Village affairs can be effected when candidates are not subjected to the influence of any political machine and are free to act for the best interests of the Village without control of any political boss." Moreover, it proclaimed its belief "in the selection of candidates, regardless of party affiliation, chosen solely on the basis of qualification." That same year one Citizens' candidate denounced the Democrats as "part of a political machine that is being built to control all forms of government." In 1935 the local newspaper warned that the village government was about to "come right under the heel of a major party organization" and deplored the recent "knock 'em down and drag-em" contests, which were "something far and away from what a purely local municipal election should be." Amid the partisan battle of 1936, the newspaper still clung to the "belief that local government would best be conducted, not on party lines but upon village lines" and warned of "a move to obtain control of the village government by political units," which was "going to mean remote control of the village."[19]

The village of Hempstead's Republican-Democrat clash proved only an isolated anomaly, for village elections in Nassau County and elsewhere in emerging suburbia were to remain nonpartisan. Democrats continued to claim that the Nassau Republican organization intervened behind the scenes, but overt partisanship was taboo. Suburban villagers did not want "remote control" by "political machines," but instead viewed the village as a refuge from the vulgar realities of the outside world and sought to ensure that it did not fall prey to those realities. Village parties were appropriate for village politics, for the village was removed from the national scene and its life was not to be tainted by exposure to the national organizations.

Yet the absence of national party battles did not necessarily result in political tranquillity. To the distress of those who sought harmony and cooperation in suburbia, municipal candidates sometimes engaged in bitter battles for power. For example, vigorous contests were the norm in Oakland County's Berkley, leading a local newspaper to label that community a "politically quarrelsome village." Saint Louis County's University City fluctuated between quiescence and heated competition. In 1931 Mayor Eugene Ruth won reelection unopposed, but two years later he faced three opponents. Commenting on the change, the *Saint Louis Post-Dispatch* noted: "Politics in University City has graduated from the class of former years, when candidates filed perfunctorily and, if opposed at all, waged polite campaigns." On election day the Civic Voters' League defeated Ruth, and the polling was marred by the alleged theft of about four hundred ballots by an overzealous poll watcher. In the 1935 election, however, normalcy returned with the incumbent winning reelection unopposed. Even in the small, elite Nassau County community of Great Neck Estates, there was occasionally sharp political competition. In 1926 the *New York Times* reported that in Great Neck Estates, "where previous elections seldom saw more than twenty voters going to the polls," a New York City lawyer defeated the Neighborhood Association's candidate "after a spirited contest which brought out 365 votes."[20]

In scores of suburban villages, however, competition was rare or nonexistent. Year after year candidates ran unopposed and no one seemed concerned that elections were mere formalities, deciding nothing. For example, in March 1927 thirty Nassau County villages elected officials but there were contests in only seven of them, and one year later thirteen of the thirty-four villages had contested elections.[21] Likewise, in Saint Louis County single-slate elections were commonplace. Candidates in many of the smaller villages seemingly never faced opponents. In April 1941 seventeen Saint Louis County villages elected trustees, but in only nine of the communities was there any contest. Two years later eight county municipalities chose mayors in the April elections; none of them faced a challenger.[22] In suburban municipalities, the much-vaunted nonpartisan elections were, then, often no elections at all. If there were no vital issues facing the villagers and few ambitious individuals seeking what little glory or power village office conferred, then there was no contest.

In a nation that had long lauded two-party politics as a necessary ingredient to healthy democracy, the uncontested elections might have been seen as a perversion of the political process. But in suburbia the lack of competition was no disgrace and was often praised as a virtue. The suburban village was supposed to be a haven of consensus and neighborliness in contrast to the abrasive heterogeneity and cold-hearted exploitiveness of the big city. In the minds of some suburbanites, one-party rule by a coterie of high-minded citizens was actually one of the crowning achievements of their community.

This was the case in Nassau County's upper-middle-class municipality of Garden City. At the time of its incorporation in 1919, Garden City adopted what was known as the Gentleman's Agreement or Community Agreement. According to this agreement, in each of the village's four sections the property owners' association would meet to select the nominees to represent that section on the village board of trustees, and these nominees would run unopposed in the ensuing election. Usually the candidates were persons of proven experience, having held positions in the property owners' associations. Moreover, they were not expected to seek office. Instead, they were supposedly drafted to do their duty by neighbors who recognized their civic devotion and competence. "On the theory that municipal housekeeping of a village has nothing to do with political issues," explained the village report for 1946, "the nominees usually are chosen from a list of civic-minded men who, regardless of party affiliation, have served their apprenticeship by years of work in the Property Owners' Associations of their sections and who have thereby won the respect and trust of their neighbors." This system seemed to satisfy Garden City residents, for after twenty-seven years of village government, the village report was able to boast that "at no time ha[d] there ever been more than one ticket placed in nomination for the offices of mayor and trustee." Thus "partisanship and disunity ha[d] been avoided," and candidates had been "selected on their merits without political pressure."[23]

The nearby village of Lawrence likewise rejected two-party competition for consensual rule by persons of proven civic distinction. There the five-person Independent Village Nominating Committee selected the single slate of candidates to appear on the ballot. The committee itself was self-perpetuating, with the members choosing their own successors. Decade after decade, the committee determined the best people to hold office, and the electorate accepted its judgment without challenge.[24] In Lawrence as in Garden City, village politics was not a competitive free-for-all for power or self-aggrandizement. Instead, the political process aimed at discovering a consensual slate of public-spirited citizens who would strive for the good of the community as a whole. Division and conflict were big-city traits. In the suburban village community and cooperation were the goals.

Moreover, this consensual politics existed not only in Nassau County but in other emerging suburban areas. For example, in DuPage County a number of municipalities relied on a single-party system of village politics. In 1930 the Civic Betterment Party won control in upper-middle-class Glen Ellyn, and for the next four decades it remained unchallenged. Before each village election the Civic Betterment Party conducted an open caucus, later referred to as a town meeting, at which the party slate was chosen, and the candidates on that slate were automatic victors in the general election.[25] In the early 1930s community leaders in nearby Hinsdale formed the Community Caucus, consisting of representatives from each organization in the village. This caucus selected a village ticket, which was assured of victory on election day.[26] Beginning in 1944 residents in adjacent Clarendon Hills applied the same caucus system in their village.[27] In the suburban village political homogeneity was as sought after as social homogeneity, and the consensual nonpartisan politics of these DuPage County communities conformed to this ideal.

Volunteerism was another foundation stone in the ideology of the suburban village. Participation in village government was not an occupation; it was a civic duty. The model suburban villager was, then, expected to volunteer his or her services to the community. Paid party ward heelers and professional politics were big-city phenomena. Government by volunteers was the goal of village idealists in Glen Ellyn and Garden City.

In many communities village officers were not even paid, for salaries were deemed to corrupt the political process. In 1936 the *Hempstead Sentinel* explained this tradition of volunteer service, observing that "there ha[d] always been the feeling that although men were chosen by election to fill important places on the governing body of the Village, the task was a return of good will service to the community in which they lived." Moreover, the newspaper feared "that putting officials on the payroll increased the hazard of the local offices becoming mere political pawns." The village report of Garden City, likewise, contended that unpaid service implied a purity of motive preferable in the suburban municipality. "With nothing to gain, in a material way for themselves," the report observed, "[village officers] can act with complete disinterestedness for the good of the Village as a whole."[28]

This idealization of the spirit of volunteerism was commonplace in suburbia. Volunteer fire departments were a feature of many suburban villages, and local newspapers reported an endless array of organizations taking advantage of those eager to donate their services. Proud boosters of DuPage County's Clarendon Hills were even to label their community "the village of volunteers."[29]

Harnessing this volunteer spirit were the community or civic associations that played a significant role in the government of many suburban areas. These associations often were founded before the incorporation of their communities and were instrumental in the effort to achieve municipal status. Once incorporation was attained, the civic associations acted as watchdogs of the municipal governments, ensuring that mayors and councils adhered to the basic principles on which the community was founded. They prodded village officers to provide needed services and to protect property values and the suburban way of life. In a typical statement of purpose, Nassau County's Matinecock Neighborhood Association pledged to do "the things which should be done in every community, no matter how small, to make the neighborhood a better place to live in." A publication of the Residents' Association in Oakland County's Huntington Woods discussed the problems of street paving, fire protection, and the single-family residential restriction, all of which "required very definite and positive action." And during the early 1940s the Munsey Park Civic Association of Nassau County dedicated itself to researching "the scope and enforceability of restrictions" in order to keep the developer Levitt and Sons from building inexpensive homes in the upper-middle-class village. Moreover, association meetings offered residents an opportunity to voice their complaints. The president of the Freeport Civic Association of Nassau County claimed his group brought "matters of great importance before their members, debating them, deciding what in their opinion was the best course to take and letting their wishes be made known at the proper time."[30]

Through the civic associations, suburban residents could, then, fight city hall. These organizations reinforced the sense that the suburban municipality was not to be a clone of its big-city neighbor. It was to be a small-scale polity that encouraged participation and fostered volunteer action. Nonpartisan and devoid of professional politics, the village with its volunteer associations was intended to be responsive and open to the average suburban homeowner.

Reality may have deviated from the ideal, and there were certainly many apathetic suburbanites who did not flock to civic association meetings and possibly did not know civic associations existed. Moreover, entrenched community leaders dominating community caucuses or associations might well have proved a greater hindrance to meaningful participation in the political process than any big-city boss or bureaucrat. In some communities one-party politics might have produced a suburban oligarchy rather than participatory democracy. And even when there was competition in village elections, the voter turnout was often low. Many suburbanites simply did not fit the concerned-citizen, dedicated-volunteer mold. But the suburban dream exercised a powerful influence on those who migrated to the metropolitan fringe. Suburban villages valued homogeneity, both political and social, and miniature government of the type unknown in New York City or Chicago. Even those who voted irregularly and did not know who was village mayor probably would have bridled at the thought of substituting a government similar to that of the big city. The suburban ideal sounded good even to those who did not live up to it.

Villages, however, were not the only pieces in the puzzle of suburban government. Suburbia was served as well by an increasing array of special districts, governmental units created to provide only a single service. Thus there were sewer districts dealing with the drainage of outlying areas, refuse districts to handle the garbage, mosquito abatement districts to eliminate pesky insects, and fire districts to battle blazes. Many reasons justified creating these districts. Often they were the only means for providing services to a populated but unincorporated area. For example, the Illinois Constitution of 1870 required counties and townships to impose uniform rates of taxation throughout their territory. Consequently, they could not impose special taxes on individual subdivisions that required special services. If the county was to collect the garbage in one populated but unincorporated area, the cost of this service would have to be paid from the taxes imposed countywide, on farmers as well as commuters. Yet through the creation of a special district, a subdivision with special needs could obtain services without burdening the population of the county or township as a whole. In some cases drainage districts were desirable because the natural drainage pattern of an area did not conform to the existing political boundaries. The facts of nature recommended that neighboring municipalities and unincorporated areas join in a single district. State-imposed debt and taxation limits on municipalities also encouraged creation of special districts. If a municipality was approaching such limits, citizens might have to resort to the creation of a special district to handle any additional costly governmental functions. For a number of reasons, then, special districts proved either convenient or necessary.

The result was a proliferation of such units. In heavily suburbanized Nassau County, the number of special districts almost doubled, from 87 in 1920 to 173 in 1933. By the latter date there were 53 lighting districts to provide street lighting, 52 fire districts, and 38 water districts to supply water to suburban homes and businesses. DuPage County was not quite as prolific in the creation of special districts, but a state report from 1934 discovered 120 separate taxing units, including municipalities, high school and grade school districts, park districts, and sanitary districts. By the mid 1940s Saint Louis County had 42 special districts offering sewer, water, drainage, and fire protection services as well as an additional 89 school districts. California's Orange County remained largely agricultural and unaffected by suburbanization, but already by 1935 it had 81 special districts dealing with everything from cemeteries to sewer maintenance. Oakland County did not rely on special districts, yet by 1932 even that county encompassed 227 independent units of government with taxing and debt-incurring authority. Besides supporting 24 municipalities, Oakland County residents paid taxes to 177 school districts.[31]

By the 1930s this abundance of governmental units was the subject of increasing criticism and complaint. According to a survey of Nassau County's government, "There are so many local jurisdictions that it was not possible to prepare a map of the county or even of one town[ship] showing local unit boundaries." This investigation found that within a single area of 120 acres, 24 governmental units exercised authority, "or one for every five acres of ground." Though Oakland County had only 227 units of government as compared to Nassau's total of 307, a 1932 study of the Michigan county likewise complained of "too many and too small units of government."[32] Having escaped from the governmental giantism of the big city, suburbanites seem to have gone to the other extreme, opting for miniature polities with overlapping jurisdictions that confused many taxpayers and angered some.

Encompassing a broader expanse of territory than most special districts or municipalities were the townships. Suffolk, Nassau, Oakland, and DuPage Counties were divided into townships with governmental service functions, whereas in Saint Louis and Orange Counties townships were not governing units. In the Missouri county they were simply voting districts, comparable to city precincts, and in Orange they were merely judicial districts, each with a justice of the peace. Suffolk had ten townships, Nassau three, Oakland twenty-five, and DuPage nine. The townships in the latter two counties generally conformed to the federal survey townships, each covering a uniform thirty-six square miles. Long Island's townships averaged more than twice that area, though they varied considerably in size. In Suffolk, Nassau, Oakland, and Du-Page Counties, townships exercised a number of governmental functions for the unincorporated areas within their boundaries. Their exact duties differed according to state law, but the construction and maintenance of roads and the administration of relief for the needy were two of the most common and significant responsibilities.

Much criticized by experts in public administration and good-government reformers as unnecessary relics of the horse-and-buggy era, townships were on the defensive by the 1930s and seemed an endangered governmental species. Yet like the multitude of village governments, the townships touched a chord deep in the ideological heart of America. In the popular imagination they represented a simpler rural existence and Jeffersonian grass-roots rule. Though they were remnants of the rural past, they thus fit into the suburban ideal of small-scale neighborly government. Attempts to eliminate them could arouse the same fears of centralized, impersonal government that stirred the souls of suburban villagers. Despite repeated discourses on the obsolescence of the township, it was, then, not as vulnerable as some believed. It had a secure niche in the emerging suburban ideology, and as long as small and simple were deemed good, the township would survive.

Townships were significant not only as providers of services but also as units of representation for county government. The principal governing body of Nassau, Suffolk, Oakland and DuPage Counties was the board of supervisors, composed of the supervisors from each township. The supervisor was the township executive, responsible for administering that governmental unit, but he or she was, in addition, the township's spokesperson on the county board. In some counties cities enjoyed representation on the county board as well. For example, in 1932 there were fifty-seven members of Oakland County's Board of Supervisors, twenty-five of them township supervisors and thirty-two representatives of the county's cities. Each township had one member on the board, but the city representatives were apportioned on the basis of population, with the largest city, Pontiac, having eight members. In Nassau County two supervisors represented the most populous township of Hempstead, whereas each of the other two townships was represented by one supervisor and the two cities of Glen Cove and Long Beach had one member each. Voting power on the board, however, was apportioned according to population. Thus each Hempstead supervisor cast sixteen votes out of a total of fifty, but the much less populous cities had only one vote each. In other words, Hempstead township's representatives cast 64 percent of the votes on the county board.[33]

The counties that these supervisors governed were far different from the villages of the suburban ideal. Whereas the village was a haven from the world and its government was dedicated to preserving and protecting its special status, the county was part of the larger world, an arm of the state and a link between the locality and the state capital. From the founding of the nation, the county had been deemed an agent of the state, created to impose the will of the state on localities. Its sheriff enforced the laws made in Albany and Springfield, its courts applied state legislative dictates, and its assessors and collectors were responsible for raising the state's revenues. Throughout American history it had been more of an administrative tool of the central government than a local policymaking body. Though it exercised some welfare functions and maintained some rural roads, the county traditionally had not engaged in the expansive provision of services characteristic of America's largest municipalities.

Moreover, the county was the principal unit of representation in state legislatures. Legislative districts generally conformed to county boundaries and each county usually had at least one representative in the state legislature. In the legislative proceedings, that representative was identified as the member from his or her county and he or she was regarded as the spokesperson for the county in the state capital. Thus the county was the instrument whereby the state imposed its will on the locality and whereby the locality expressed its concerns to the state.

Traditionally, then, the county was a conduit to the outside political authorities. In contrast, the ideal suburban village was a walled preserve, protected by zoning ordinances and municipal status from the threatening forces of the world. The county faced outward; the village looked inward. The county kept the door open to the world; the village tried to close it. Consequently, the rules of politics for the county differed markedly from those for the village. Whereas village politics was nonpartisan, at the county level Republicans openly battled with Democrats. County officials ran on partisan tickets and party conflict was often sharp and bitter. The only exception was in Orange County, the nonpartisan tradition being particularly strong and pervasive in California. Elsewhere suburban villagers who abhorred partisan politics at the municipal level lined up loyally behind national party candidates in county elections. The same Garden City residents who kept party competition out of their village elections and strived for political consensus and homogeneity in municipal government voted a straight Republican ticket in county, state, and national elections and were among the most reliable mainstays of the Nassau County Republican Party organization. Likewise, many Glen Ellyn devotees of the Civic Betterment town meeting never failed to rally behind the GOP in a county contest. Politically the village was a world apart from the county, state, and nation, and the political culture appropriate for the villages of Garden City and Glen Ellyn was inappropriate for higher levels of government.

Powerful political organizations with armies of loyal party workers underscored the deep partisanship at county levels. Suffolk's Republican organization was long regarded as having a secure stranglehold on the county, and in the mid-twentieth century DuPage County's Republican Party was a GOP counterpart to Chicago's powerful Democratic machine. On election day DuPage County leaders could produce reliable Republican majorities as effectively as Chicago's organization piled up votes in the Democratic column.

The most successful and durable political organization, however, was Nassau County's Republican Party. Before World War I the township of Hempstead had been loyally Republican, but in the townships of North Hempstead and Oyster Bay Democrats were able to win some victories. In 1915 G. Wilbur Doughty secured control of the Nassau Republican organization and put an end to any Democratic chances for electoral success. Until his death in 1930 Doughty efficiently produced the votes on election day and made Nassau a seemingly insuperable GOP stronghold. Following a struggle for power in the early 1930s, Doughty's nephew J. Russel Sprague secured unchallenged control of the organization and proved an even more effective leader than had his uncle.

Though Franklin Roosevelt's popularity put Democrats in office elsewhere in the nation, Nassau County, if anything, grew even more Republican during the 1930s, and any GOP candidate for governor or president could rely on Sprague for a bumper crop of votes on election day. In fact, he was a powerhouse in national politics from the mid 1930s to the 1950s, chairing the New York state delegation to the Republican national convention in 1936 and winning appointment to the Republican national committee in 1940. As a close political advisor to New York's Governor Thomas Dewey, he was a leading figure in Dewey's presidential races of 1944 and 1948. In 1943 Nassau County's district attorney predicted, "No man living will exert so much influence on the election of the next President as Russ Sprague." By 1948 most astute observers were not dismissing such statements as hyperbole. Sprague was clearly a person to reckon with. During the presidential campaign of that year a political commentator in the *New Republic* characterized Nassau as "the most Republican county of the United States" and Sprague as "the power behind the Republican candidate." *Harper's* identified him as one of the "Triumvirate" who controlled the national Republican Party and most influenced the thinking of candidate Dewey.[34]

Dewey's defeat in 1948 did not destroy Sprague. In 1952 he helped Eisenhower win the GOP nomination and was influential in the selection of Richard Nixon as vice presidential nominee. Moreover, during the Eisenhower administration, Nassau County congressman and Sprague disciple Leonard Hall served as national chairman of the Republican Party.[35] From the mid 1930s through the mid 1950s, as Nassau went so went the Republican Party. No county exercised so much influence on the GOP as Nassau.

Moreover, Doughty and Sprague built their political empire, in part, by consciously placing the GOP in the role of great suburban defender. Nassau's Republicans constantly characterized themselves as the chief bulwark against the forays of New York City's notorious Tammany Democratic machine. As early as 1904 Republicans were warning that it would be "safer to keep the Tammany Tiger out of Nassau County," and in succeeding decades the GOP instilled in the minds of local voters the fear that a Democratic victory would mean annexation by New York City.[36] Doughty and Sprague made clear that Democrats stood for the big city and its values. Republicans were the party of the suburbs and the GOP would man the barricades to fight any attempt to make Nassau the sixth borough of New York City. In the end, though, the Sprague organization was as much a machine as the hated Tammany. Actually, Sprague had an even tighter grip on his domain than did the big-city bosses. As one observer noted, "Tammany is sometimes defeated in New York; Sprague is never beaten in Nassau."[37]

Along the suburban fringe, there was, then, a dual political culture. At the village level partisanship along Republican and Democratic lines was unacceptable. The party boss was anathema and the political machine was deemed one of the horrors of the big city. Even Russel Sprague publicly regretted partisan interference in municipal politics, though his Democratic foes doubted the sincerity of his public proclamations. During the Republican-Democratic contest in Hempstead village in 1936, Sprague attended local Republican meetings but made clear that never before had he interfered in a village contest and he implied his distaste for having been forced to do so.[38] Yet the county was an open battlefield for the two national parties. Sprague himself proved that suburbia could nurture powerful party organizations that could deliver the votes and wield clout in Albany and Washington.

During the coming decades this schizoid view of politics would continue to prevail, and any reform of the governments of suburbanizing counties would have to take it into account. The suburban ideal of the village haven would have to be respected; voters who had migrated to suburbia to invest and live in such havens would not permit structural reforms in government to destroy their dream. Already in the 1930s, academics, journalists, and political leaders were complaining about the multiplicity of governmental units, the overlapping jurisdictions, the lack of coordination in the delivery of services, and the general inefficiency and confusion of suburban government. Something had to be done. But whatever changes were made could not violate the political realities of the bifurcated suburban world.

REFORMING SUBURBAN GOVERNMENT

Responding to the proliferation of both people and governments in emerging suburbia, some policymakers during the 1920s and 1930s began to work for change. As populations doubled and more municipalities and special districts cluttered the map, many leaders believed the structure of government had to adapt. There had to be greater coordination and cooperation among government units and some overarching authority to deal efficiently and effectively with problems common to the entire suburban region. While recognizing the devotion to grass-roots rule in the small municipality, a number of reform-minded individuals suggested the creation or strengthening of broader units of government that could unite the governmentally fragmented fringe.

Oakland County, for example, demonstrated a growing interest in cooperative action. During the 1920s the municipalities of Royal Oak, Huntington Woods, and Pleasant Ridge had formed the North Woodward Association to cooperate in the transmission and storage of water purchased from the city of Detroit. Moreover, in 1927 an amendment to Michigan's constitution authorized the creation of metropolitan districts comprising two or more adjacent municipalities or townships. These districts were empowered to deal not only with water supply but also with sewage disposal and the provision of light, power, and transportation services. In the early 1930s in densely populated southeastern Oakland County a number of municipal leaders seriously considered organizing such a district to administer a proposed multimillion-dollar drain project, and in April 1930 representatives of two townships and six municipalities gathered in the Royal Oak city hall to discuss the matter.[39] At the meeting a state legislator described the "super-municipality" that could be created, but not until 1942 was the Southeastern Oakland County Sewage Disposal System organized to cooperatively handle the sewerage problems of eight municipalities and three townships.[40]

Meanwhile, in 1932 Professor Thomas Reed of the University of Michigan and the National Municipal League conducted a survey of Oakland County's government at the request of some prominent citizens who believed that to discard the "archaic form" of county government "adapted to the horse and buggy era . . . would be the largest possible step towards economy." A nationally renowned expert on local government, Reed concluded: "There are too many municipalities in the south[eastern] corner of the County, suburban to Detroit— too many councils, mayors, managers, and too much general overhead—the taxpayer paying a high price for an 'independence' which means in most instances very little to anyone except the local politicians." Reed's recommendations, however, did not deal with cities and villages but instead urged creation of a single executive to administer county government, the transfer of a number of functions to the county, and the abolition of townships.[41] Expressing the typical view of academic experts of the era, Reed proposed centralization of authority in the larger county unit and the elimination of small units whose continued existence violated all accepted principles of efficient public administration.

Reed expressed his views further at a meeting before one hundred interested citizens in Royal Oak. According to the Royal Oak newspaper, Reed claimed, "Michigan local government, efficient in the days of ox carts and single track dirt roads, have become wasteful and unwieldly in this 1932 age of automobiles." Moreover, the newspaper reported that the "possibility that in the near future the Detroit area must be assembled under one central government was hinted by Dr. Reed." "Citizens of this area may find it advisable to unite parts of Wayne, Macomb and Oakland county under one government," Reed bluntly told his listeners.[42] Needless to say, Reed's prognostications won over few Royal Oak residents to the cause of reform. Reed knew the textbook formulas for governmental efficiency but had little understanding of the suburban commitment to small-scale government in homogeneous communities. The automobile had not made the township or village irrelevant. Instead, the automobile enabled thousands of commuters to escape from the big city of Detroit to the townships and villages of Oakland County, where they found governments more closely approximating their ideals.

Suburbanites were not to accept Reed's radical visions of the future. Yet in Oakland County and elsewhere cooperative action was acceptable if it would reduce the cost and improve the quality of such basic services as water supply and sewage disposal. Suburbanites sought the neighborliness and tranquility of village life but they also wanted the conveniences and comforts of the city. Consequently, they were willing to compromise the absolute independence of their municipalities through intermunicipal contractual agreements or the creation of agencies for coordinated action. In coming decades much of the political debate in suburbia centered around achieving the proper balance between what was deemed desirable cooperation and the much-vaunted separatism of the suburban village ideal.

Elsewhere in the nation the first signs of a new centralization of authority arose that could bring some unity to fragmented suburbia. For example, Du-Page County was assuming some new and unusual powers that seemed to promise a strengthened role for the county in suburban government. As early as 1917 the Forest Preserve District of DuPage County was organized to acquire and maintain a county park system. DuPage was only the second county in Illinois, and the fifth in the nation, to assume responsibility for the creation of a network of parks. Then in 1933 DuPage became the first county in Illinois to adopt a zoning resolution. Two years later DuPage was instrumental in securing a county zoning act from the state legislature.[43] With this state authorization, the county was able to dictate land uses in unincorporated areas and influence the pattern of suburban development in northeastern Illinois.

In 1936 the DuPage County Taxpayers Council, a private reform group, hired a professional consulting firm to recommend further changes in county rule. This firm sharply criticized the twenty-five-member board of supervisors, which exercised both legislative and executive roles, and urged a reduction in the number of such elected officers as sheriff, clerk, auditor, and recorder of deeds. In place of the existing ramshackle framework of government, the consultants proposed "a small board of three or five members, with legislative powers only, and with management centered in a chief executive." Moreover, they urged the abolition of townships, characterizing them as "uneconomical units" adding "to the confusion, complication, and lack of centralized planning and control of government within the county."[44] Thus the consultants echoed Reed's Oakland County report prepared four years earlier. Townships were supposedly obsolete and concentration of executive authority in a single county manager appeared essential to modernized government. DuPage residents were not yet willing to accept such changes, but purported experts and reform-minded citizens believed more rational and centralized administration was necessary if the county were to adapt effectively to suburbanization.

Meanwhile, Californians were pioneering in the expansion of county powers. In 1921 Orange County initiated free library service to residents in unincorporated areas; three years later it began providing public health services throughout the county in both incorporated and unincorporated territory; in 1927 the board of supervisors took charge of the newly created Orange County Flood Control District; and in 1933 a county building department was organized to regulate building practices in unincorporated areas.[45] Both Orange and DuPage Counties were broadening their role as a provider of services, engaging in the operation of libraries, park development, zoning, and building inspection, all responsibilities traditionally associated with municipalities. Though municipalities within the counties retained their authority to provide these same services, the larger unit of the county was expanding its responsibilities and becoming a possible future competitor of the smaller units.

The most marked changes in county government and the pattern of suburban rule, however, took place in Nassau County. Labeled America's fastest-growing county during the 1920s, rapidly suburbanizing Nassau seemed most in need of an overhaul in government. Throughout the 1920s and the first half of the 1930s, the county's leaders and residents struggled with the problem of adapting the governmental framework to the soaring population growth. In the end, they fashioned a new structure that balanced demands for centralization and the deep-seated desire for small-scale, grass-roots rule. Moreover, this new structure would be a model for other suburbanizing counties.

The campaign for change began in 1914 with the organization of the Nassau County Association. A good-government group of concerned citizens, the association investigated the state of local government and concluded that marked reforms were necessary. The association secured state legislative authorization for the appointment of a commission to propose changes in Nassau's governing structure, and the county board of supervisors proceeded to create such a commission and select its members.

In 1918 the commission submitted its final report. Summarizing the criticisms and recommendations heard at public hearings, the report concluded that "there was a unanimous demand for radical changes in the system of government in the towns and the county, and in particular for a greater centralization and responsibility of authority." Centralization of authority and responsibility was, in fact, the chief theme of the report, and the commission members confessed a belief that "as a purely theoretical proposition," incorporating the entire county as a city "would give the county a form of government better suited to its needs than would otherwise be possible under the restrictions of the existing constitution." As a practical matter, however, the commissioners realized that the creation of a city of Nassau would have limited voter appeal, so they suggested less drastic reforms. Yet they still asserted that "the governmental problem confronting the county [had to] be viewed from the broader standpoint of the county as a single municipality." The commissioners contended that "many governmental functions analogous to those exercised by a municipality" could and should be bestowed upon county government.[46] In other words, the commission believed that ideally Nassau's government should be centralized and resemble city government with countywide provision of services. Recognizing the impossibility of this, the commissioners argued that the county's government structure could at least more closely resemble the supposedly proven principles of efficient municipal administration.

Consequently, the report proposed the creation of the office of supervisor at large, comparable to that of mayor. According to the commission, "Political thought and experience have established no principle of municipal government more firmly than that . . . efficient and economical administration . . . requires a single-headed chief executive with adequate power of supervision and control over its finances and over the officers in charge of the various departments."[47] With authority to appoint a broad range of county officials, draft the county budget, and veto measures of the board of supervisors, this supervisor at large would fill the requirement for a strong executive. The commission also proposed shifting some responsibilities from the townships to the county and endowing the county with sole authority over health and welfare functions. It further recommended the creation of a county police force comparable to big-city law enforcement agencies.

The commission's proposals, however, were not implemented at the time, and they certainly offended some county residents. In the subhead of its article on the report, the *New York Times* announced that the reformed structure "Would Govern Long Island County Like Big City." This was a red flag to many of Nassau's citizenry, who had recently escaped from the big city. As one doubter noted, "many of the new settlers of this section have come out here from the city to avoid the high taxes of the metropolis."[48] The commission report of 1918 proposed many reforms that would later be adopted, but the bugaboo of big-city government would continue to be an obstacle in the path of those seeking centralization of authority.

In 1921 New Yorkers approved a state constitutional amendment that permitted Nassau County and suburban Westchester County, north of New York City, to adopt new forms of government. Though the amendment had a winning margin of only 361 votes in Nassau, reform-minded residents soon set to work to realize the proposals of 1918.[49] In April 1922 the board of supervisors appointed a bipartisan commission, chaired by William Pettit, to draft a new county charter. This body generally agreed with its predecessor and proposed the creation of a county president as well as the transfer of health, welfare, and tax assessment duties from the townships and municipalities to the county. Moreover, it recommended the formation of a county police department and a county planning and zoning board to regulate land use in all unincorporated areas. The proposed charter also included certain provisions designed to halt the continued fragmentation of Nassau County into myriad municipalities. Under the new framework of government, a community would not be able to incorporate without first obtaining the consent of the township board. To further limit incorporations, the Pettit commission charter authorized the creation of "village districts," which would be able to provide some services but would remain subject to the control of the township and county authorities. They would offer communities a semblance of village government, but, in fact, they would be districts of the larger units and not independent municipalities.[50]

When the proposed charter was unveiled to the public, it stirred some fears and doubts. Ratification of the charter was a two-step process. First, it was presented to the state legislature for approval, and then it had to win the approval of Nassau's voters in a local referendum. In April 1923, however, just a month after its submission to the legislature, the state representative from the north side of the county announced his opposition to immediate legislative action, claiming that the charter needed further consideration.[51] Others proved hesitant as well and submitted a long list of suggested revisions to the Pettit commission document.[52] Consequently, the county referendum on the charter was postponed until November 1925.

Meanwhile, the leaders of the county's powerful Republican organization turned against the charter, and by the fall of 1925 the chorus of complaints was mounting. County Attorney H. Stewart McKnight led the attacks, which centered on the charter's supposed threat to the much-vaunted "home rule" of municipalities and townships. According to a local newspaper, McKnight claimed that "the charter would mean the surrender by Towns, villages and cities of their inalienable right to local government." Moreover, he raised the familiar specter of annexation to New York City to frighten any undecided Nassau residents into voting no. "If the people adopt this charter," McKnight claimed, "it would be saying to the people of the State, 'we have become so compact that the town, village and city government is antiquated and no longer meets the needs of the county and we must have a central county government.'" Then McKnight asked, "What argument can be advanced to any Legislative Committee of the State—what appeal could we make to stand between us and the City of New York if we say we have no use for local government?"[53] In other words, the only excuse for Nassau County remaining outside New York City was the preference of Nassau's citizenry for decentralized village and township rule. If voters denied this preference, Nassau would have no reason for a continued separate existence.

Defending his handiwork, William Pettit denied that the charter was a sword aimed at the heart of home rule. In a debate with McKnight he presented himself as a staunch supporter of the "beautiful structure of village government." In the charter campaign Pettit further emphasized that the proposed framework would achieve efficiency and economy in government. According to Pettit, centralization of authority would result in more effective administration and less waste of the taxpayers' dollars.[54] It would not hand Nassau over to the grasping big city.

On election day, however, the voters sided with McKnight, defeating the charter by a better than two-to-one margin. Moreover, in each of the three townships, the vote was equally lopsided. Throughout the county, then, the electorate rejected the proposed centralization of authority. The rhetoric of home rule was more appealing. In an election postmortem, a local newspaper recognized the prevailing dread of bigness when it concluded that "there very probably was a fear on the part of the voters that a new great political machine was in the making." It also recognized that before any changes in local government were possible, reformers had to "overcome the nightmare of communities" that they would be forced "to surrender all the asserted privileges of home rule."[55]

The battle of 1925 revealed the problems reformers faced. In suburbia village home rule was a much-valued commodity and voters were not likely to bargain it away in exchange for vague promises of improved administration. If the framework of suburban government was to change and the overarching authority of the county was to be enhanced, proponents of reform would have to tread lightly on the privileges of Nassau's many municipalities and demonstrate clearly to voters that they could have economy and efficiency as well as the small-scale governments they valued. Balance was vital. Suburbanites would not tolerate too much centralization or the total triumph of bigness. For the sake of convenience and lower taxes, they might accept an increased concentration of authority, but the countervailing weight of the village had to be preserved.

Meanwhile, reformers were able to secure some piecemeal change aimed at strengthening the role of the county. For example, in 1925 a county police department was created to patrol unincorporated areas and any villages that chose to avail themselves of the service. By 1934 the department had 459 employees and policed 72 percent of the area of the county and 52 percent of its population, including twenty-six incorporated villages.[56] The larger municipalities retained their own police forces, but a number of recently incorporated miniature villages relied on the new county department. Thus even without charter reform, one element of the proposals of 1918 and 1923 was achieved.

Yet criticisms of the existing structure of rule were mounting and pressure for yet another charter proposal was strong. Among those urging reform was New York's Democratic governor Alfred E. Smith. In a special message to the legislature in 1926, Smith contended that "intelligent people generally agree[d] that the existing forms of government [could not stand] up much longer under the pressure" of suburbanization. Like the proponents of the proposals of 1918 and 1923, Smith urged the creation of a county executive and the centralization of certain functions at the county level.[57] Two years later in a speech before the New York City Bar Association, Smith went even further. "Within the next five years Nassau will have to be a city," Smith told the assembled attorneys. "It cannot stand up. The old form of town government was only good in the sparsely settled sections of the State, but when they commence to build you cannot do it." Speaking of the problems created by the governmental fragmentation of Nassau, Smith declared, "You cannot build a little sewer where this city ends and then have the fellow on the other side of the street without any sewer." In 1930 now former Governor Smith repeated the assertion that Nassau should be incorporated as a city. A Nassau County real estate developer, however, responded to the ex-governor, expressing the suburban viewpoint that Smith ignored. "The people of Nassau County want decentralization rather than the opposite," this developer observed. "The fact that Nassau County is composed of a number of individual villages governed by the residents themselves is one of its strongest selling points."[58] Nassau was thus caught between demands that it become a city and the desire to remain a collection of villages.

Faced with mounting criticisms from state political leaders, in 1932 Nassau countians formed yet another charter committee. Known as the Cuff Committee, after its chairman, Thomas J. Cuff, this supposedly bipartisan committee was too closely linked with the Democratic party to win the favor of many good Republicans and its handiwork was the object of bitter partisan conflict. Like previous proposals, the Cuff charter favored the creation of a county executive and the consolidation of authority at the county level, but it also eliminated representation by township on the county's governing board, recommending instead that board members be elected from seven districts. With their strong township organizations, the Republicans benefited from representation by township and regarded the district proposal as a Democratic grab for power. Moreover, in the minds of some, the districts resembled wards and thus smacked of the big city. The whole charter seemed designed to weaken the traditional townships and make Nassau more like a city.

New York's state legislature approved the Cuff charter, even though one of Nassau's Republican state representatives, Leonard Hall, attacked it as an attempt to introduce "Tammany corruption" into suburbia. The proposed charter, however, also required the approval of Nassau's electorate. The referendum was scheduled for November 1935, and during the weeks prior to the vote Republicans leveled their rhetorical guns at the hated document. One opponent warned that though the charter labeled the "seven sub-divisions of the county unit as districts," they were actually "'wards' in every evil sense that the word implie[d]." This critic claimed that the "proposed wards would develop sectionalism and retard the growth of a county consciousness." "They will fasten future gerrymandered districts upon our county," he continued. "They will breed logrolling, a kind of logrolling that has been notorious for the piling up of public debts."[59] *Logrolling, gerrymander,* and *wards* were all words associated with "dirty" politics, and now the Democrats were supposedly trying to introduce these political viruses and destroy the vitality of townships created by colonial forefathers more than two hundred years earlier. Moreover, the legal counsel for the more recently created village of Plandome concluded that the proposed charter threatened "the home rule taxing power of the villages and would increase the burden of taxpayers residing in villages." According to Republicans, Democrats eager for partisan gain were endangering both the village and the township. Faced with this threat, Russel Sprague cautioned voters, "Don't be stampeded into change for change's sake."[60]

It was hardly surprising when the electorate in the heavily Republican county rejected the Democratic-tainted charter. More than 41,000 Nassau residents cast ballots against the document, whereas 27,000 voted for it. The need for reform was still evident but partisan sentiments helped scuttle yet another charter proposal. A year earlier the *Nassau Daily Review* had concluded, "There is political electricity in the atmosphere whenever either Republicans or Democrats propose a change in county government."[61] The referendum of 1935 proved the truth of this statement.

Rather than appear to be obstinate naysayers opposed to any change, the Republicans had already begun work on their own charter plan prior to the Cuff referendum. In January 1934, the Republican-controlled board of supervisors hired Professor Thomas Reed to survey Nassau County government. In Nassau as in Oakland County, Reed found "the number of villages and districts . . . excessive" and urged efforts "to regulate the formation of new villages and districts and to reduce as far as possible the number . . . existing." Moreover, he believed that as the area developed and attracted more residents, the townships would inevitably "lose ground to the county on the one hand and to the villages on the other." Yet in the end he accepted practical realities and recognized "the necessity for the continued existence" of the townships and villages.[62] In fact, his list of recommendations for change were not radical but instead were familiar to Nassau political leaders. Like past charter committees, Reed favored a county executive and the transfer of all authority over welfare, health, and tax assessment to the county.

Having received the report, in late 1934 the board of supervisors then appointed another charter commission. As chairman of the county board as well as Republican party chieftain, Russel Sprague was the leading figure pushing the GOP into the camp of governmental reform. Sprague realized that reform could improve the quality of government, but he also recognized the partisan necessity for action. "We had to do a real job of getting a good new charter," Sprague declared, "or the Democrats would be back at it again with another of their own and we'd be on our way out."[63] If there was going to be reform, Sprague was dedicated to making sure that it was reform advantageous to the Republicans.

In January 1936 the new charter commission presented its proposed charter to the public. Its provisions followed the recommendations of Thomas Reed and embodied a number of reforms that had appeared in every previous plan. Like its predecessors, the commission proposed an elected county executive to act as chief administrative officer of the county with a qualified veto over the actions of the board of supervisors. A two-thirds majority of the board could override the executive veto. Moreover, the executive was to prepare the annual county budget for submission to the board of supervisors. As had often been suggested, the county would assume full charge of welfare, health, and assessment functions. This meant a shift of some authority from the municipalities and townships. For example, under existing law each of the sixty-five municipalities as well as the three townships either employed or had the authority to employ a health officer to administer each unit's public health services. The charter would eliminate this dispersion of responsibility and concentrate authority in a county board of health. In addition, the proposed charter would abolish township justices of the peace and create a new system of inferior county judges. And the charter authorized the formation of a county planning commission charged with adopting a master plan to guide the physical development of the county. Townships and municipalities retained planning authority, but the county could veto any changes in the zoning of property within three hundred feet of a municipal or township boundary. In other words, the county had authority to regulate boundary areas so that municipalities would not zone their fringes in a manner incompatible with the land use pattern of neighboring cities or villages. One municipality would not be able to locate factories adjacent to another municipality's expensive residences.[64]

Equally significant were the omissions from the proposed charter. It did not include any mention of "village districts" or other novel local units that might be deemed a threat to existing municipalities. One local newspaper reassured its readers, "The proposed new charter does not suggest any tearing down of either the present Towns or Cities nor of the incorporated Villages."[65] Moreover, the townships and cities remained the basis of representation on the county's governing board. There were no districts as in the Democratic plan and nothing reminiscent of big-city wards. Instead, the charter retained the traditional mode of representation, and nothing in it could be deemed to weaken the Republicans' township organizations. In other words, the charter did not threaten the power of the GOP nor endanger the continued existence of the suburban villages.

The commission proposed, then, reform, but not radical reform. It did not assault the local bastions of the Republican party nor did it seriously bruise the suburban ideal of small-scale, grass-roots government. It reflected Russel Sprague's realistic assessment of the problem. According to Sprague, the charter was based on "the theory of the 'two layers' of government." "In the lower layers," Sprague explained, "there were to be retained or preserved to the several communities such as the special districts, villages, two cities and three towns, complete control and power over those functions of government which were closest to them, which they knew the most about and which they genuinely desired to have continued under the authority of their respective inhabitants." This ensured "the preservation of 'home rule' to the separate communities." County government was to constitute the upper layer. "This county governmental layer was to be brought up to date," according to Sprague. "It was to be made businesslike in full sense, designed to meet the needs and demands of a continuously fast-growing population." Whereas the charter preserved the lower layer, it reformed this upper layer so as "to give the greatest number of governmental improvements and services possible for each tax dollar."[66]

Thus the villages and towns, which represented tradition and the antithesis of the big city, were perpetuated at the same time the county was transformed into a governmental dynamo suitable for an up-to-date, rapidly urbanizing area. The charter offered both old and new, small scale and big scale. Moreover, it built upon the traditional roles of the village and county. The villages could remain inward-turning, defensive, and quaint, with village greens reminiscent of the past and exclusionary zoning to guard against an unwanted future. The county, however, was given new strength to confront the harsh realities of growth and dense population.

Sprague admitted that the charter was a compromise, but it was a desirable compromise that could win voter approval. According to Sprague, "experience has indicated that the more comprehensive, ideal or perfect a proposed change of municipal government may be the less is the likelihood of its adoption at the polls."[67] The proposed framework did not offend too many residents nor threaten their interests. Its reforms had been discussed for twenty years and were familiar and thus less frightening. It was, then, a realistic solution.

New York's state legislature approved this carefully balanced document, and a local referendum on the proposal was held in November 1936. During the weeks prior to the election Nassau County's leaders lined up in support of the charter. The Republican party organization mobilized to win ratification, and a long list of local notables added their endorsement.[68] Exploiting once again the long-standing fear of the big city, Sprague urged the charter's "adoption as not only the best document of the kind yet presented but as positive guarantee against future annexation to New York City without consent."[69] The county's Democratic leader, John S. Thorp, predictably opposed the Republican handiwork, attacking the charter as "a tax-eating Frankenstein" that would cause the county to regress into the "twisted maze of antiquated government." Criticizing the continued governmental fragmentation of Nassau County, Thorp argued, "Freezing into organic law all existing governmental units and political subdivisions makes a bad condition worse."[70]

Freezing existing units may have been bad government but it was good politics. On election day Nassau's voters endorsed the Republican compromise by a substantial margin, with 57,000 in favor and 37,000 opposed. The charter passed, however, only because of the better than two-to-one support in the Republican bulwark of Hempstead township. In the two northern townships where wealthy estate owners feared county reassessment of their property, the charter failed to win majority support.[71] Yet the opposition of estate owners was to no avail. After two decades of discussion and debate, the county was to have a new framework of government.

The first executive under the new charter was, predictably enough, Russel Sprague. Elected in 1937, he was to serve five consecutive three-year terms, stepping down at the close of 1952. Under his leadership, authority was highly concentrated, for he was not only county executive but remained unchallenged boss of the Republican organization. He could dictate who served in county and township offices, and Sprague loyalists filled the payrolls at both levels. Sprague's county budgets always passed the board of supervisors without revision, and according to one account, from 1938 to 1948 fewer than ten "no" votes were cast at board meetings. In 1938 a Republican publication proudly boasted that board meetings were "characterized by unanimity of opinion and celerity of action."[72] Ten years later, a journalist reiterated this point when he reported that "controversy [was] absent from the public deliberations of the county board." The *Nassau Review-Standard* likewise testified to the authority of the county's executive, claiming that "clock-like precision and steam-roller effect" characterized government under Sprague. Writing in 1951 of Sprague's uncontested sway, another journalist observed, "The only corporations that are administered as smoothly as Nassau County are dummy corporations." Sprague clearly determined county policy and he brooked no opposition. "Sprague did not take dissent kindly," noted one insider in county politics. "No one disagreed with him and survived."[73]

Thus even though the government of Nassau appeared fragmented, authority was actually highly concentrated in the hands of the dominant party chieftain. During his long tenure as county executive, Sprague personally centralized the government of Nassau. He made a career of warning about the depredations of Democratic bosses in New York City, but he wielded a power that any Tammany politico would have envied.

Sprague, in part, owed his strength to an acute understanding of the political facts of life in suburbia, upon which he fashioned his governmental framework. Suburbanites clung to the village ideal and would fend off any attacks on small, neighborly, homogeneous communities. Yet they wanted the best services at the cheapest prices, so they would compromise for the sake of economy and efficiency. With his two-layer theory, Sprague negotiated the acceptable compromise, and throughout his years in politics he was careful to adhere to the terms of this compromise. Though Democrats continued to claim that Sprague was a force behind the scenes in the politics of some villages, the county executive remained outwardly dedicated to nonpartisan municipal contests and refused to publicly dictate village policy. Moreover, during his years as executive he never attempted to abolish the township governments, and special districts continued to proliferate in number. In 1948 a critic could still complain that there were "eight or ten times as many 'autonomous' units of local government as there [were] movie theatres in the county."[74] Unlike his Democratic foe John Thorp, Sprague realized that the perpetuation of existing governmental units was what the electorate wanted, and attacks on those units were fraught with peril. Similarly, unlike Democratic Governor Smith, he never urged the incorporation of Nassau as a city. Nassau residents sought to escape the city, and anyone interested in winning elections on Long Island had to remember that basic fact. Sprague knew the dreams and fears of his suburban domain, and he fashioned a governmental system to satisfy his constituents and thereby perpetuate the power of his GOP organization.

Moreover, Sprague's creation was to serve as a model for American suburbia. His compromise between centralization and decentralization was to be repeated in fringe areas throughout the nation. Like Sprague, reformers in Oakland, DuPage and elsewhere would seek to balance the suburban village ideal against the need for strengthening the overarching authority of the county. This balance was the key to Sprague's successful formula, and it would remain the preeminent feature of government in suburban and post-suburban areas of the future.

3

The Emerging Post-Suburban Pattern, 1945–1960

In May 1958 the Area Development Council of the Long Island Association sponsored publication of "Long Island Looks to the Future," a twenty-page supplement to the Sunday edition of the *New York Herald Tribune*. This promotional tract was intended to present "the case for Long Island," not only as a place of residence and recreation but as a site for business. Advertisements in the supplement pointed out why any "business or industry [would] profit by a Long Island location," and the lead article lauded "the almost fantastic growth of Long Island's commerce," which made Nassau and Suffolk Counties "just about the most sought-after piece of real estate outside of . . . Manhattan." Yet the boosterish supplement did not neglect traditional suburban advantages, heaping lavish praise on the home life and leisure activities of the two counties. An advertisement for Nassau proclaimed that county "a better place than ever to live, work and play," with "gracious living" as well as great attractions for business. Throughout the supplement the prevailing theme was the advantages of balanced development. According to their promoters, Nassau and Suffolk offered a balance between the traditional suburban virtues of domesticity and leisure and the more urban assets of jobs and profits. "It's Fast-Growing in Industry, and Wonderful for Recreation" announced the headline in one article, and another said of Long Islanders of the late 1950s, "Working Near Home Gives Them More Leisurely Life."[1] An ideal mix of work and leisure was what Nassau and Suffolk purportedly offered.

The *Herald Tribune* supplement of 1958 was, in fact, a proclamation of the revised suburban ideal of the postwar decades. Whereas the theme of escaping to country villages dominated the sales pitch of suburban promoters of the prewar era, by the late 1950s many believed that the ideal suburb had to be more than a haven and refuge. It needed to offer a balanced way of life, including home, recreation, and work. During the decade and a half following World

War II, retailing and manufacturing moved to suburbia as did millions of home buyers, and "Long Island Looks to the Future" not only accepted this wave of commercialization but embraced it enthusiastically. Though still satellites, Nassau and Suffolk seemed on their way to becoming hubs. But unlike the traditional hubs of New York City, Boston, or Chicago, they supposedly would achieve an enviable balance, combining the best of the urban and the suburban. Manufacturing plants would produce handsome tax revenues but not billows of smoke, stores would offer convenience but not foster congestion, and everyone would be able to enjoy their backyard patios just minutes away from their places of work. The ideal of the suburban retreat survived, but by the late 1950s it was increasingly tempered by a belief that commerce and industry were potential friends rather than foes. Through planning and proper development, these urban elements would not destroy suburbia but enhance it.

Just as suburban leaders increasingly sought a balance between home and commerce, so they also continued to struggle for the correct combination of centralized and decentralized rule. During the fifteen years following World War II village governments proliferated along the metropolitan fringe as more communities sought the advantages of municipal autonomy. The ideal of grass-roots rule remained very much alive, and many refugees from the big city valued their small-scale governments as much as they did their crabgrass-free lawns. Both were symbols of the good life on the fringe. But at the same time practical necessity seemed to dictate the creation of some overarching authority to coordinate the mass of suburban polities. Village government remained a key element of the suburban dream but enhanced county authority was deemed necessary to check the forces of fragmentation that threatened to run amuck. Throughout the nation suburbanites were adapting their forms of government and strengthening county rule just as Russel Sprague and his Long Island disciples had done a few decades earlier. In the postwar era these compromises in the structure of government were as much a part of the metropolitan scene as was the emerging compromise between residence and business.

Both the forces of centralization and commerce were, then, compelling suburbanites to deviate from the traditional suburban ideal and to adopt a way of life closer to that of the big city from which they had escaped. Yet the appeal of village rule and the dream of the residential refuge remained powerful, and during the postwar decades commercial promoters and political centralizers could only go so far before angry suburbanites applied the brakes. The result was a delicate balance between suburban and urban, a balance that eventually would become a leading characteristic of the post-suburban world of the late twentieth century. This emerging post-suburban pattern was alien both to the nation's big cities and to the outlying upper-middle-class havens of the prewar era. But as early as the 1950s signs were already indicating the direction of future post-suburban development.

The emerging pattern was so unprecedented that it lacked a name, and in the late 1950s some struggled to apply an appropriate label to the new phenomenon. Recognizing that their retailing hub was neither exactly urban nor suburban, the developers of a giant Long Island shopping center invented the term *co-urban* to describe the novel hybrid. Moreover, they labeled the increasing number of noncommuting suburbanites who lived, worked, and shopped in Nassau and Suffolk Counties as *co-urbanites*. [2] This was a pioneering attempt to name the strange new world on the metropolitan fringe, but the label would not survive. *Technoburb* and *edge city* would eventually supplant *co-urban,* but the shopping center developers were perceptive enough to realize the change that was occurring. Already Nassau, Suffolk, Oakland, and Saint Louis Counties seemed less deserving of the title *suburban.*

CREATING A CO-URBAN AMERICA

The period 1945 to 1960 was the heyday of suburbanization in the United States. Outward migration proceeded at an unprecedented rate, and ranch and split-level dwellings spread across the countryside to house the millions of Americans drawn to suburbia. Magazine articles and books analyzed this centrifugal wave of population, and many commentators derided the bland homogeneity supposedly bred by the new suburban developments and the rape of nature that accompanied the construction of endless rows of outlying homes. In the minds of some observers, suburbanites were a shallow-minded horde of conformists who valued the look-alike tract house, the station wagon, and the television set above all else, and who threatened the very foundations of urban civilization. Millions of Americans, however, viewed the new homes along the metropolitan fringe as a dream come true. For them a three-bedroom house on a quarter-acre lot was not a symbol of decline but a sign of success. It represented the good life. No matter whether one believed suburbia was good or evil, no one could deny that it was attracting an increasing share of the American population. During the postwar era, the metropolitan periphery was clearly assuming a new significance in American society.

This boom is evident in the population figures for Suffolk, Nassau, Oakland, DuPage, Saint Louis, and Orange Counties. As seen in table 3, between 1950 and 1960 Orange County more than tripled in population, Suffolk and DuPage more than doubled, the number of inhabitants in Nassau rose more than 90

TABLE 3. Population and Density of Population, 1950 and 1960

County	1950		1960	
	Population	Population per Square Mile	Population	Population per Square Mile
Suffolk	276,129	299	666,784	723
Nassau	672,765	2,243	1,300,171	4,334
Oakland	396,001	452	690,259	787
DuPage	154,599	467	313,459	947
Saint Louis	406,349	818	703,532	1,416
Orange	216,224	277	703,925	900

Sources: Bureau of the Census, Census of Population, 1950, 1960 (Washington, D.C.: U.S. Government Printing Office, 1952, 1961).

percent, and the rate of increase in Oakland and Saint Louis Counties was better than 70 percent. During the 1950s Nassau surpassed the million mark in population, and by 1960 all but DuPage could claim a population over a half million. With better than four thousand people per square mile, Nassau was as densely populated as many cities, and open space was at a premium in eastern Saint Louis, southeastern Oakland, and northern Orange Counties. At the close of the 1950s mile after mile of housing subdivisions, stores, schools, and factories blanketed each of the counties.

One community after another experienced phenomenal growth rates. In 1951, 55,000 newcomers arrived in the Nassau township of Hempstead, boosting the population about 12 percent in a single year. In 1950 the adjacent township of Oyster Bay had fewer than 67,000 inhabitants, but from 1953 through 1956 it acquired 30,000 new residents annually. The Oakland County city of Oak Park, with 5,200 residents in 1950, tripled in population during the next three years, and a Detroit newspaper observed that "almost overnight thousands of new homes grew like mushrooms after a warm summer rain." Orange County's Anaheim doubled in population from 1950 to January 1955, rising from 14,556 to 30,059, and then doubled once again between January 1955 and December 1956. The booming community claimed to be "the fastest growing city in the fastest growing county in the nation." Nearby Buena Park had welcomed an average of fewer than 100 new residents each year during the first half of the twentieth century; then in the 1950s the annual average soared to 4,000. A plan of the city reported that "almost overnight the farming area was inundated with humanity and an unorganized urban character emerged." The Orange County community of Fullerton was yet another boomtown. In 1955 a local newspaper commented on that city's "amazing growth," reporting a population rise of 31 percent in a single year. "All but the most extreme guesses were exceeded by the preliminary report on Fullerton's current population," the newspaper enthusiastically announced.[3]

Breakneck growth was, indeed, destroying the bucolic past and imposing an increasingly urban character on each of the counties. In 1960 the annual report of the Orange County Planning Commission observed, "The county exceeds eleven states in population and is the fastest growing major county in the nation." "We are growing now at the rate of almost 100,000 people a year!" boasted an Orange County supervisor at the onset of the 1960s. In 1958 a proud Long Island industrialist had said of Nassau and Suffolk Counties, "We have more people than Baltimore, Cleveland, St. Louis, Washington, Boston, San Francisco or Pittsburgh . . . , and there is no indication that we have reached the saturation point." Meanwhile, the *Naperville Clarion,* "DuPage County's Oldest and Best Weekly," was announcing that its home county was the fastest growing in Illinois.[4] In each of these counties, boosters spoke in superlatives about the recent development and future prospects of their communities. Despite continued paeans to a semirural, suburban way of life, explosive growth was the reality that awed and amazed everyone along the metropolitan periphery.

Throughout the postwar years, this awe-inspiring wave of development devoured thousands of acres of farmland, destroying the very meadows and groves that had lured so many to the fringe. From 1950 through 1957, in Oakland County alone forty-five square miles of land were platted, an area twice the size of Manhattan. During the 1950s development consumed an equal amount of land in DuPage, reducing the inventory of agricultural land in that county by 22 percent. Between 1950 and 1954 in rapidly urbanizing Nassau County, the agricultural domain fell from 27,000 acres to 13,000 acres, with farms accounting for less than 7 percent of the county's area by the latter date. In 1958 one commentator predicted, "There probably will be no agriculture on Long Island to speak of by the turn of the century."[5]

The most dramatic monuments to the sweeping transformation of suburbia were the expansive new communities planned and constructed by a single developer which sprang up in a few short years. Not satisfied with a simple housing tract covering a few dozen acres, some developers envisioned the creation of whole new cities of houses, stores, churches, and schools. For example, in 1957 DuPage County builder Jay Stream found himself in a clash with the city of Naperville over plans to lay out a subdivision in that municipality. Naperville's uncooperative city clerk finally asked Stream, "Why don't you go build your own town?"[6] Stream accepted the clerk's challenge and began construction of a whole new community, which he named Carol Stream after his daughter. It was to be an independent municipality with separate zones designated for residential, commercial, and industrial development. Moreover, it would include apartment buildings as well as the typical suburban expanse of single-family housing. In the late 1950s Albert and Jack Kaufman of Surety Builders were likewise planning an entire new community in southern DuPage County, to be known as Woodridge. The first homes went on the market in 1958 and the Kaufmans expected to build three thousand structures housing 10,000 to 12,500 people within the following three years. They did not meet this ambitious goal, but by 1965 the new town could boast of more than 5,000 residents, with the number rising rapidly.[7]

The most spectacular and famous of the instant communities of the postwar decades, however, was Levittown, in Nassau County. Begun in 1947 by Levitt and Sons builders, it was completed four years later when the last nail was pounded into the 17,447th home. By the mid-1950s 82,000 residents inhabited the 7.3-square-mile tract, which only a decade earlier had been an expanse of potato fields. Moreover, the Levitts constructed seven shopping districts and nine swimming pools to satisfy the retailing and recreational needs of the thousands of homeowners.[8] Many commentators criticized the modest look-alike tract homes that the Levitts sold to former apartment dwellers, but most of the purchasers were enthusiastic converts to the new suburban way of life. A refugee from a one-room apartment said of his previous existence: "That was so awful I'd rather not talk about it. Getting into this house was like being emancipated."[9] In 1957 a survey of Levittowners found that 94 percent would recommend the community to their friends.[10]

But Levittown suffered one major flaw that few could ignore. It lacked industry and the tax revenues that industry could provide. Manufacturing plants paid more in property taxes than they cost in services. For residences, however, the opposite was true, especially if the residences housed school-age children. That was the case in Levittown and many similar suburban communities. In 1957 more than half of all Levittowners were under the age of seventeen, and between 1947 and 1957 enrollment in School District Five, which encompassed most of Levittown, rose from 47 students in a three-room schoolhouse to 16,300 pupils in fourteen newly constructed buildings.[11] Thus Levittowners had to support a program of breakneck school expansion, but they had no industry to help pay the cost. Homeowners had to foot the onerous bill alone.

Between 1946 and 1957 the property tax rate in School District Five soared from 28 cents per $100 of assessed valuation to $6.057 per $100. By the latter date the district's rate ranked second among the sixty-two districts in Nassau County. In 1955 one Long Island publication noted, "Many residents who left

New York City because of high taxes, and because they wished to live and raise their families in a suburban atmosphere, are beginning to wonder if they have merely leapt from the frying pan into the fire."[12] Fiery confrontations at annual school budget meetings reflected the tension over high taxes. For example, in May 1957 the District Five meeting erupted into a near riot and its first session was broken up by the fire department, which regarded the disorderly gathering as a fire hazard. When it reconvened three days later, three thousand taxpayers packed the school auditorium and overflowed into the gymnasium. This meeting lasted from 7:30 in the evening to 6:15 the following morning when those present approved the annual budget and a hefty tax hike. This exercise in grass-roots democracy culminated a year of rancor during which charges of Communist influence in the schools added to the already mounting bitterness over the heavy tax burden.[13] In any case, harmony did not prevail in suburbia, and contributing to the dissatisfaction was the lack of industrial taxpayers to relieve the burden of governmental expenses.

The emerging postwar generation of suburban leaders did not ignore the lesson of Levittown. Clearly, the prewar dream of tranquil homesteads far removed from commerce and industry would prove too expensive a proposition for most suburbanites. It was a luxury within the price range of only the wealthiest commuters, who could pay the bills for quaint, semirural municipalities. With a baby boom producing thousands of new pupils for the public schools, a growing number of suburban residents could not afford to snub commerce and industry. Balanced development was increasingly vital if tax levies were to remain reasonable.

Some also favored business development in order to boost job opportunities in the suburbs. Commuting to the central city was costly, inconvenient, and generated mind-boggling traffic jams. Employment close to suburban homes would reduce the number of commuters and further the economic self-sufficiency of the fringe areas. In 1955 the chair of the Long Island State Park Commission Robert Moses urged the creation of jobs in an address on "The Future of Nassau and Western Suffolk." "Suburban industry among other things," Moses predicted, "will reduce the number of commuters in serge and seersucker who spend nights and weekends with families they hardly know. . . . The suburbs will be self-contained units tied in many ways to the Big City, but in other respects completely independent. That is as it should be." That same year the Saint Louis County Planning Commission also promised to "make it possible for the people of St. Louis County to have a proper place of work near their residential area," and by the beginning of the 1960s this same planning body was explaining the need "to shorten the home-to-work trip" so that "the executive and the worker [could] reduce his travel time" and "minimize the daily peak hour capacity of highways and other transportation facilities."[14]

In fact, throughout the 1950s planners and suburban leaders in general were making it clear that manufacturing and commerce had to be part of suburbia; past dreams of isolation from the workplace were no longer tenable. In its 1951 annual report the Saint Louis County Planning Commission observed, "The modern trend is to zone *for* industry rather than *against* industry." According to the commission, "the zoning ordinance of the future should be permissive rather than prohibitive." Three years later "a plan of progress" for the Orange County community of Anaheim noted the need for "an adequate industrial and commercial district" to ensure a "continued balanced economy." In the 1956 "General Development Plan" of the Oakland County city of Clawson, the commission observed that new industry offered "the best prospect of increased tax base. More industry will help achieve a high level of municipal services without a proportionate increase in tax burden for the residential owner. Its benefit will be felt by every taxpayer." In 1957 a Suffolk County real estate broker testified, "New industries, businesses and service organizations are being sought and welcomed by all communities, much with an eye to helping with the tax load." According to an official of nearby Oyster Bay, in Nassau County, that township's comprehensive zoning plan was "designed to accomplish three major objectives: protect homeowners, attract desirable industry, and provide a practical balance among residences, business, and industry." The 1959 plan for the DuPage village of Itasca likewise was dedicated to "securing a balance between residential and non-residential development to strengthen the economic base or source of tax revenue available to provide community facilities."[15]

Even older upper-middle-class residential suburbs, which had developed in the 1920s and 1930s in accord with the prewar ideal, were having second thoughts about excluding business. In 1958 consultants working for the University City Plan Commission in Saint Louis County noted that it had been "the more or less established policy of the city and its inhabitants to preserve the residential character of the municipality and to minimize manufacturing and industrial development." "However, in order for the city to maintain an adequate tax base and at the same time continue as a high-grade residential suburb," the consultants urged, "there should be a carefully worked out plan for limited development of light industry." They told University City residents, "The major consideration favoring an expansion of local industry is the desirability of broadening the local tax base to help maintain public services like schools, water, street improvements, and police and fire protection."[16] Known as the "Gold Coast" of DuPage County, the elite community of Hinsdale had never emphasized business development, but in 1958 that municipality's plan commission also "recommended that a careful study of the economic tax base be undertaken with the intent being to find ways of broadening the base and substantially increasing tax revenues."[17] By the beginning of the 1960s few suburban towns and villages were so affluent that they could ignore their tax base. For the multitude of fringe municipalities the manufacturing plant was a boon, not a bane.

During the postwar years, many suburbanites welcomed industrial tax receipts but still dreaded the appearance of smokestacks on the horizon. Yet certain innovations in industrial planning made manufacturing more palatable to these foes of industrialization. Most notably the concept of the industrial park minimized the clash between traditional suburban ideals and the emerging desire for tax revenues and a balanced economy. Industrial parks were carefully planned, attractively landscaped districts of light manufacturing. In these restricted developments, the design of the industrial plants and the surrounding shrubbery and lawns were intended to dispel the traditional stereotype of the ugly, soot-begrimed factory. The parks were laid out to be as inoffensive as possible to nearby homeowners, and the very use of the term *park* to describe a manufacturing area was a sop to suburban sensibilities. Developers of industrial parks aimed at selling fringe communities on the idea that factories need not pollute the air or threaten residential property values. If masked by shrubbery and separated from residences by landscaped buffer zones, the factory could fit into the revised suburban ideal of the postwar years.

Suburban observers recognized that the industrial park was at least a partial answer to the dilemma confronting them. In 1957 a Suffolk County newspaper editorialized that industrial parks were "likely to meet the least resistance from those who [were] still in opposition to industrialization of this area," and it noted that Islip township was fortunate in having sites for a number of parks that could "offer employment to local people without harming the residential character of the community. The plant being erected on such a site these days—under the rigid restrictions of the town's industrial code—is a far cry from the smokestack factory of yesteryear." That same year a publication of Nassau's Hofstra College observed, "In view of the necessity to diversify Long Island's economy and to achieve a better balance in land uses, the industrial park . . . promises to be a vital contributor in terms of greater employment opportunities and a more equitable sharing of local taxes. One of its chief attractions is that it need not clash aesthetically or otherwise with the existing suburban nature of Long Island's two Eastern Counties."[18] The following year an account of Long Island industry reported that "Nassau and Suffolk Counties

TABLE 4.   Number of Manufacturing Employees, 1947–1963

County	1947	1954	1958	1963
Suffolk	13,213	41,410	32,139	43,507
Nassau	25,725	69,327	79,274	97,613
Oakland	44,566	57,624	47,522	66,528
DuPage	2,863	5,554	7,784	15,655
Saint Louis	10,347	38,544	48,215	68,110
Orange	6,100	15,755	31,161	96,885

Sources: Bureau of the Census, County and City Data Books, 1952, 1962, 1967 (Washington, D.C.: U.S. Government Printing Office, 1953, 1962, 1967).

abound[ed] with these industrial parks," which were designed to "fulfill their vital role in community life without incurring the hostility of neighboring homeowners." A Saint Louis County planning report said much the same thing when it observed, "The use of the industrial park is one of the best methods of meeting the demands of industrial growth and still retaining the amenities of St. Louis County."[19]

Throughout the postwar era industrial parks and landscaped manufacturing plants were increasingly common features of suburbia. Manufacturers needed extensive tracts of land for their expanding plants and sufficient open space was not available in the central cities. Thus a move to the suburbs became imperative. As seen in table 4, between 1947 and 1963 manufacturing employment rose markedly in each of the six counties along the metropolitan fringe. The number of industrial employees soared sixteenfold in Orange County, almost sevenfold in Saint Louis County, and better than fivefold in DuPage. In four of the six counties the rate of increase in industrial employment was considerably greater than the rate of population increase, and in Suffolk County the two figures were approximately equal.

Only in Oakland County did the growth in manufacturing employment lag behind population growth. Because of the concentration of motor vehicle manufacturing in Pontiac, Oakland began the postwar era with a strong industrial base, which grew erratically during the following two decades, rising and falling with the fortunes of the American automobile industry. Yet the industrial growth of Oakland County far outpaced that of the Detroit metropolitan area as a whole, with the number of manufacturing employees in Oakland rising more than 12 percent between December 1956 and March 1963, whereas the number of such workers declined 20 percent in the metropolitan area.[20] Moreover, despite the ill fortunes of a recession-plagued auto industry, manufacturing employment rapidly increased in the suburban areas of Oakland outside of Pontiac. By 1958 more production workers were employed in the emerging suburban townships and municipalities of Oakland than in the city of Pontiac.[21] While the older industrial hub of Pontiac lost plants, other communities attracted them. For example, in 1954 the Ford Tractor Division moved to the upper-middle-class residential community of Birmingham, and four years later Ford opened a giant Lincoln-Thunderbird plant, employing 3,000 persons, in rural Wixom.[22]

In other suburban areas federal defense spending boosted the emerging industrial economy. The chief element of Long Island's manufacturing sector was the aircraft industry, which first boomed during World War II, suddenly transforming Nassau and Suffolk into major arsenals. Led by Republic Aviation, Grumman Aircraft, and Sperry Gyroscope, federal defense contractors remained the mainstay of manufacturing in the Long Island counties, and Suffolk residents were especially vulnerable to fluctuations in cold war military spending.[23] Saint Louis County was the home of the giant McDonnell Aircraft Company, which was the largest of the growing number of industries developing around Lambert Field, the metropolitan area's principal airport. Orange County similarly benefited from the aerospace boom. In 1951 Northrop Corporation's electronics division moved to Anaheim, and six years later Hughes aircraft located its ground systems division in the Orange County community of Fullerton. Moreover, local leaders realized that this was only the beginning. According to an Anaheim planning report of 1957, "Most of those engaged in electronics anticipate a very large scale expansion in the next five to ten years." Their anticipations proved correct, for employment in the electronics industry in Orange County soared from 11,000 in 1957 to 42,000 in 1964.[24]

By the early 1960s, then, the so-called suburbs were becoming hubs of industrial development. In 1961 one Long Island booster proudly observed that more people worked in the two thousand manufacturing plants of Nassau and Suffolk Counties than "in the industries of eighteen of our states." As early as 1955 Saint Louis County planners were already pointing out that their county was no longer simply "the living room for the metropolitan area or the dormitory community." Instead, during the previous decade there had been "a dispersion of industrial location within St. Louis County warranting complete restudy of traffic and transportation, public utility services, public works facilities, etc."[25] A commercial revolution was sweeping across the cluster of residential havens on the fringe, and commentators in New York, Missouri, and elsewhere recognized that suburbia would never be the same again.

Another manifestation of that commercial revolution was the growth of retailing along the metropolitan periphery. In each of the six counties retail sales figures soared as suburbia captured a larger share of the metropolitan area shoppers. In 1948 the total value of retail sales in the city of Saint Louis was about four times as great as the figure for Saint Louis County; fifteen years later the county almost equaled the city in cash value of sales. During the late 1940s Nassau County ranked seventh among New York counties in retail sales; by the early 1960s it had moved into third position even though it ranked only fifth in population.[26] By 1960 Oakland County was grabbing more than its proportionate share of sales in the Detroit metropolitan area. In 1950, with 13.1 percent of the metropolitan population, Oakland accounted for 10.8 percent of retail sales, but ten years later, with 18.4 percent of the area's inhabitants, it garnered 19.9 percent of the retail dollars spent.[27]

The most obvious physical monument to this retailing boom was the suburban shopping center. Oakland County was in the forefront of shopping center development, and its Northland Center in Southfield won nationwide attention. Built by the J. L. Hudson Company, Detroit's largest department store, Northland opened in 1954, offering shoppers nearly 1.5 million square feet of retailing space plus parking for 9,500 cars. A three-story Hudson's store ringed by ninety-five smaller shops attracted thousands of customers, and from its beginning the center's developers envisioned Northland as a magnet for further commercial investment and as the hub of a new suburban downtown.[28] One publication from the 1950s accurately described Northland as "a regional shopping center that transplant[ed] downtown to the suburbs." Moreover, local boosters recognized that the complex offered Southfield the advantages of a big city. In 1959 the city manager observed proudly of Northland, "It's got more shopping area than downtown Flint, and more parking space than downtown Grand Rapids."[29]

The center also proved a boon to the Southfield city treasury, accounting for 16.45 percent of the community's assessed valuation in 1959. In large part because of the giant shopping complex, the city of 30,000 residents enjoyed a considerably lower tax rate than many of its neighboring municipalities. Other Oakland communities attracted retailing investment as well, with ten additional shopping centers opening in the county from 1954 through 1959.[30] But none rivaled Northland Center.

Nassau County's premier shopping center, Roosevelt Field, opened in 1956. With a 300,000-square-foot branch of Macy's department store, 77 other retail outlets, and 11,000 parking spaces, Roosevelt Field matched Northland Center as a retailing complex. The developers of the Nassau shopping complex also laid out an adjacent industrial and office zone, making Roosevelt Field, like Northland Center, a multipurpose business hub.[31] Moreover, the same year that Roosevelt Field opened, twenty-two additional shopping centers were built in booming Nassau County. The largest of them were Mid-Island Center in Hicksville and Green Acres Shopping Center in Valley Stream, which together with Roosevelt Field attracted a multitude of shoppers who formerly had commuted to New York City for the purchase of clothing and accessories.[32]

Saint Louis County experienced a similar rise in retailing. In 1948 the Famous-Barr department store pioneered a policy of decentralization when it opened a branch in the county seat of Clayton. Famous-Barr had expected annual sales of $3 million, but in its first year the suburban branch produced $10 million instead.[33] Such figures were a green light to other Saint Louis retailers. It was obviously time to move to the suburbs. In 1955 Westroads Shopping Center opened in Richmond Heights, two years later Crestwood Plaza in Crestwood welcomed its first customers, and by 1961 the county could boast of four shopping centers of more than 350,000 square feet.[34]

Besides factories and shopping centers, Orange County benefited from yet another form of commercial endeavor, the theme park. In 1954 Walt Disney Company purchased a tract of orange groves in Anaheim and the following year Disneyland opened to visitors, bringing nationwide fame to the previously obscure municipality in northern Orange County. "On opening day," reported *Life* magazine, "a mob of small and large fry started lining up at 2 A.M., eight hours before the turnstiles began clicking." Within its first six months the theme park drew one million customers, and by the late 1950s it was being touted as "the biggest tourist attraction in California and the West, among the biggest in the nation." In 1959 Disneyland employed 3,650 workers and surrounding hotels and restaurants provided jobs for additional Orange County residents. Moreover, for the city officials of Anaheim the theme park was a source of more than amusement, paying an average of over $1 million annually in local taxes during its first twenty years.[35] Though not as spectacular an attraction as Disneyland, Knotts Berry Farm in nearby Buena Park proved another magnet for tourists and a lucrative source of tax receipts.

With nationally famous attractions drawing millions of tourists, an ever-growing number of shopping centers, thousands of retail and manufacturing employees, burgeoning industrial parks, and endless rows of freshly minted tract houses, suburbia no longer seemed so much like suburbia. Little wonder that observers were already attempting to coin a new word for the phenomenon they witnessed. Roosevelt Field did seem more "co-urban" than suburban; it was more of a competitor of the central city than a subordinate. It was not urban nor did it conform to the traditional suburban ideal. It would have been equally out of place in the mock English country villages of the prewar realtors' dreams and in midtown Manhattan or downtown Chicago.

The signs of the "co-urban" world were omnipresent by the late 1950s. Traffic reminiscent of the big city clogged suburban highways, bringing expletives to the lips of harried drivers. In 1957 in the previously tranquil Suffolk County village of Port Jefferson, the local newspaper reported that traffic was "one of [the] port area's most serious problems," and a planning committee said of the traffic tangle, "If strong steps are not taken at this time, . . . the existing shopping areas in Port Jefferson and Port Jefferson Station will decline." That same year an industrial survey of Long Island reported that "a critical transportation problem [was] now in existence. . . . The traffic problem is a deterrent to industrial expansion and other desirable land use." Urbanlike congestion also emerged as the number of multifamily dwellings increased. Whereas the number of single-family dwellings constructed in Nassau County fell from approximately 30,000 in 1950 to 6,800 in 1959, the number of new units in multifamily structures rose from 1,600 in 1950 to over 2,600 in the last year of the decade. From 1951 through 1953 an average of 254 multifamily dwelling units were built in Saint Louis County but the figure for 1958 through 1960 was 1,271. The rate of construction for single-family structures, however, remained relatively constant. In DuPage County the same phenomenon prevailed, with apartment buildings arising in communities previously dominated by single-family tract homes.[36]

Moreover, a growing share of the population was spending both night and day in suburbia. Writing of Nassau and Suffolk Counties, the *New York Times* observed that "before the war commuters exceeded those locally employed by better than 3 to 2" but in the postwar era the proportion had been reversed. "Local employment now provides jobs for 335,000 persons," the *Times* reported in 1957, "while 175,000 persons are commuters." Indeed, by the late 1950s reverse commuting from New York City to Nassau and Suffolk was an increasingly significant fact of metropolitan life. A survey in 1958 found 64,300 persons commuting outward each workday from homes in New York City to jobs in suburban Long Island.[37]

According to the federal census of 1960, in Suffolk, Nassau, Oakland, and Orange Counties a majority of those residents reporting their place of employment worked within their home counties. With 73 percent and 68 percent respectively, Orange and Suffolk Counties led in the proportion of noncommuting residents. Only in DuPage and Saint Louis Counties did commuters still constitute a majority of the working population, and even there more than four of every ten employed residents earned their living within the counties.[38]

These signs of change did not mean that suburbanites were yielding to the onslaught of urbanization without complaint or reservation. During the postwar era they remained staunchly dedicated to suburban ideals, though many realized the need to adjust and adapt these ideals. For example, in the 1950s Garden City residents fought to modify plans for the Roosevelt Field complex on the eastern edge of their village. They forced the developers to provide a seventy-foot landscaped buffer strip between the development and village residences. Moreover, the village forbid brightly lit signs in the portion of Roosevelt Field that lay within Garden City's boundaries, and on this tract the developers could build only office structures of no more than three stories. Writing of the compromise, a local chronicler concluded, "Garden City, although still sensitive to the situation, was becoming increasingly aware as time went on that there had been no satisfactory alternative." Likewise, in 1958 in the Oakland County residential suburb of Pleasant Ridge, city officials would agree to the sale of municipal property along a major commercial thoroughfare only if the land was used for "professional and administrative offices."[39] Drive-ins, gas stations, and strip shopping outlets were not welcome in Pleasant Ridge. Garden City and Pleasant Ridge sought to remain as gardenlike and pleasant as possible, but they would adjust enough to new realities to allow properly designed office blocks buffered by tasteful landscaping. The protected residential refuge remained very much a part of the suburban ideal, but an increasing number of communities would tolerate an occasional office building and some taxpaying commerce.

By 1960, then, many suburban leaders sought the best of both the urban and the suburban. They continued to laud the green open spaces of suburbia and the merits of the single-family home in a carefully restricted subdivision. But at the same time, commerce was moving outward from the central city and offering the tempting advantages of tax revenues and jobs. Southfield, Michigan, was to become an archetypical edge city and perhaps better than anyone else, its city manager summed up the emerging amalgam of goals that underlay much suburban development by the beginning of the 1960s. In 1959 he boasted, "Give us 15 years, and we'll be the biggest city in Oakland County." But in the same interview he said of his community, "That's what makes this such a wonderful place to live—the openness and greenness. There's no asphalt jungle in Southfield. We don't want to carry this 'togetherness' stuff to extremes."[40] Southfield's leaders would not eschew growth nor would they block development. Commerce paid the municipality's bills and another Northland Center was always welcome to the city treasurer. But openness and greenness had to be preserved, and suburbanites did not want a community where residents lived on top of one another. The emerging pattern was one that embraced traditional suburban ideals but tempered them with new realities. Eventually

TABLE 5. Number of Municipalities, 1940–1960

County	1940	1950	1960
Suffolk	27	27	27
Nassau	65	65	65
Oakland	24	25	38
DuPage	18	18	28
Saint Louis	41	84	98
Orange	13	13	22

Sources: Bureau of the Census, Census of 1940, 1950, 1960 (Washington, D.C.: U.S. Government Printing Office, 1942, 1952, 1961).

this delicate balance of openness and development and commerce and residence would produce the post-suburban world of the late twentieth century.

PROLIFERATING MUNICIPALITIES

During the 1940s and 1950s suburbia proved almost as fertile a field for the growth of new governments as it was for new shopping centers. The proliferation of governmental units evident in the prewar era continued, arousing consternation among those who thought there were already too many municipalities along the metropolitan fringe. As seen in table 5, the number of municipalities increased markedly in four of the outlying counties. Saint Louis gave birth to an especially large brood of village and city governments, with the number rising 140 percent between 1940 and 1960. From 1945 through 1950, the rate of production reached an extraordinary peak, with the incorporation of forty-two new municipalities in the Missouri county during this six-year span. Political fragmentation did not proceed at such an explosive pace in Oakland, DuPage and Orange Counties, but still the number of municipalities was on the rise.

Owing to a change in New York state law in the 1930s, township governments and special districts acquired new authority to provide local services that previously were the responsibility of villages and cities. Consequently, incorporation was no longer such an attractive option for residents of Nassau and Suffolk Counties, and the number of Long Island municipalities remained unchanged between 1940 and 1960.[41] Yet devotion to small-scale governmental units did not wane and was expressed in the multitude of new special districts created in those counties. From 1945 to 1955 the number of nonschool special districts in Nassau County climbed from 199 to 268, and in Suffolk between 1950 and 1960 the figure soared from 246 to 407.[42] Some of these were administered by the township governments and were primarily taxing districts with no independent governing boards. But all of Nassau's 41 fire districts and all of the 110 fire districts in Suffolk County had separate boards of commissioners elected by the voters of the districts.[43] In most of these districts the grass-roots tradition of volunteer fire companies survived as suburbanites rejected not only bigness but also the impersonal paid professionals associated with urban administration. Though the county was approaching a population of one million, in the mid 1950s most of Nassau still relied on protection from seventy volunteer companies composed of nine thousand men.[44]

The proliferation of governmental units along the metropolitan fringe was, in large measure, a product of the persistent desire to protect the village life style as well as the growing competition for lucrative tax sources. Fondness for the restricted village remained a powerful sentiment in suburbia, spawning scores of new independent municipalities. From New York to California, the long-standing goal of keeping offensive influences at bay motivated many postwar community leaders to opt for the protection that incorporation afforded. Yet the desire to grab or preserve revenue sources was another common motivating factor of incorporation battles. Homeowners in unincorporated areas did not wish to lose commercial mother lodes to tax-hungry adjacent municipalities eager to annex shopping centers or factories, and the only way to keep the tax receipts for their own use was to incorporate. Most suburbanites wanted to retain the advantages of the prewar residential suburbs, but many also sought the revenues that postwar commercialization produced. These dual factors fueled the many incorporation free-for-alls of the 1940s and 1950s.

Nowhere was the complex mix of motives so evident as in Southfield Township in southern Oakland County, where a battle over the creation of governments rocked local politics for most of the 1950s. On the one hand, some parts of the township wanted the semirural peace and charm associated with the prewar ideal. But on the other hand, the creation of Northland Center and other commercial resources led to attempted tax grabs by nearby municipalities and to incorporation efforts aimed at thwarting these grabs. It was a clash with many combatants, and it led to the partition of the township into multiple municipalities designed to serve different needs.

The battle over partition of the township began in December 1950 with a conflict between those who favored incorporation of the entire township and those who wished to incorporate as a separate municipality one segment of the township known as Lathrup Village. Lathrup Village was a thousand-acre subdivision laid out in the 1920s by Louise Lathrup Kelley. It was a carefully planned and restricted residential community; all homes had to be constructed of stone, brick, or masonry, with an attached garage. There were few businesses and no factories within the community, and Kelley and many village residents wanted to keep it that way.[45] "During the work day, a lot of us are in direct contact with big business, modern improvements, the hustle and bustle that makes big wheels go round," explained one advocate of incorporation. "When we come home, we like to be removed from all the hub-bub and pressure of getting big things done in a hurry. The desire is for relaxation in a quiet, friendly, rural village atmosphere." One townshipwide municipality would destroy this, for, according to a Lathrup leader, "within 10 years of normal development, its entire area will become a closely built up community with city improvements and a big-city atmosphere." Advocates of municipal autonomy sought to keep their "small community as an informal, friendly village with the minimum of government, with the minimum of officials, and with the minimum of big business."[46]

To ensure this goal, Lathrup Villagers gathered signatures on incorporation petitions and rushed to the county courthouse in Pontiac to file their documents before their foes working for townshipwide incorporation could file conflicting petitions. The Lathrup Villagers won the race by twenty minutes. When the Southfield Township forces arrived with completed petitions, they met Louise Lathrup Kelley's husband coming out of the courthouse, where he had just deposited his community's documents.[47] The county considered incorporation petitions in order of submission, so it gave the Lathrup request priority and authorized an election in the village to determine whether a majority of the voters approved municipal status. After some delay, in May 1953 the community's electorate endorsed incorporation, distancing themselves from Southfield Township and the forces of high-powered development it seemed to represent.[48]

By spring 1953 the situation was becoming more complex in the remainder of Southfield Township, for the completion of Northland Center was imminent and other commercial projects were anticipated. Rather than seeking to escape this commercialization, some tax-poor communities sought to embrace it through the incorporation or annexation of the area surrounding the shopping hub. The city of Oak Park, to the east of Southfield Township, began circulating petitions for the annexation of a two-and-a-half-square-mile block of land that included Northland Center.[49] Meanwhile, residents of the Magnolia and Southfield Park subdivisions organized the Southfield Citizens' League, which collected signatures on petitions to incorporate the southern part of the township, including the shopping center, as a separate municipality.[50] And Southfield Township officials still hoped to incorporate the entire township, excepting Lathrup Village, as a city. A township supervisor complained: "We don't want our township broken up into small pieces. Most of them will not have a stable tax base that way." To make matters more confusing, the city of Berkley contemplated annexation of a tract of east-central Southfield Township. "The time is now right for an attempt at annexation," explained the president of the Berkley Chamber of Commerce.[51]

As in the Lathrup Village contest, time was of the essence, for the first petition filed took precedence. When the county courthouse opened at 9:00 A.M. on May 14, 1953, the leaders of the Southfield Citizens' League presented their petitions. The county clerk, however, refused the documents since the league did not have the $500 filing fee. The league then launched an hour-long telephone campaign to raise the money, but at 9:25 A.M. the city manager of Oak Park presented his annexation petitions to the clerk, thus beating the Citizens' League by better than a half hour.[52] Oak Park's prompt action failed ultimately to produce the desired treasure trove of taxes, for in September 1953 voters rejected the Oak Park annexation bid, leaving Northland Center in unincorporated Southfield Township.[53]

Meanwhile, the annexation and incorporation attempts were frightening residents in the northern part of the township into action. The community of Franklin valued its quaint semirural environment and its large, uncrowded lots. Its principal developer George Wellington Smith had, in fact, advertised the community as "the town that time forgot."[54] Smith and his affluent lot purchasers wanted the town to remain forgotten to all but the wealthy few who could afford solid-gold charm and serenity. They certainly did not want it discovered as a possible site for shopping centers or manufacturing plants. Consequently, Franklin residents sought the zoning protection afforded by municipal autonomy, and in November 1953 the local citizenry voted by a three-to-one margin to incorporate their village.[55] The preamble of the village charter read, "We, the residents of Franklin, . . . wishing to preserve our simple, rural way of life and the identity of historic Franklin; do hereby ordain and establish this Village of Franklin Charter."[56] "A simple, rural way of life" remained the ideal of the General Motors and Ford executives whose homes sprawled across Franklin and who could afford to eschew tax-producing commerce.

Other communities in northern Southfield Township soon followed Franklin's example. The adjoining community of Bingham Farms filed for incorporation in January 1955 and in June its voters approved the creation of the new municipality. As its name implied, Bingham Farms enjoyed a rural ambiance, which its residents sought to preserve. "What it lacks in size," observed a 1970 account of the village, "it more than makes up in scenic splendor." It was a community with "large tracts of rolling land with beautiful trees," and its residences were "all characterized by a quiet, understated elegance." Like its Franklin counterpart, the Bingham Farms charter spoke of preserving a "simple rural way of life," and to that end the residents sought their independence from the remainder of Southfield Township.[57]

By the close of 1958 the partitioning of the thirty-six-square-mile township was complete. Fearful that Southfield authorities would allow excessive commercialization and dense development, the northern community of Beverly Hills opted for separate incorporation in April 1958, after having repeatedly thwarted the efforts of Southfield leaders to create a municipality that included both Beverly Hills and the remainder of Southfield.[58] With all of the northern Southfield communities having declared their independence, the southern two-thirds could now proceed to incorporate as the city of Southfield.[59] Following the creation of the municipalities of Lathrup Village, Franklin, Bingham Farms, Beverly Hills, and Southfield, only a minuscule 117 acres remained outside any municipal boundaries and subject to the control of the township government.[60] Thus what had formerly been a single governmental entity now included five independent municipalities plus a small remnant governed by the township.

The balkanization of Southfield was not unique. In Farmington Township, immediately to the west of Southfield, incorporation conflicts dominated local politics during the late 1950s. In 1958 the city of Farmington attempted to annex approximately eight square miles of surrounding Farmington Township and thereby broaden its industrial tax base through absorption of prospective factory sites and capture of the township's largest taxpayer and chief manufacturing plant, the Star Cutter Company. City officials argued that the municipality "desperately need[ed] new undeveloped land areas into which it [could] expand and grow" and the "well-planned development of the surrounding area [would] provide additional industrial commercial growth to help carry the tax burden and pay for . . . schools."[61] Residents of the township responded with a number of defensive incorporation attempts. An area of estate-size lots quickly chose to incorporate as the village of Quakertown, thus preserving its "simple rural way of life."[62] A large section of the township also petitioned to become the municipality of Farmington Woods, and incorporation proceedings simultaneously began in another area known as Clarenceville. The backers of the Farmington Woods proposal claimed that they sought incorporation to preserve the "residential-rural" nature of the area.[63] Those who wished to perpetuate township control of the territory, however, attacked the proposed "city" of Farmington Woods and asserted that continued township rule would ensure "preservation of the suburban character of [the] community, [and] freedom from

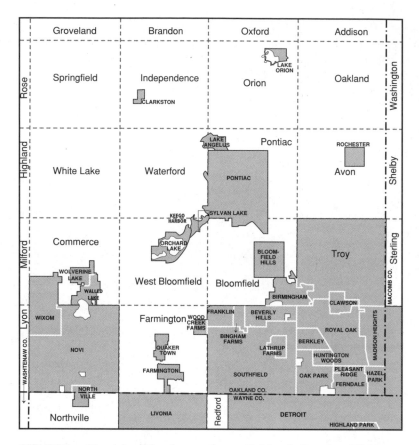

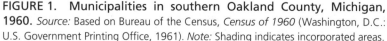

FIGURE 1.   Municipalities in southern Oakland County, Michigan, 1960. *Source:* Based on Bureau of the Census, *Census of 1960* (Washington, D.C.: U.S. Government Printing Office, 1961). *Note:* Shading indicates incorporated areas.

exorbitant taxes, overcrowded schools, city noise, and numerous other detrimental factors." After much debate, in August 1958 voters defeated the city of Farmington's annexation attempt, and in November the incorporation proposals for Farmington Hills and Clarenceville likewise both failed to win the endorsement of the electorate.[64] Consequently, most of Farmington Township remained unincorporated, but the battle over municipal status would resume in later years.

To the west, in Novi Township, the grab for tax resources was similarly stirring conflict. In 1957 Ford Motor Company opened a giant plant in the northern part of the township and the unincorporated village of Wixom suddenly opted to become a municipality, with boundaries that included the lucrative factory. Novi Township challenged the incorporation in the courts but lost. Meanwhile, the municipality of Northville expanded into the southern section of the township, annexing a tract of potentially tax-rich territory. Aroused by the dangers of an eroding tax base, the remaining township chose to incorporate in 1958, thus opting for municipal autonomy before any further marauders could deprive it of land.[65]

Throughout Oakland County the story was the same. In 1955 a remnant of Royal Oak Township chose to incorporate as the city of Madison Heights because its residents feared loss of their tax resources through annexation raids. Speaking of adjoining communities, one advocate of incorporation noted, "They will grab all the valuable tax land, leaving the township without any major industrial areas to balance the tax rate."[66] That same year the city of Troy incorporated because of a similar fear that its Oakland neighbors would slice off the most lucrative tracts and leave Troy residents devoid of revenue.[67] Some residents wanted restricted rural charm and beauty with no commerce or tract housing. Others wanted shopping centers and factories to pay the municipal bills. Both goals, however, produced the same effect—a proliferation of new governmental units.

Moreover, the Oakland scenario was repeated elsewhere. Throughout the nation defensive suburbanites chose to create new municipalities. In 1956 in DuPage County, the community of Lisle incorporated not only to secure better streets and drainage but also, according to a local newspaper, to ensure the "protection of local zoning laws and a local building code." Referring to the campaign for incorporation, the newspaper reported, "Proponents pointed out that the village will be able to enforce a more strict building code which would curb slum-like development."[68]

Meanwhile, in Orange County dairy farmers were creating municipalities to protect their businesses from encroaching residential and commercial development. In 1955 agriculturalists in the northeastern section of the county feared annexation to the city of Buena Park and in defense incorporated the two-square-mile city of Dairyland. If Buena Park had absorbed the farms of Dairyland, its city council would have zoned the malodorous, fly-ridden cow barns out of business. But the rulers of the new municipality zoned its entire territory for "heavy agriculture," allowing the farmers to milk their Holsteins in peace. At the time of its incorporation that city was reported to have "a population of 600 people and about 60,000 cows," and appropriately, the municipal council adopted as the city motto, "United to Preserve."[69]

In fall 1955 Buena Park's threatened annexation of a wedge of land in the

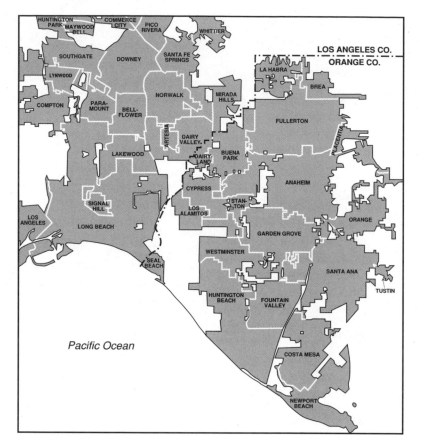

FIGURE 2. Municipalities in northern Orange County, California, 1960. *Source:* Based on Bureau of the Census, *Census of 1960* (Washington, D.C.: U.S. Government Printing Office, 1961). *Note:* Shading indicates incorporated areas.

heart of the unincorporated community of Cypress inspired additional incorporation campaigns. The southern dairy farming section of Cypress considered incorporating separately as Dairy City and much of the remainder petitioned to become the city of Cypress. Moreover, some residents actually supported annexation to Buena Park and circulated petitions in favor of that option.[70] The *Fullerton News Tribune* reported that "a state of confusion reign[ed]" in Cypress as local residents did not know whether they were about to become residents of the cities of Dairy City, Cypress, or Buena Park or remain in unincorporated Orange County. Finally in 1956 the area incorporated as Dairy City, but residents quickly changed the name to Cypress. According to a county newspaper, many incorporation advocates opposed the name "Dairy City" because "they wanted to avoid the implication that the new city would be reserved primarily for cows."[71] Yet during its early years Cypress, like Dairyland, was primarily a "cowtown" sympathetic to agricultural interests.[72] Thus, in California as elsewhere, incorporation proved a handy device for anyone wishing to thwart potential foes. It protected the herdsmen of Orange County and those fearful of "slum-like" development in DuPage County as well as the country gentlemen and anxious taxpayers of Oakland County.

In Saint Louis County this protective device was carried to extremes. Under Missouri law, municipalities could annex unincorporated territory without the approval of the voters in the area to be absorbed. Consequently, about the only way to halt annexation to an adjoining municipality was through incorporation, and this legal fact of life was responsible for the extraordinary municipal birthrate in Saint Louis County during the 1940s and early 1950s. To protect themselves, residents of the most miniature communities opted for independent municipal status. In 1946 residents of a tract of only eleven acres chose to incorporate as the village of MacKenzie, and by 1951 twenty-six of the county's municipalities had areas of fewer than one hundred acres.[73]

Midget municipalities were especially numerous in the northern half of the county, leading to mind-boggling confusion. In 1950 the municipalities of Wellston, Bel-Nor, and Hanley Hills all filed petitions to annex the same territory, but meanwhile residents of the disputed tract submitted incorporation papers to the county court seeking to create the independent municipality of Greendale. That same year Wellston and Hanley Hills also attempted to annex land that was incorporated as the city of Pagedale. Writing of the confusing spectacle, the Wellston newspaper observed: "It appears that someone eventually will have to get around to unscrambling it. . . . And if everybody gets incorporated, a map maker who tries to make a map of each town in a different color is going to run out of colors."[74]

Wellston's editor was not the only one to criticize the political melee among existing and prospective municipalities. During the 1950s one commentator after another attacked the division of suburbia into an ever-increasing number of government units, emphasizing the inefficiency and conflict resulting from such fragmentation. In 1952 the Saint Louis County Planning Commission published a report titled *Let's Get Together,* presenting "the advantages of an integrated community." "Even long-time residents of St. Louis County are confused by [the] jigsaw puzzle of numerous incorporated areas," the report observed. "There are cities within cities and boundaries as irregular as lightning streaks." According to the county planners, "We are facing disintegration as a

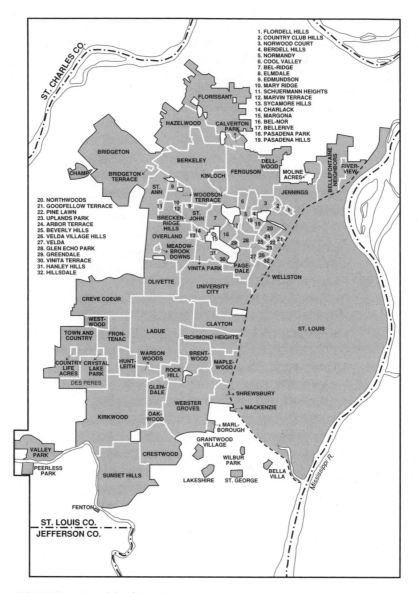

FIGURE 3.   Municipalities in western Saint Louis metropolitan area, 1960. *Source:* Based on Bureau of the Census, *Census of 1960* (Washington, D.C.: U.S. Government Printing Office, 1961). *Note:* Shading indicates incorporated areas.

county community unless we can work together." A few years later the county planning commission reiterated its conclusion, warning that the "trend toward a multiplicity of incorporated areas" could "lead to waste and administrative and political chaos."[75] In 1958 a report on "the proposed consolidation of the municipalities of Ladue, Frontenac, and Huntleigh Village" also referred to "the multiplicity of municipal governments" as "one of the most serious problems of St. Louis County." Urging union of the municipalities, the report concluded, "Residents of the three communities, by consolidating, would form a government better able to provide efficiently and economically the municipal services they need and want."[76]

Long Islanders were hearing many of the same arguments. In 1959 a political scientist attacked the "jungle of governments" in Nassau and Suffolk Counties, claiming that Long Island residents had created a governmental "jig-saw puzzle of such complexity that coordination . . . [was] impossible to accomplish."[77] The situation was especially confusing in Suffolk County, where quite literally no one knew where some of the multiplicity of special districts began or ended. "Many of these districts have never been mapped," a survey of Suffolk reported in the early 1960s. "In fact, two towns[hips] have neither maps nor written descriptions for 20 per cent of the districts."[78] Local government in Suffolk County thus remained uncharted, its boundaries and limits as yet unknown to cartographers.

In Michigan and California, too, fragmentation was a dirty word among friends of good government. Some Oakland County leaders sought to exploit fears of fragmentation to win support for incorporation of townshipwide municipalities. For example, in 1957 the threat of fragmentation led to a campaign to incorporate all of Waterford Township. "I feel that something has got to be done to hold the township together," observed one resident. "If incorporation is the answer, then I'm all for it." A 1958 study of local government in Southern California found that "the pattern of confusion, duplication, and overlapping units" was most evident in Los Angeles County but reported that Orange County was "on the threshold of a similar expansion in numbers and types of governments."[79] Alert to the problem, California's governor Edmund Brown in 1959 charged a commission to find answers to the questions, "Do we have too many overlapping jurisdictions?" and "What is the danger point in proliferation of local government?"[80]

Everywhere people were questioning the proliferation of government units and asking what could be done about it. Seeking to preserve a desired way of life and capture tax revenues, suburbanites were creating new municipalities all along the metropolitan fringe. Some of these units were large but many were

miniature domains that conformed to the traditional ideal of suburban government. In municipalities of fewer than one hundred acres there seemed no lack
of grass-roots rule. Yet the emerging concern for coordination of government
policies and services, already evident in Nassau County before World War II,
was leading many suburban leaders to search for something better than un-
adulterated small-scale government. Just as suburbia needed a more balanced
economy, so it needed a more balanced government, one that maintained an
equilibrium between the face-to-face rule of the village and the professional administration of the larger regional unit. Outcries against fragmentation reflected
a demand for innovative political reforms that would keep the governmental
scale from tipping too far toward divisiveness and disunion.

STRENGTHENING COUNTY GOVERNMENT

In answer to criticisms of fragmentation, a growing body of suburban reformers favored a restructuring of county government similar to that which had
occurred in Nassau County in the 1930s. Nowhere were the demands for reform greater than in splintering Saint Louis County. For years Saint Louis-area
newspapers and civic groups had attacked the structure of county rule as out-
moded and inefficient. By the late 1940s, however, the onslaught of governmental fragmentation added to the urgency of their cries for change. Suburban Saint
Louis was becoming a hodgepodge of pint-sized polities and needed a new
framework of county government to provide a semblance of coordination and
a foundation for future cooperation.

Missouri's Constitution of 1945 gave Saint Louis Countians the green light
to proceed with change. That document authorized "any county having more
than 85,000 inhabitants" to "frame, adopt and amend a charter for its own government," and that charter could vest the county with authority to regulate "the
public health, police and traffic, building construction, and planning and zoning" in unincorporated areas. Moreover, the county would be able to "perform
any of the services and functions" of a municipality in those incorporated cities
or villages that contracted for services from the county.[81] In other words, the
constitution gave Missourians the right to transform their counties into pur-
veyors of a wide variety of municipal services, a change that might eliminate
the need for incorporating further municipalities. In addition, existing municipalities could opt to buy services from the county and thus benefit from the
economies of scale enjoyed by the larger unit. If a county took advantage of the
new constitutional provision, it could become a powerful regional government
unlike anything that had previously existed in Missouri.

During the late 1940s suburban Saint Louis residents seized the opportunity to discard their governmental structure, and in March 1946 two hundred fifty civic leaders met at the county courthouse to consider the drafting of a charter.[82] Early in 1946 the reform-minded Governmental Research Institute already was producing propaganda calling for "a home rule charter" for the county. The institute urged that suburban voters replace the existing county government "adapted to an agricultural community, with a modern government organized and empowered to handle the problems of an urban community." Not only was the county as then constituted unable "to handle the complex problems of a densely populated community," it was incapable of imposing some order on the 188 local governments within its boundaries. Under a home-rule charter, however, "machinery [could] be provided to enable many of the smaller governments to utilize the county government for the performance of common services." The result would be "a higher quality of service at a saving to the taxpayers." Moreover, the institute saw a crying need for an executive to coordinate county functions.[83] Under the existing form of government, a three-member panel, known as the county court, adopted the budget, fixed the tax rate, and determined basic policy, but a long list of elected officials operated independent of this board. The sheriff, coroner, recorder of deeds, and other such administrative officers were largely lords of their own domains. This uncoordinated dispersion of authority among a bevy of courthouse politicians was anathema to the reform mentality.

Throughout the late 1940s these same arguments would dominate discussion of a home rule charter for Saint Louis County. Repeatedly, proponents of change would speak of horse-and-buggy government ill-suited to the populous, fast-growing suburban region. Just as frequently they would cite the need to cope more effectively with the multitude of local units, and the creation of a county executive was consistently at the top of the reform agenda. Coordination, cooperation, and modern, efficient administration were the goals of the Saint Louis County reformers and their sales pitch repeated these themes throughout the charter campaign.

To realize their goals, reformers created the St. Louis County Charter Organization Committee, composed of representatives from the League of Women Voters, county chamber of commerce, bar association, farm bureau, American Legion, real estate board, and League of Municipalities. During 1947 and 1948 the committee organized a petition campaign to collect thirty thousand signatures in support of the creation of a charter commission. In January 1949 the chair of the committee announced that the petition campaign was "over the top," and by the beginning of May the county circuit and probate judges had selected a fourteen-member commission.[84] With seven Democrats and seven Republicans, the charter commission did not represent any one political interest or viewpoint. Moreover, its diverse membership included three former county officials, two farmers, one labor leader, and the past president of the Missouri League of Women Voters.[85] The *St. Louis Globe-Democrat* had suggested "that all sections of the county be represented, that the membership include lawyers, businessmen and representatives of women's interests."[86] Clearly, the circuit and probate judges accepted this advice, appointing a commission that represented a range of beliefs and concerns.

These men and women were charged with fashioning a new framework for the booming county. Throughout 1949 and into 1950 they met and heard the recommendations of various groups. Perhaps the chief point of contention was whether to create an appointed county manager, a nonpartisan, professional executive who like a city manager would administer but leave policy-making to the elected legislative board. Both the League of Women Voters and the *St. Louis Globe-Democrat* favored this reform, but it proved too bold a move for others.[87] Equating governmental change with higher taxes, the farmers were most reluctant to back reform. According to the county farm agent, farmers favored the existing form of government "with a change in the name of the county court and perhaps five members on the administrative board in place of three." The agent concluded that "farmers . . . would hold to the old order rather than favor innovations, such as a county manager."[88]

Less timid was the Wellston Chamber of Commerce, which actually suggested to the commission that the county's seventy-one municipalities consolidate such functions as traffic control, street construction and repair, police and fire protection, and "as many others as lend themselves to consolidation." Wellston's mayor testified against his constituents' radical proposal, but clearly some county residents viewed charter reform as an opportunity for combating the plague of government fragmentation sweeping suburban Saint Louis.[89]

In early 1950 the commission presented its draft of the charter. Answering demands for greater central coordination, the charter specified that an elected county supervisor would be "the chief executive officer of the County" and would appoint the heads of the eleven departments as well as being responsible for preparation of the county budget.[90] This newly created officer was, in effect, to serve as mayor of the county. A seven-person county council was to exercise legislative authority and establish basic policy. The new county government would be able to perform a broad range of municipal functions in unincorporated areas, and municipalities could contract with it for any specific service. It was, then, more powerful than traditional county governments and had the potential to become a regional supermunicipality.

Yet the document was not a radical one. It did not eliminate most of the independent elected county officers. The Saint Louis County ballot would still include candidates for sheriff, treasurer, clerk of courts, and prosecuting attorney. Moreover, the new charter extended the system of competitive civil service examinations and merit appointments only to the departments of public health, hospitals, public welfare, and parks and recreation. Political patronage could still flourish in the other departments. Significantly, the charter also did not disturb any of the existing political subdivisions of the county. All of the county's myriad municipalities were to survive intact.

Some reformers were disappointed that the charter did not impose greater change, and especially did not do more to curb the power of old-fashioned courthouse politicians. But metropolitan-area civic leaders acknowledged that the proposed framework was a great improvement over the existing system and urged voters to approve it in a referendum scheduled for March 1950. The *St. Louis Globe-Democrat* recognized that the charter was "admittedly not perfect," and the other leading metropolitan daily, the *St. Louis Post-Dispatch,* concluded, "The charter is not nearly as good as it should be, but it contains some improvements and opens the way to still further improvement."[91] Commission member Mrs. R. Walston Chubb of Webster Groves claimed that previous reform measures in Missouri had failed to win voter approval because they were "too idealistic." "We have tried to profit by their mistakes," Mrs. Chubb explained. "Under this charter, the government can be improved later when it is seen changes are necessary." Likewise, the mayor of Normandy, in the northeastern section of the county, concluded, "While the proposed charter fails by a good margin of accomplishing what the majority of people had hoped for, it is nevertheless a great improvement over our present form of county government." The Webster Groves newspaper summed up the prevailing attitude in the county, when it said of the charter: "We believe it will bring our county government up to date and at the same time, it will enable us to move forward when movement is necessary without seeking the patronage of our state legislators who may not understand our local problems."[92] Stated simply, the charter seemed a step in the right direction.

Moreover, proponents of the document repeatedly mentioned the enhanced possibility of governmental cooperation in the fragmented county. The chair of the citizens' committee supporting adoption claimed that the charter would "promote better cooperative relationships between the nearly 200 governments in providing common services." The *Globe-Democrat* noted that the charter did not "authorize the county government to interfere in the affairs of municipalities of the county, or with existing fire, sewer, and school districts." It did, however, "include provisions to encourage cooperation between the county and its municipal units." Likewise, the *Post-Dispatch* said that the new framework of government "would encourage cities and districts to seek the county's help in providing efficient common services."[93]

Though the charter might encourage cooperation, it would not facilitate annexation of suburban Saint Louis County to the city of Saint Louis. Fears of annexation were a traditional bugaboo in the county, and some proponents of the new framework of government claimed it would actually allay those fears. The former chair of the county board of election commissioners contended: "The adoption of this charter will make St. Louis county a body corporate and no part of its territory thereafter may be absorbed by another body corporate. We in the county will be free from the agitation of those living in St. Louis who would like to annex part of our territory." According to this political leader, "we today want to be free of the threat of someone wanting to take our front lawn away from us. The adoption of this charter will remove that threat or danger."[94] This observer may have exaggerated the possible effect of the charter, but he expressed the prevailing suburban bias. Cooperation among suburbanites was desirable; invasion by the big city was not.

The charter, then, represented a middle way that satisfied the suburban desire to balance local grass-roots rule and centralized, efficient administration. Local autonomy would survive and a multitude of mini-municipalities would continue to clutter the map of Saint Louis County. But a reorganized county government would offer a more efficient administration of county services as well as a range of municipal services. With municipal services available from the county, fewer localities might opt for incorporation and the rate of fragmentation might diminish. By facilitating cooperation between existing municipalities, the new county regime might also militate against the worst effects of balkanization. Yet it would not destroy any small-scale village governments. In fact, by allowing undersized municipalities to contract for services from the county, the new county charter might well perpetuate the existence of these independent but generally inadequate units of government. Finally, a strengthened county government would be better able to combat the threat from the city of Saint Louis. Thus the charter preserved the suburban ideal of local rule while offering government suitable for an urbanizing area.

The charter was so well tailored to suburban thinking that it faced no organized opposition. The newspapers claimed that the courthouse politicians and local political organizations covertly opposed the charter, though the leading Republican officeholder, county judge Luman Matthews, vigorously supported its adoption.[95] Moreover, the Republican precinct committee leaders for the elite residential areas of Ladue and Clayton Townships unanimously urged "all Republicans in St. Louis County . . . to vote in favor of the new St. Louis County charter."[96] Joining Matthews and the Republican precinct leaders in support were such diverse groups as the Florissant City Council, the St. Louis County Medical Society, the Forum of the First Unitarian Church, and the Ladies Division of the Wellston Chamber of Commerce.[97] About two hundred public meetings were held throughout the county to discuss the new framework of government, though some were poorly attended and aroused little interest. The caustic *Wellston Journal* remarked that the debate at one meeting "at times reached the heights or depths of boring absurdity," and the *Webster News-Times* said of an opinion survey on the charter: "Again it was proved that too many citizens either aren't interested or don't know."[98]

On election day those voters who did care turned out and approved the charter by an almost two-to-one margin. In eleven of the fourteen townships a majority of the ballots were cast for the charter; only three of the outlying rural townships opposed the new form of government. Support was strongest in the most urbanized, eastern portion of the county, where the margin of victory was five to one. Suburbanites in Ladue, Clayton, and University City lined up solidly behind a scheme suitable for their suburban, but urbanizing, region.[99]

In November 1950 Luman Matthews was elected the first county supervisor, and over the next decade he and the members of the county council gradually expanded the county's governing role. Actually, even before the passage of the charter, Saint Louis County had begun to assume a range of tasks traditionally associated with municipalities. In 1943 the county adopted subdivision regulations for developments in unincorporated areas, and in 1946 the county enacted its first comprehensive zoning ordinance for territory beyond municipal limits.[100] Following passage of the charter, the county extended its planning function by adopting a building code, and by 1957 the county department of public works not only performed the electrical inspections for unincorporated areas but contracted to do so for fifty municipalities and had informal agreements to provide the same service to an additional thirty-four cities and villages. Similarly, this same department was responsible for plumbing inspection in the unincorporated zone and in approximately seventy municipalities, which availed themselves of the service through contract or informal understanding.[101]

The county was also assuming responsibility for parks and recreation. In 1944 it acquired its first parkland and the following year adopted a preliminary park plan, specifying the location of fifty-one proposed recreation areas or natural preserves.[102] Just twenty years after drafting this initial plan, there were thirty-two county parks with a combined area of 3,764 acres.[103] Meanwhile, the county library system was also expanding, bringing edification and enjoyment to a growing population in both unincorporated and incorporated areas.

The new municipal role of Saint Louis County was most evident in the transformation of local law enforcement. During the first few years under the charter, the elected sheriff retained responsibility for policing the unincorporated county. A bastion of political patronage and ineptitude, the sheriff's office, however, proved woefully inadequate to perform this task. Complaints mounted and peaked following a shooting incident involving two deputy sheriffs. On June 26, 1953, at a barbecue party of courthouse employees at the El Avion roadhouse, Deputy Sheriff Nicholas Burke shot and wounded Chief Deputy William Smith. Sheriff Arthur Mosley claimed Burke, who had been "suffering from severe migraine headaches for the past year, suddenly became temporarily insane, went berserk and came into the restaurant shooting wildly."[104] Others presented different accounts, and some claimed that Burke and Smith had fought over who was a better marksman.[105] Moreover, confidence in the sheriff's office was not enhanced by Mosley's claim that it was "not necessary" to arrest the supposedly lunatic gunman following the shootout. The *St. Louis Post-Dispatch* referred to the incident as "a barroom brawl" and county voters regarded it as prime evidence of the incompetence and corruption of the sheriff's office.[106] In the minds of many county residents, an urbanizing region required an urban-style police department, not a band of trigger-happy political appointees.

Consequently, in 1954 voters approved a charter amendment creating the Saint Louis County Department of Police. Modeled after city police forces, the department was governed by a bipartisan board of police commissioners appointed by the county supervisor; the commissioners in turn chose the police superintendent. The county squad not only patrolled unincorporated areas but under contract also served some municipalities. By the beginning of the 1960s, the county provided full police services to eight municipalities and radio-dispatching service to thirty-nine additional cities and villages.[107]

Zoning, building codes, parks, libraries, and police departments were all traditionally associated with city government, but now Saint Louis County, like Nassau County, was assuming these responsibilities and becoming a producer of municipal services for both incorporated and unincorporated areas. Yet in

Saint Louis County, as in Nassau, the grass-roots units of suburban government remained intact and the suburban ideal of small-scale, village rule was not unduly compromised. By adopting Russel Sprague's two-tier scheme of government, suburban Missourians, like their counterparts on Long Island, believed they could retain the suburban ideal at the same time they achieved more efficient and effective regional administration. They rejected a sheriff's department suitable for rural America and substituted a city-style police department, but simultaneously they clung to their small-town governments and fostered the municipal balkanization of suburban Saint Louis. They were, then, both dividing and uniting, and in the process fashioning a form of government suitable for the suburban ideals and urban realities of their emerging co-urban county.

During the 1950s Suffolk Countians were also following the lead of their Nassau neighbors and molding a balanced polity to satisfy their desire for both governmental intimacy and efficiency. By the middle of the decade Suffolk's population was soaring, imposing new burdens on the county government. Moreover, state investigators were delving into county practices and exposing an unflattering record of corruption and incompetence.[108] Consequently, the leader of the county's dominant Republican Party, R. Ford Hughes, felt that restructuring the framework of government was imperative. "What we need, and ultimately will have," Hughes contended, "is a charter form of government similar to that originated and adopted by Nassau County in 1938." "Our county's government has crawled along while its residents progressed from the ox cart to the jet plane," Hughes argued in December 1955. "Now, we must get up and walk."[109]

Responding to Hughes's complaints, in early 1956 Republicans drafted a proposed charter that conformed to the two-layer theory of local government. The document provided for a county executive to ensure centralized administration, a county police department to upgrade law enforcement, and the transfer of public health duties from the townships and villages to the county. Though the document strengthened central authority, the forces of decentralizing grass-roots rule strongly influenced the final version of the proposed framework of government. The five less-populated, rural townships of eastern Suffolk were dedicated to ensuring that each of the ten townships, no matter its population, would continue to have one vote, and only one vote, on the county board of supervisors. Thus the balance of power with the five western suburban townships, where 80 percent of the population lived, would be maintained. When a leader of Islip Township, with 119,340 inhabitants, suggested apportionment on the basis of population, Supervisor Evans Griffing of

Shelter Island Township (population 1,230) rose in defense of the interests of his fragment of the county. Suspicious of centralizing reforms that might threaten township authority, Griffing expressed a familiar sentiment when he said, "Home rule is the best rule."[110] Griffing won the battle, and the proposed charter retained the traditional composition of the board: one supervisor from each township, regardless of population.

The eastern townships also insisted that the board of supervisors appoint the proposed county executive rather than allowing the county's voters to elect that official. Because of the numerical supremacy of voters in western townships, easterners assumed that an executive elected at large would always be from the western half of the county and would give that area an upper hand in county government. Consequently, the final document provided for an appointive executive with no authority to veto acts of the board of supervisors or break tie votes of the ten-member board. The executive would administer but would not have policy-making authority and would not enjoy an independent electoral base.

The planning and policing provisions of the proposed charter also reflected the parochialism of many Suffolk Countians. The original draft of the charter empowered the county planning department to devise a master plan, and all township plans would have to conform to this county blueprint for development. Moreover, the county was to assume responsibility for zoning.[111] Both of these centralizing provisions were deleted from the final version after spokespersons for the townships and villages objected vigorously. The final charter proposal also specified that a county police force would be established only if five adjoining townships voted in favor of such a force. If they did so, only those townships would be subject to the county police and pay for its support. In other words, naysaying residents in the eastern half of the county could keep their township law enforcement agencies and avoid centralized policing.

The proposed charter would, then, enhance central authority to a degree, but it embodied numerous concessions to placate the county's local units. Township and village governments would not disappear and they would still be able to zone their domains as they wished. But the charter did seem to offer new opportunities for countywide coordination of services and supposedly would update Suffolk's antiquated structure of government.

A creation of the county's Republican leaders, the charter was not popular with Democrats. Yet in order to be adopted, it had to win the approval of the state legislature and the Democratic state governor as well as a majority of Suffolk's voters. In March 1956 the legislature endorsed it, but the next month Democratic governor Averill Harriman vetoed the charter. Justifying his veto, he claimed the charter was too limited in its reforms. According to Harriman, the county needed a more thoroughgoing overhaul, including the creation of a powerful elected executive with the authority to break ties on the board of supervisors. Moreover, apportionment of the board should have been on the basis of population. Thus the governor deplored the concessions granted to the townships and urged the creation of a bipartisan committee to draft a more radical document. Partisanship clearly played a role in Harriman's veto, and Republican leader Hughes attacked it as "political persecution" and "petty vindictiveness."[112] The veto was to begin a two-year battle as the Democratic governor sought to coerce the Republican county into taking more drastic action.

Suffolk leaders responded to Harriman's action by creating a new nineteen-member charter commission, including four Democrats, to draft a revised document for submission to the 1957 session of the state legislature. The framers of this second charter sought to answer some of Harriman's objections and specifically recommended an elected executive. Suffolk Countians, however, would not yield on the apportionment of the board of supervisors. Equal representation by township had to be retained, and by early 1957 Harriman seemed willing to concede this point.[113] Yet the representatives of the eastern townships on the board of supervisors proved more intransigent than the governor. When the revised document was submitted to the board in March 1957, these easterners convinced a majority of the board to amend the proposed charter to eliminate the elected executive and to provide again for appointment of the county chief.[114]

Predictably, Governor Harriman repeated his veto of the previous year, dooming the revised document. Just as predictably Suffolk County Republicans roundly condemned the governor for denying Long Islanders the right to govern themselves. Hughes referred to Harriman's veto as "repulsive," and a Suffolk County newspaper angrily editorialized: "Our pampered, demagogic, multi-millionaire play-boy Governor has done it again. He vetoed the new edition of the Suffolk County Charter over which men of far greater integrity, character and intelligence have been sweating blood for two years." This irate journal could only conclude, "It is perfectly obvious that Governor Harriman is still playing his petty politics to the hilt."[115]

Following the second veto a volunteer citizens group known as the Suffolk County Citizens Charter Committee assumed the task of revising once again the proposed charter. This group forthrightly favored a strong elected executive with veto power, the authority to break ties on the board of supervisors, and responsibility for appointing county commissioners and department heads. The executive would, then, be comparable to a strong city mayor, and the creation of such an office was a marked deviation from the traditional structure of county rule. In February 1958, by a six-to-four vote, the board of supervisors approved this draft. One of the eastern supervisors defected and joined the five westerners to form the majority. But the remaining four easterners remained bitter and did not concede defeat easily. One western supervisor said of the battle: "It was a beaut. The east end feels an elected executive will lead to their doom." An eastern supervisor argued that the proposed county executive would exercise "almost dictatorial" powers, and Shelter Island's Supervisor Griffing concluded, "I can only hope that the people of the county will see fit to repudiate at the polls what the board is doing here today."[116]

In the words of one local newspaper, this third draft of the charter was "tailored to meet Harriman's approval," and in 1958 the governor was finally amenable to submitting the proposal to Suffolk County voters for their approval.[117] Not only did the document authorize an elected executive, it provided for the creation of a county police department if at least three contiguous townships approved such a change. Like the drafts of 1956 and 1957, it also eliminated township and village health officers, assigning responsibility for public health solely to the county. Moreover, any township or village zoning measure affecting property within five hundred feet of a village or township boundary or a state park or parkway had to be submitted to the county planning commission for approval. Land use planning would remain largely a township and village responsibility, but the county would act as a mediator to review zoning changes in borderland areas.[118]

Both political parties endorsed these provisions and during fall 1958 opposition to the proposed charter was confined to the eastern townships. A newspaper in the western end of the county praised the creation of "a county police force to replace the many law enforcement agencies that ha[d] been tripping over one another's toes for years." Another western newspaper likewise lauded the establishment of a county police department "to simplify and unify the existing 27 law enforcement agencies now extant in the county and confusing to all except the shrewd law breaker."[119] Proponents of the charter repeatedly referred to "streamlined government" and "good business sense" when commenting on the reforms.[120] The charter would supposedly eliminate waste, duplication, and inefficiency and finally bring Suffolk County's archaic government into the twentieth century.

On election day an overwhelming majority of the Suffolk County electorate agreed with this analysis. The final tally recorded 88,000 votes in favor of the charter and only 33,000 votes against. Support was especially strong in the western half of the county, where voters in densely populated Islip Township approved the document by a five-to-one margin and approximately 80 percent of the electorate in Babylon Township lined up behind reform. Each of the five more heavily populated western townships supported the charter by substantial margins, but each of the less populous eastern townships rejected it, with four of every five voters in tiny Shelter Island casting a negative ballot. Moreover, all five of the western townships voted to transfer law enforcement duties to a county police force whereas the five eastern townships were to retain their local constabulary.[121]

Residents of the heavily populated suburban areas of Suffolk County thus opted for change and for increased central authority. But the degree of change was limited, with the county's twenty-seven villages, myriad fire protection districts, and ten townships retaining most of their authority. The Suffolk charter simply adjusted county government to changing realities; it did not overturn the existing structure of rule or violate long-standing suburban ideals. Moreover, the long and difficult conflict between easterners and westerners in Suffolk was indicative of the strength of localism in suburbanizing counties. Even moderate adjustments could raise cries of tyranny in townships fearful of being shortchanged by reform. Townships and villages were alert to the dangers confronting them, and in Suffolk as well as Saint Louis County, proposals for change confronted a wall of suspicion. Moreover, if suburban political leaders seemed to be moving too far in the direction of centralized control, then this wall would become a barricade blocking reform and protecting parochialism.

Whereas Saint Louis and Suffolk Counties followed the example of Nassau and adopted charters outlining a new structure of government, other suburban counties proceeded with piecemeal reforms that likewise centralized authority to achieve some coordination among the many municipalities along the metropolitan fringe. For example, in 1949 Oakland County established a county planning commission, only the second such body to be created in Michigan. The board of supervisors appointed a special committee to consider the formation of a planning commission, and in its report this committee emphasized the need "for a central agency to coordinate and make plans for the future growth and development of the County as a whole." According to a member of the board, this report "further pointed out that many County problems [were] inter-related with problems of other local communities, and that because of the extensive growth of the County the importance of water, sewage, and land use and development would become more acute every day."[122] In other words, in Oakland as in Saint Louis and Suffolk Counties, officials were recognizing that fast-paced development demanded coordination among the local government units and that the county needed to assume the role of coordinator.

During the following decade, the Oakland County Planning Commission actively sought to realize the goal of coordinated, planned development. Starting with an annual appropriation of $6,000 in 1950, the commission's budget rose to almost $109,000 by 1962. In the course of that period, it drafted a subdivision guide, prepared reports on the county's water resources, conducted zoning forums to educate township officials about land use planning, compiled parking studies for a number of communities, investigated the potential for retailing development in the county, and issued information bulletins to municipal zoning officials. Thus it did not focus solely on land use but also surveyed the provision of public services and monitored the economic development of the county.[123] By the early 1960s it had clearly convinced local officials of the need for central coordination and countywide planning. In 1962 the chair of the board of supervisors observed: "We have found that master planning is essential. Services and facilities must be provided on an area basis and built with sufficient capacity for future potential use."[124]

During the 1950s Oakland County took further action to minimize the adverse consequences of fragmentation. Especially serious in the relatively flat, humid county was the problem of drainage, which no single municipality was competent to solve. Following heavy rains, water filled basements, flooded streets, and caused the existing inadequate sewers to back up. Among the traditional county offices in Michigan was that of Drain Commissioner, but under existing state laws that official could not readily correct the problem in the fast-developing county.[125] Consequently, in 1957 Oakland's board of supervisors pushed a bill through the legislature authorizing a county department of public works. This county agency had the authority to construct and maintain water supply and sewerage systems if requested to do so by county municipalities. Moreover, if a municipality's drainage problems posed a hazard to adjoining communities, the county department of public works could extend sewerage lines into the offending municipality without that community's permission. According to a planning commission report from 1960, the department of public works served "local units of government within the county which [were] unable to solve their sewer and water problems individually" and thus found it "expedient to have this work undertaken by a central organization on a large area basis."[126] Drainage and water supply problems transcended municipal boundaries and required action by a broader countywide agency. The department of public works was intended to serve that regional function.

Within a few years the department was proving its value. By 1960 it was already planning or constructing sewer projects to drain 47 percent of the county's area.[127] Faced with a multitude of separate municipalities unable to shoulder the task, the county had taken charge and coordinated a multimunicipal approach. The first director of the public works department recognized the need for centralization to counter the governmental fragmentation in the county. In 1958 he told county business leaders that "the sanctimonious veil of home rule" had resulted in the "defeat of proposals that could [have led] to the solution of area problems." Moreover, he claimed that Oakland Countians had had their "heads in the sand for many years insofar as planning and developing . . . basic facilities on an area basis [were] concerned." But now the department of public works seemed to usher in a new era of county coordination. In 1959 a local newspaper observed: "The DPW is a new attempt in county services and county leaders have long talked about it as a model for extension of services into other experiments in area government."[128]

Like their Michigan counterparts, Orange Countians did not opt for a wholesale reconstruction of their governmental framework. Though California's constitution permitted counties to fashion their own government structures through home rule charters, Orange County voters chose to retain the noncharter format specified by the general laws of the state. Despite this seeming reluctance to change, Orange County authorities were gradually assuming a broader role during the 1950s to ensure coordinated countywide action. This was evident in the work of the county planning commission. In 1956 the commission formulated a master plan for arterial highways and during the late 1950s county planners worked closely with their municipal counterparts to update the scheme. In 1960 the commission praised the highway program as "a good example of City-County cooperative effort."[129]

Such cooperative effort was a major theme of the commission's programs of the late 1950s. In 1957 the county planning director initiated the City County Planning Directors Group, which held monthly luncheon meetings devoted to bridging the gaps that separated the various governmental units in Orange County. According to the county planning commission report, "These gatherings provide an opportunity for the exchange of ideas, planning procedures and techniques for the mutual benefit of all concerned and promote fellowship and acquaintance on a first name basis in a group having a common interest." Moreover, the county planning director, county road commissioner, and four representatives of cities selected by the Orange County League of Cities constituted a street-naming committee to achieve some uniformity in the county's street names. Forty-two of the arterial highways had 129 names, with different municipalities applying different names to the same thoroughfare.[130] Again the goal was to impose some unity and alleviate the confusion arising from governmental fragmentation.

The county planning director also spearheaded the development of a countywide park scheme. In May 1960 the planning commission recommended that the county establish a regional park program, and in December the board of supervisors responded by creating the Regional Parks Advisory Committee, chaired by the planning director.[131] Rather than just review subdivision plats submitted by developers or consider zoning variances, Orange County planners were increasingly attempting to assume the role of regional coordinator and ensure a unified countywide approach to recreation and park development as well as highway and street construction.

In Orange County as in Oakland, Suffolk, and Saint Louis Counties, then, the fifteen years following World War II witnessed not only the splintering of suburbia into multiple municipalities but also a concurrent trend toward central coordination to achieve better services and more effective administration. A governmental balance of power was developing in these counties, a balance that was to become characteristic of emerging post-suburban areas. In the minds of many, suburbia may have seemed an irrational crazy quilt of defensive municipal fragments jealous of their authority. But the increasingly durable threads of county coordination were holding these fragments together, and gradually, as the post-suburban polity emerged, the pattern of authority would appear less crazy and more attractive to perceptive eyes. A pragmatic solution to conflicting demands was developing. Residents of Oakland County could indulge their preference for a five-way division of Southfield Township while, courtesy of the county department of public works, still enjoy a system of sewers equal to those in the city of Detroit. Saint Louis Countians could maintain their miniscule municipalities and contract with Saint Louis County's police department for radio-dispatching service. Along the metropolitan fringe, citizens were negotiating a compromise that might allow them the benefits of both small-scale and large-scale administration.

4

Maintaining the Balance of Power

During the late 1950s and the 1960s the emerging balance between governmental fragmentation and central coordination faced a serious challenge. Academics, journalists, and reform-minded politicians viewed the multitude of suburban governments as a national disgrace threatening the quality of metropolitan life. They repeated the standard arguments about wastefulness, duplication of services, and inefficiency, but the apparent decline of the older central cities added a special urgency to their diatribes against suburban government. By the 1960s New York City, Detroit, and Saint Louis were aging badly, with blight spreading through their neighborhoods so rapidly that urban renewal agencies were falling further behind in the effort to bring new life to the city core. Moreover, television coverage of race riots and reports of rising crime rates reinforced the prevailing sense of urban debacle. Supposedly the government barriers between the central cities and suburbs were contributing to this decay and chaos, and only a united effort by all metropolitan residents, regardless of jurisdiction, could handle the emerging urban crisis.

Books, articles, and editorials thus called for governmental unification of metropolitan areas not only for the sake of efficient administration but more important, to save the endangered cities. Political scientists and reform pundits ridiculed the small-scale villages fostered by the traditional suburban ideal and called for a new inclusive metropolitan vision and a willingness among Nassau residents to admit that they in fact lived in the New York City metropolis and among Webster Groves homeowners to view themselves first and foremost as Saint Louisans. Even the federal government attempted to blackmail suburbanites into believing themselves responsible for the central city's ills as well as for the problems of their own villages. Federal funding was to depend on metropolitan-wide cooperation and a renunciation of suburban parochialism. So-called experts, the media, and Washington, D. C. were sending the same message to the residents of Garden City, Southfield, Glen Ellyn, and Ladue. Eschew the delicate governmental balance that preserved the autonomy of the fragment and embrace metropolitanism.

By the close of the 1960s, however, the forces of metropolitan reform had failed. Attempts to strengthen the ties between Nassau and New York City, Oakland and Detroit, and Saint Louis County and Saint Louis city were to fail, as suburbanites successfully rejected the best advice of experts and bureaucrats and unequivocally made it clear that they were not residents of the central city and did not wish to be regarded as such. They fended off the forces of metropolitanism and in the process declared their independence anew. In the late 1960s the residents of the fringe counties thus retained their belief in small-scale, intimate government. Metropolitan-wide rule appeared more unrealistic in 1970 than in 1960 as suburbanites kept cooperation with the central city to a minimum.

While not surrendering to the forces of metropolitan unity, fringe dwellers were curbing their proclivity for governmental balkanization. During the 1960s, lawmakers successfully aborted the birth of additional units of government and fewer new municipalities appeared along the metropolitan rim than in earlier decades. Thus the tendency toward fragmentation was checked but at the same time metropolitan unity was thwarted. By the late 1960s, the middle way that was to characterize the emerging post-suburban metropolis was more evident than ever before. Long Islanders, inhabitants of Saint Louis County, and their counterparts in Orange County were devoted neither to infinite governmental splintering nor to metropolitan giantism. Rather, they continued to tend toward an intermediate position, which balanced the small-scale and intimate against the large-scale and coordinative.

Meanwhile, the life style and economic development of Suffolk, Nassau, Oakland, DuPage, Saint Louis, and Orange Counties were also increasingly balanced. These areas remained bastions of white-collar homeowners dedicated to green lawns, clear air, and good schools, but commercial growth continued to bolster the independent economic base of the counties. An increasing number of office buildings joined shopping malls and factories in fringe municipalities. The six counties were growing less suburban and more post-suburban and as they did so the arguments underlying the extreme options of fragmentation and metropolitanism seemed less convincing. The image of the country village where every voter knew the mayor and council members personally and volunteered to extinguish fires was increasingly incongruous in a suburbia of corporate headquarters and one-hundred-store malls. Despite many outlying residents clinging to the traditional suburban image, the six counties were no longer semirural refuges where village rule alone was sufficient. Yet at the same time they were no longer adjuncts of the central city and subordinate components of a single metropolis dependent for its economic vitality on the central-city downtown. The counties were developing into something new, and neither village nor metropolitan-wide government totally suited them.

EXECUTIVE CITIES

"Mid-America's New Executive City"—by the late 1960s that was the new label applied to Saint Louis County's Clayton.[1] No longer just a community of fine homes and carefully manicured lawns, its flashy glass office towers, high-rise hotels, and lofty apartment buildings were symbols of the changing status of the once-traditional suburb. It was a full-fledged center of business, a community where business executives not only lived but also worked. Yet during the 1960s other executive cities were emerging along America's metropolitan fringe. In the 1950s factories and retailers had migrated to suburbia, but now office developers were doing likewise in increasing numbers. Corporate headquarters and slick office buildings were beginning to dot the suburban landscape, another sign of the growing obsolescence of the term *suburban*. The standard image of the split-level house, station wagon, and freckle-faced children survived, but it was an image increasingly out of line with what was happening along the urban rim.

Though office employment was growing in outlying areas throughout the nation, Clayton deserves credit as America's first full-fledged edge city. As early as 1952 the Brown Shoe Company moved its corporate headquarters to the Saint Louis County community, and in the course of the 1950s 2- and 3-story office blocks proliferated along Clayton's streets.[2] In 1958, however, city leaders ushered in a new era when they repealed a 5-story height limit and permitted the building of high-rise structures in the community's business district.[3] During the early 1960s developers took advantage of the change, completing a 13-story office building in February 1962 and the 16-story Pierre Laclede Building a year later. The latter office tower proved so successful that a 23-story companion structure was erected in the late 1960s.[4] High-rise apartment buildings added further vertical accents to the Clayton landscape, and in 1966 the *St. Louis Post-Dispatch* reported that the community's skyline "no longer blended into the county's amorphous urban sprawl, but now appeared more like a little Tulsa or perhaps an Omaha, than just another incorporated outskirt of St. Louis."[5] A year later the chamber of commerce boosted that Clayton was "known for its high rise business district and high rise quality apartment buildings." But by 1968 the developers' dreams were soaring even higher, with one investor proposing an office center with one 30-story and two 20-story buildings.[6]

By the mid 1960s Clayton, in fact, had developed into a major office hub. A wide range of businesses filled its new towers and approximately one hundred of the nation's five hundred largest corporations had offices in the Saint Louis County community. At the beginning of 1966 Clayton could boast of fifty office buildings with a combined floor space of over two million square feet, equal to one-third of the total office space in downtown Saint Louis. Two years later a scholarly study of Clayton proclaimed it "a new metropolitan focus in the St. Louis area" and "an urban sub-capital" that supplemented the Saint Louis central business district.[7]

Yet high-rise office towers did not spell doom to high-priced residential neighborhoods. Clayton's city council was dedicated to preserving the elite residential reputation of the community and in the city's annual reports were repeated references to the "protection of residential areas" and "the containment of the Central Business District."[8] As early as 1960 the city manager assured the local citizenry that commercial development had "not been at the sacrifice of [Clayton's] fine residential community character." Similarly, the city's proud mayor reported, "Farsighted and comprehensive planning has protected our fine residential areas while permitting desirable business development." The city council refused permits to construct a motion picture theater and to expand the local Ramada Inn when those projects were deemed to "adversely affect residential quality."[9] As the mayor and city manager noted, the city's rulers were not about to trade the traditional advantages of the community for unrestrained commercial growth.

In fact, Clayton leaders sought and achieved both business and residential wealth. In its annual report for 1966, the city government proclaimed Clayton to be the "image of a balanced community," and four years later the report described the town as "a balanced community with excellent schools, fine homes, exceptional recreation and cultural facilities and a distinguished office and business center." Yet it was only balanced in terms of having the best of both commerce and residence. It certainly was not socially balanced. As the chamber of commerce boasted, it was truly an executive city, where executives worked and with neighborhoods where only executives could afford to live. According to the 1970 census, within Saint Louis County only the two census tracts in elite Ladue could claim a higher mean value of owner-occupied dwellings than could central Clayton. Moreover, the east and west ends of Clayton were also well above the county average in terms of wealth.[10] Clayton was, then, a community composed primarily of the hub and outer ring of the traditional city. The intermediate concentric circles that included the lower- and middle-income neighborhoods were largely missing.

With its skewed social and economic profile, Clayton was the embodiment of the post-suburban dream. Having more than its fair share of mansions and high rises, it successfully captured the residential and commercial wealth of the metropolis. Post-suburban areas sought to combine the tax base of the central business district with the advantages of the traditional upper-middle-class suburb. As early as the 1960s Clayton had achieved that lucrative mix.

But Clayton was not the only community experiencing a rise in office construction and an influx of commercial wealth. The phenomenon was also evident on Long Island. Between 1959 and 1965 the number of office jobs in Nassau County rose 41 percent whereas manufacturing employment grew by less than 20 percent. Moreover, by the late 1960s planners were predicting that office employment would double in Nassau by the year 2000 whereas manufacturing jobs would increase only about 25 percent.[11] Nassau was, then, attracting an increasing number of offices, and new low-rise office blocks were especially prevalent in the center of the county near the Roosevelt Field shopping mall.

In the mid 1960s, however, Long Islanders were dreaming of far grander developments. Mitchel Field, a former air base in the heart of Nassau County, was now available for development, and in 1965 C. McKim Norton, president of the Regional Planning Association, a private planning organization, suggested that the abandoned field and its environs become the site of a new "center for the suburbs." What he proposed was "a green Rockefeller Center suited to the suburbs," including shopping, offices, and cultural facilities, to serve as a focus for the sprawling, amorphous suburbia of Long Island. Recognizing that a post-suburban transformation was already underway, he told Long Island business leaders, "Even though we keep using the word 'suburbs,' they aren't suburbs anymore—they aren't 'sub' to any 'urb.' Suburbanites once depended on a central city for services which now must be supplied out among one-family houses." According to Norton, "the only way to get them [services] at top quality is in centers—not one-purpose shopping centers but new combined centers, uncrowded and green, suited to the new life that these new urban areas symbolize." The Regional Plan Association's report on the proposed Nassau Center expanded on Norton's vision of the future. "Nassau Center can be something new, combining the best of the urban and suburban world—if the right degree of concentration and greenness and the relation of each activity to the others are attained."[12]

Though *Newsday* reported that the proposal for a "'downtown center' in Nassau County won the support . . . of the Long Island Association, a businessmen's group," the redevelopment of Mitchel Field proceeded slowly over the succeeding years and never realized the dream of Norton or the Regional Plan Association.[13] The proposal, however, was a classic post-suburban manifesto. It recognized that the suburbs were no longer truly suburban, but it also sought to create a future that balanced the traditional advantages of suburbia with the best of urban life. The proposal sought to replicate that great symbol of urban success, Rockefeller Center, but the Nassau version was to be a "green" Rockefeller Center, a center that did not pave over nature or crowd out sylvan beauty. The emerging post-suburban vision demanded "the right degree of concentration and greenness," a perfect balance between the village and the city, between flora and concrete.

Meanwhile, a similar vision was emerging in Southfield, the pioneering post-suburban community of Oakland County. As early as 1955 the Bendix Corporation constructed its general offices and research center in Southfield, and Standard Oil and Reynolds Aluminum followed suit with low-rise regional offices later in the decade.[14] Freeway construction in the 1960s hastened Southfield's development with the city having the good fortune of being at the juncture of some of the metropolitan area's leading highways. By 1964 Mayor James Clarkson was boasting of Southfield as "a Hub City with one of the largest expressway interchanges . . . , with 26 ways to go in the United States."[15]

With ample vacant land and optimum automobile access, Southfield became a favorite for developers of office buildings. In 1960 Eaton Yale and Towne transplanted its offices to the community, three years later the west tower of Northland Towers was completed adjacent to Northland Shopping Center, and an identical east tower was renting office space by 1966. Meanwhile, Federal Mogul had migrated to Southfield and was joined in the late 1960s by 3-M Investment Company, Merrill-Lynch-Pierce, and a high-rise building housing IBM's regional office.[16] With its mother lode of taxable commercial structures, Eight-Mile Road was nicknamed the "Gold Coast." Moreover, in the mid 1960s Mayor Clarkson predicted that "Northwestern Highway, already beautified by some of the foremost creative industries and office centers in the world, [would] be further silhouetted against the skyline by the erection of high-rise apartments; Northland Center and its Pointe [would] be fully developed and completed—making this a 'Golden Triangle Center.'"[17]

Office construction peaked in 1967 and 1968, with building permits for almost 1.3 million square feet of office space being issued during the latter year. The Detroit riot of 1967 accelerated the outward migration of business from the racially tense central city, and Southfield was the fortunate beneficiary. By 1971 Southfield was being called "Detroit's new downtown," with over 8.2 million gross square feet of existing office space or space under construction.[18]

Though still dwarfed by the 22 million gross square feet of space in Detroit's central business district, Southfield's office inventory continued to grow, ensuring that city a place of significance in the emerging post-suburban world.

By 1970 Southfield was, then, no longer a bedroom suburb; instead it was a commercial hub providing jobs for people from throughout the metropolitan area. Whereas 26,518 gainfully employed persons resided in Southfield, 42,305 people worked there, including 11,352 commuters from Detroit. By comparison, only 8,262 Southfielders journeyed to a workplace in the central city.[19]

Yet in Southfield as in Clayton, residents were not willing to kowtow unthinkingly to the forces of economic growth. When in 1969 promoters of a new domed stadium for the Detroit Tigers and Lions sought a site in the booming community, local homeowners rose in rebellion. "Southfield stadium jeered by residents" read the headline in the *Detroit News,* and a spokesperson for the stadium promoters had to promise a gathering of concerned presidents of neighborhood associations, "We aren't going to shove this down your throats."[20] The city of Detroit was vying desperately to become the site of the new major-league stadium. But Southfield residents feared the traffic and the resulting burden on local police and fire services. Unlike Detroit, Southfield was not willing to make major sacrifices in order to become a big-league city. Instead, it favored development only if that development was lucrative and did not detract from the advantages of suburban life.

Farther west, in DuPage County, the planned community of Oak Brook was winning recognition as yet another post-suburban pioneer. The father of Oak Brook was Paul Butler, heir to the Butler Paper Company fortune. A devotee of polo, Butler accumulated extensive land holdings in eastern DuPage County on which he raised his horses. In the 1950s, however, Butler's property became the site of one of the major interchanges in northeastern Illinois, the crossing of the East-West and Tri-State tollways. Recognizing that his land could support more than polo ponies, Butler embarked on the creation of a prestige development, including only the finest in residences, retailing, hotels, and offices. In 1964 he joined forces with Del Webb, an Arizona developer, and together they sought to fashion the ideal executive city.[21]

During the 1960s the rate of change was rapid. At the time of the community's incorporation in 1958, it had a little more than one hundred inhabitants; according to a long-time resident, it was known as "Horse Town" and "it was all prairies, groves, and polo fields."[22] Ten years later the 154-acre office park laid out in 1960 was 60 percent developed and included twenty-three low-rise structures of one to three stories as well as five high-rise buildings of six to twelve stories.[23] In 1958 American Can Company had been the first to establish offices in the community, but by the early 1970s Oak Brook could boast of the world headquarters of the McDonald's hamburger chain, the food research facilities of both Swift and Armour, and a long list of regional offices for Fortune 500 corporations. In 1974 it had 5 million square feet of office space and there were plans for the construction of 2.5 million more.[24] With the opening of Oakbrook Center in 1962 it also became one of the shopping meccas of northeastern Illinois. Initially anchored by the Marshall Field and Sears department stores, the shopping mall later would attract such posh retailers as Neiman-Marcus, Saks Fifth Avenue, and I. Magnin.[25] In the Chicagoland area, Oak Brook was to become synonymous with executive-class retailing.

But it was also to become an enclave of upper-crust residences. Carefully restricted subdivisions such as York Woods, Brook Forest, Steeplechase, and Ginger Creek became home to the most affluent DuPage Countians. Through restrictive convenants Paul Butler imposed architectural and aesthetic standards aimed at ensuring only the most tasteful and expensive development. Rumors circulated that Butler even controlled the type of draperies that hung in Oak Brook living rooms.[26] Once the neighborhoods were established, homeowner associations assumed responsibility for enforcing the restrictions that made Oak Brook an ideal residence for executives. By 1970 Oak Brook ranked first among DuPage County communities in median value of owner-occupied homes, its figure being more than double that of the county as a whole.[27]

With a 1970 population of 4,118 spread over approximately 5,000 acres, Oak Brook also retained an unusual amount of open space. At the heart of the community was the 550-acre International Sports Core, which offered residents an eighteen-hole golf course, three swimming pools, tennis courts, and extensive equestrian facilities, including seven polo fields.[28] In 1970 as in 1958 Oak Brook was a horse town, for Butler had achieved the remarkable feat of attracting corporate headquarters without sacrificing polo. By the early 1970s twenty thousand employees of the mall and offices crowded Oak Brook's major thoroughfares, but along these same roads were signs warning, "Yield to Equestrian."[29] This mix of the horse and the high rise, the semirural and the urban, was basic to Oak Brook and was evident in community institutions. Though its impressive tax base was able to support a first-class professional fire department, the Oak Brook Volunteer Firemen's Association survived to aid paid firefighters and to perpetuate the traditional village spirit of volunteerism so cherished by suburbanites.[30]

With office towers, Marshall Field's, exclusive residential subdivisions, and unparalleled leisure and recreation facilities, Oak Brook came as close to the post-suburban ideal as any community on earth. "To a remarkable degree," commented one observer in 1974, "Oak Brook has maintained its 'village' atmosphere while reaping the benefits of being a suburban 'downtown' for the region." In accord with the traditional suburban ideal, it was an exclusionary sylvan refuge, but it was a refuge both for big business and wealthy homeowners. This commentator correctly summed up the cardinal principle underlying the development of the community when he wrote, "Only two classes are welcome in Oak Brook—rich people and rich corporations."[31]

In California's Orange County new post-suburban communities were also arising, but on a scale that dwarfed little Oak Brook. Development could proceed on a grand scale in Orange because the vast ranches in the southern part of the county had never been partitioned. Consequently, in the early 1960s huge tracts of land remained in the hands of a single owner or corporation, standing ready for the creation of expansive new communities. Most notable of the holdings was the Irvine Ranch, which sprawled across 130 square miles, encompassing approximately one-sixth of the county's area.

Before 1960 the Irvine Company had permitted the development of some relatively small tracts at the fringe of its holdings, but at the beginning of the decade its vast ranch remained largely intact, an undisturbed domain of orange groves, vegetable fields, and grazing cattle. Faced, however, with growing pressure to develop the land, in 1960 the company hired planner-architect William Periera to lay out a ten-thousand-acre community around the proposed campus of the newly created University of California-Irvine, and four years later Periera assisted in formulating a plan for the thirty-five thousand acres constituting the ranch's southern sector. Central and northern sector plans also followed as the company adopted a comprehensive blueprint for the development of its holdings.[32]

True to the emerging post-suburban model, the Irvine lands were to include tax-producing commerce as well as homes attractive to those seeking the suburban way of life. The company's leading office and retailing development of the 1960s was Newport Center, advertised as "a 622-acre complex of financial, business and medical office buildings, stores, restaurants and apartments in the epicenter of America's fastest growing area."[33] At its core was Fashion Island, an upscale shopping mall, which promoters described as a "vast forum of tree-lined plazas and sculptured fountains intertwine[d] among four major department stores and more than 50 exquisite shops and restaurants."[34] Nearby was the Financial Plaza of Newport Center, where two nine-story office buildings were completed in 1969. That same year ground was broken for the $10 million, sixteen-story Avco Financial Center, which would further enhance Newport Center's growing reputation as a post-suburban downtown for the southern half of Orange County.[35] Meanwhile, the Irvine Industrial Complex was attracting manufacturing and research facilities to the former ranch lands. By the close of the 1960s, 280 industrial companies had located in the 3,100-acre complex, providing jobs for more than 14,000 people.[36]

Even though the Irvine Company was planning to create a full-scale city that eventually would include 430,000 residents, towering high rises, and giant factories, it did not wholly eschew the traditional suburban ideal of the small-scale and the intimate. Basic to the Irvine plan was the goal of creating a city composed of distinct residential villages that, according to one report, would "imbue the residential environment . . . with a sense of place and identity to which residents [could] relate on an intimate scale." The villages were to range in size from fewer than six hundred to more than two thousand acres and include schools and shopping facilities. Moreover, each was to have "a unique theme or focal point which differentiate[d] it from all other villages."[37] This theme could be derived from a natural feature of the village, such as a canyon or bluff, or from its proximity to a golf course or water.

To further re-create the village atmosphere of the ideal traditional suburb, the company also organized homeowner associations charged with maintaining the neighborhood park and recreation facilities as well as enforcing architectural controls. Homeowners elected the association's governing board, which supposedly would speak for the neighborhood and enhance the sense of grass-roots rule.[38] Thus the Irvine Company sought to fashion a city of villages with the intimacy of the small town and the participatory government of friends and neighbors so intrinsic to traditional suburban ideology.

Other large-scale developments in southern Orange County sought to achieve the same mix of community neighborliness and commerce. Laid out from 1965 on, Mission Viejo was an eleven-thousand-acre project with an expected ultimate population of ninety-five thousand middle- and upper-middle-class residents.[39] Yet the developers of this giant real estate scheme emphasized instilling community identity in the new residents so that the project would not be just an anonymous collection of thousands of homes. To achieve this, the Mission Viejo Company built the community around an early California Spanish theme. All buildings conformed to the company's version of early California architecture and preferably had earth-colored stucco walls and tile roofs. Moreover, the community celebrated Cinco de Mayo, the Mexican national holiday, and when the development company asked residents for suggestions to rename the local newsletter, it reminded them, "Since Mission Viejo reflects the tradition of Early California and its Spanish heritage, a name indicative of this influence could be a strong contender."[40] Yet the community also included a

TABLE 6. Population, Population Density, and Percentage of Resident Work Force Employed in County, 1970

County	Population	Population per Square Mile	Percentage of Employed Residents Working in County
Suffolk	1,124,950	1,211	64%
Nassau	1,428,080	4,942	59
Oakland	907,871	1,047	64
DuPage	491,822	1,486	50
Saint Louis	951,353	1,907	57
Orange	1,420,386	1,816	74

Source: Bureau of the Census, *Census of Population: 1970* (Washington, D.C.: U.S. Government Printing Office, 1973).

three-hundred-acre industrial park, which attracted its first occupant in 1969, an engineering and manufacturing facility for electronic computers expected to employ more than fourteen hundred persons.[41] According to the local newsletter, this high-tech facility was "to be built of adobe-style concrete block," thereby conforming with the prevailing Spanish theme.[42] Like other emerging post-suburban communities, Mission Viejo sought to attract commercial facilities and places of employment. But commerce was not to disrupt the suburban sense of community created through a unifying fantasy of romantic old California. In a community like Mission Viejo, the computers had to be manufactured in an adobe-like structure.

On Long Island, in Oakland, DuPage, and Saint Louis Counties, and in Southern California, the emerging post-suburban communities were, then, balancing the urban and the suburban. They were creating a world in which corporate headquarters adjoined polo fields and high-rise office towers arose within walking distance of elite residences. In this new world computer plants were to be sheathed in charming adobe and Rockefeller Centers were to be swathed in greenery. The best of the central city and the suburb were to be combined in an incongruous mix, a post-suburban compound that was becoming increasingly popular among developers and residents along the metropolitan fringe.

Moreover, a growing number of Americans were experiencing this transformation of metropolitan life. As seen in table 6, by 1970 Suffolk, Nassau, and Orange Counties each had more than one million residents while Oakland and Saint Louis Counties were not far from the million mark. Even diminutive DuPage County could boast of almost a half million inhabitants. Whereas the population of the nation as a whole rose 13 percent during the 1960s, the population of Orange County soared 102 percent, Suffolk's count increased 69 percent, and the figures for DuPage, Saint Louis, and Oakland Counties rose 57 percent, 35 percent, and 32 percent respectively. Moreover, in each of the six counties population density exceeded one thousand people per square mile. With almost five thousand people per square mile, Nassau was filled to capacity, having virtually no additional undeveloped tracts. The bucolic open spaces that had lured early residents to the fringe areas were disappearing, and urbanization was proceeding without respite.

Indicative of the post-suburban trend was the growing percentage of people who both lived and worked along the metropolitan fringe. By 1970 in each of the six counties, at least 50 percent of employed county residents who reported their place of work were employed within their home counties (see table 6). And in every county but Suffolk this percentage had risen during the previous decade. Even in Suffolk, New York City was no longer the destination of the largest number of commuters; instead post-suburban Nassau had surpassed Gotham as a source of employment for Suffolk Countians. The white-collared, pinstriped commuter who boarded the train each day and migrated to an office in Manhattan or the Loop was not the predominant species in such areas as Nassau, Suffolk, or DuPage. This type was in the minority in the pioneering post-suburban counties.

The 1970 census data, however, only confirmed what was evident to anyone driving along the highways of Long Island, Southeastern Michigan, or Southern California. Those who were able to move along the traffic-clogged thoroughfares observed new office buildings arising at every interchange or major intersection. Shopping malls were growing larger, and manufacturing plants were releasing an increasing number of workers onto the highways at five o'clock each evening. With more greenery and parking, the relatively spacious layout of the post-suburban metropolis differed from that of the central city. But the office towers, department stores, and research laboratories announced to any observer that the executive-city model of Clayton and Oak Brook was definitely supplanting the prewar ideal of the suburban village.

CHECKING GOVERNMENTAL FRAGMENTATION

Not only did the 1960s witness the emergence of executive cities that achieved a lucrative balance between commerce and residence. During these same years the local governmental structure also continued to adapt to the persistent need for balancing grass-roots village government and centralized, areawide administration. According to many political leaders and experts, in the past the governmental scales had tipped too far toward the side of the pint-sized village and

TABLE 7.   Number of Municipalities, 1960 and 1970

County	1960	1970
Suffolk	27	29
Nassau	65	66
Oakland	38	38
DuPage	28	36
Saint Louis	98	95
Orange	22	25

Sources: Bureau of the Census, Census of Population, 1960, 1970 (Washington, D.C.: U.S. Government Printing Office, 1961, 1972).

the fragmentation of suburbia. In the 1960s, however, the emerging post-suburban counties corrected this perceived imbalance and backed away from the rampant balkanization that had produced scores of municipalities in prewar Nassau County and postwar Saint Louis County. Though small-scale, intimate rule still appealed to many residents along the fringe, the splintering of the political scene into minuscule municipalities for every few hundred residents was no longer acceptable. To achieve the advantages of coordination and cooperation, lawmakers along the metropolitan rim were now prepared to halt the border wars and divisive incorporation battles that had characterized earlier decades. The mad rush to the courthouse to file annexation or incorporation petitions before one's rival was a phenomenon disappearing from suburban practice.

The result was a drop in the rate of new incorporations. As seen in table 7, during the 1960s no new municipalities were created in Oakland County, the number of Long Island village governments rose only slightly, and in Orange County there were only three new incorporations. In Saint Louis County, the number of municipalities actually fell by three, owing to the consolidation of some existing units. (By comparison, during the 1950s fourteen new municipalities had appeared in Saint Louis County, thirteen in Oakland, and nine in Orange; see table 5, in chapter 3.) Though the number of municipalities that were fully or partially in DuPage County increased by eight, this figure is misleading. Actually only two new municipalities, Warrenville and Darien, were incorporated. Six municipalities, which were primarily in adjoining counties, annexed small tracts in DuPage, thus inflating the total number of municipal governments. In none of the counties was there an explosion of new governments of the type experienced in previous years.

In part, this change reflected the growing importance of subdivision associations as defenders of property values and regulators of suburban behavior. These homeowner associations increasingly offered the defenses desired by suburbanites and reduced the necessity for incorporation. Miniature private governments were thus filling the role previously played by public governments. But the decline in the birthrate of municipalities also was a consequence of changing legal procedures. In one state after another, lawmakers were fashioning a legal environment more hostile to the proliferation of governmental units.

Nowhere was the change so dramatic as in Saint Louis County, that once-prolific mother of municipalities. As early as 1951 the county council drafted a policy to restrict further incorporations. The council specified that henceforth incorporation petitions had to present detailed information about the proposed municipality, including the projected first-year budget of the city or village, and copies of the petition had to be transmitted to the county counselor, highway engineer, clerk, and planning commission for their perusal. These officials or bodies were then to approve or disapprove the petition, and if any of them expressed disapproval, incorporation would require a positive vote by at least five of the seven county council members.[43] Yet under Missouri law the validity of the council's efforts to curb the creation of new municipalities was doubtful. That same year the county counselor told the county legislators, "The County Court (or Council) is not authorized to deny incorporation to any area that reasonably constitutes a city or town merely because it decides that no more municipalities are advisable." Moreover, the counselor concluded that a negative opinion by the planning commission, highway engineer, or other county officer could not block an incorporation effort. "If the area is properly the subject of incorporation," he contended, "the petition must be granted whether they [the various county officers] approve or not."[44]

Of greater significance in checking the rate of incorporation were major changes in Missouri's annexation procedures. In Saint Louis County fear of annexation had been a leading motive for incorporation. Under Missouri law, a municipality could annex new territory unilaterally, without the approval of the residents of the tract to be absorbed. One could block a proposed annexation only by submitting an incorporation petition for the disputed territory prior to the filing of the annexation measure. Thus the permissive annexation laws had spawned scores of new municipalities as residents seized upon incorporation as their best defense against absorption. By curbing the annexation threat, Missouri would clearly slow the pace of new incorporations and limit metropolitan fragmentation.

Recognizing this, in 1953 the Missouri legislature adopted the Sawyers Act, which offered new protection for areas threatened with annexation. Under the new law, cities could still annex without the approval of residents of the area to be absorbed, but before proceeding with an annexation, municipalities had to submit a petition to the county circuit court for a declaratory judgment authorizing the annexation. The petition had to demonstrate that the boundary change was "reasonable and necessary to the proper development of said city" and that the annexing city could "furnish normal municipal services of said city to said unincorporated area within a reasonable time after said annexation." Moreover, the burden of proof was on the annexing city.[45] In other words, the Sawyers Act provided for judicial review of the reasonableness of an annexation proposal and forced the annexing city to prove that a boundary adjustment was necessary.

With the county council dedicated to resisting further incorporations and the Sawyers Act providing a judicial forum for determining the validity of boundary changes, the birthrate of new cities and villages dropped markedly after 1953. Only four additional municipalities were created between that date and 1960. But some irregular incorporations were still possible. For example, in 1959 developer Bill Bangert engineered the creation of the village of Champ as a means for developing an industrial park through the issuance of tax-exempt municipal revenue bonds. At the time Champ included only fifteen residents and Bangert was clearly exploiting the permissive incorporation laws for the purpose of personal profit.[46] The *St. Louis Post-Dispatch* labeled Champ "a promotion that grabbed one of the prime commercial locations in the then unincorporated area," and Missouri's attorney general challenged the validity of the incorporation, claiming that Champ was formed "for and exist[ed] for a private and not a public issue."[47] Missouri's Supreme Court, however, upheld the incorporation, permitting the creation of yet another unit of government in Saint Louis County.

During the early 1960s, though, the Missouri Supreme Court generally offered little support for the forces of fragmentation and took action that markedly strengthened the foes of metropolitan divisiveness. The tribunal acted most notably in the case of the *City of Olivette v. Graeler.* In 1957 the predominantly residential community of Olivette sought to annex 303 acres on its western boundary. Saint Louis County had zoned this acreage for industrial and commercial development, and Olivette's land grab was at least partially motivated by the municipality's desire to rezone the tract as residential and thus protect its western flank from the incursions of commerce. The land bordered on the existing Monsanto Company headquarters and laboratories in adjoining Creve Coeur, and county planners claimed it was ideally suited for industrial plants, which would enhance the county's tax base and employment opportunities.[48] The case thus represented a classic conflict between county planners concerned about the broader welfare of the area and parochial municipal leaders dedicated to exclusionary zoning, no matter the consequences to the county as a whole.

In the county circuit court, Judge Noah Weinstein ruled against Olivette, arguing that the county charter of 1950 had, in effect, incorporated the county and thus precluded municipalities from annexing any further county territory.[49] On appeal in September 1960, the state supreme court rejected Weinstein's contention that the entire county was incorporated and ruled that annexation of county territory was possible. But the court asserted, "The interest of the county as a community must be weighed against the claims of the city." In ruling on the annexation of sections of the county, "attention should be given to the needs of the area for municipal services, whether they are adequately cared for [by the county] and whether they should be supplanted by those of the city."[50] The supreme court then returned the annexation proposal to the circuit court for further consideration. According to the high tribunal, the county charter did not automatically preclude annexation, but the circuit court had to weigh the county's interests against those of the municipality and determine if landowners in the disputed tract had anything to gain in terms of services from annexation to Olivette.

In 1961 the county circuit court reheard the dispute and issued a decree authorizing the boundary change.[51] Again the decision was appealed to the state supreme court, and in 1963 that tribunal thwarted Olivette's plans for annexation. In a ruling that reflected the growing opposition to metropolitan fragmentation, the court observed, "This race for annexations has become somewhat unseemly." It claimed that the county was "able to furnish all normal municipal services" to the area that Olivette sought to annex and thus annexation offered nothing to the property owners of the tract. Moreover, "in this instance, the interests of the 'county as a community' outweigh[ed] the claims of Olivette."[52] In other words, the county would suffer from the annexation and its land-use plans would be threatened. Olivette could present no compelling interest that would outweigh this loss; consequently, Olivette had to yield. The court also recognized that Saint Louis County was not a typical Missouri county but had to be considered as a special case. It did provide municipal services and was not "an interim device, intended merely to operate during a transition period and until the areas had developed so as to be susceptible of municipal government." Defending the county against the forays of parochial municipalities, the court concluded, "So long as the County has an effective county organization, it should not be whittled away to a mere shell by annexations which have as their prime purpose the acquisition of more city taxes."[53]

Together the two *Graeler* decisions of 1960 and 1963 greatly enhanced the opportunity for county coordination of boundaries and limited the likelihood of further fragmentation. If the county could prove that its interests outweighed those of the annexing municipality, then the county could stymie the annexation scheme. Moreover, in the *Graeler* rulings and later decisions as well, the Missouri Supreme Court showed little sympathy for selfish municipal land grabs. For the next two decades the courts vetoed annexation proposals aimed primarily at enhancing the tax revenues of municipalities. Such boundary changes were deemed unreasonable and unnecessary and thus invalid. Given the *Graeler* rulings, Saint Louis County now enjoyed the upper hand in boundary adjustment disputes. County opposition to an annexation proposal generally doomed that proposal to defeat. In 1963 an expert on the municipal law of Missouri concluded, "Although it is doubtful that the second *Graeler* decision will entirely inhibit future annexations by St. Louis County municipalities, it is nonetheless clear that for all practical purposes such municipalities now have a very heavy burden to meet in establishing not merely that the particular annexation is reasonable and necessary with respect to the municipality and the area to be annexed, but also that it is consonant with the interests of St. Louis County as a whole."[54] Henceforth, in boundary disputes the interests of the whole would prevail over the interests of the fragment.

Meanwhile, in 1963 the Missouri legislature amended the Sawyers Act to require approval of the voters in the area to be annexed prior to annexation. Eschewing unilateral boundary adjustments, Missouri's lawmakers now mandated concurrent majorities in both the annexing city and the tract to be absorbed. Thus the legislature and the supreme court together eliminated the threat of annexation that had earlier balkanized local government in Saint Louis County. During the 1960s municipalities seeking boundary changes suffered repeated defeats, both at the polls and in the courts. The county's most populous municipality, Florissant, lost a number of battles in the courts, and audacious little Champ could no longer pursue its selfish plans unobstructed.[55] When the virtually uninhabited village attempted to annex two tracts totaling one thousand acres for further industrial development schemes, the Missouri Supreme Court proved an insuperable obstacle. "On the whole record, . . . both annexations are unreasonable," the court held in 1969. "The village of Champ is not bursting at the seams. It is not growing into either area. . . . It has no present facilities or demonstrated future abilities for providing any sort of municipal services to the areas sought to be annexed."[56]

While the supreme court was blasting the ambitions of Champ, some within the state legislature were attempting not only to slow the rate of new incorporations but to consolidate existing governmental units. Repeatedly during the

1960s, legislators submitted bills that would require consolidation or disincorporation of all county municipalities having a population under two thousand. The legislature never adopted the measures, but these bills aroused consternation since they threatened the existence of about half the villages in Saint Louis County.[57] Missouri lawmakers did, however, reduce the barriers to municipal consolidation. Until 1961 state law required that mergers win the approval of two-thirds of those casting ballots in each of the merging municipalities. That year the requisite margin of approval was reduced to a simple majority.

Meanwhile, within Saint Louis County some were also urging a reduction in the number of municipalities. In 1967 County Supervisor Lawrence Roos added his voice to the chorus decrying fragmentation and called for the compulsory consolidation of the thirty county municipalities having fewer than one thousand inhabitants. If compulsory mergers proved impossible, Roos urged that at least the county council and county planning commission should assume the initiative in proposing, studying, and submitting schemes for consolidation.[58] Some, however, were not willing to wait for county action. In 1967/68 a group called the Citizens Advisory Council for Consolidation and an University of Missouri study proposed the merger of the municipalities of Manchester, Winchester, Ellisville, and Ballwin. Repeating the arguments that foes of fragmentation had been presenting for decades, the university report claimed, "The consolidation . . . offers the best practical approach for citizens to take planned action to see that their governments are modernized to provide maximum services."[59] Moreover, proposals for the consolidation of Ferguson and Berkeley and Ferguson and Bridgeton stirred some interest in the northern half of the county.[60]

Though the forces of consolidation were taking the offensive, the defenders of localism proved formidable foes. Speaking for the suburban cities and villages, the St. Louis County Municipal League opposed the bills to establish minimum population limits, claiming that ability to provide municipal services rather than number of inhabitants should be the standard used to determine whether a municipality should survive. Vincent A. Bayer, mayor of Greendale (population 1,100) and chair of the league's merger committee, observed: "My study of cities in the county has led me to believe that it is true that many do not provide adequate services. But some smaller ones do a good job and some larger ones do not."[61] The league's president seconded this position, claiming, "It is not necessarily bad to be small any more than it is necessarily good to be big."[62] Even the *St. Louis Post-Dispatch* expressed opposition to the idea of forced consolidation or disincorporation, arguing that there was "no need to eliminate any municipality that [met] its obligations to the county as a community." If the city or village adequately provided basic services, "why condemn it to extinction?"[63]

Plans for the merger of Manchester, Winchester, Ballwin, and Ellisville aroused similar criticisms. "In the smaller community people know their elected officials better and participate more closely in city government," argued the mayor of Manchester. Expressing a view often repeated along the metropolitan fringe, his honor told reporters, "If they [suburbanites] liked the cold impersonal attitude of big city government they would have moved to or stayed in St. Louis."[64]

Faced with such opposition, the merger movement made little headway. Manchester, Winchester, Ballwin, and Ellisville remained separate municipalities as did Ferguson, Berkeley, and Bridgeton. In 1962 little Meadowbrook Downs consolidated with Overland, and two years later Marvin Terrace merged with Saint John as did Elmdale in 1965.[65] Thus the number of municipalities declined but the great majority of governmental units survived. A continuing devotion to grass-roots rule was sufficient to stymie wholesale mergers. Fragmentation abated in the 1960s but consolidation advanced only slightly.

Though suburban Californians were not as prolific producers of municipalities as their Saint Louis counterparts, they too were attempting to curb the forces of fragmentation during the 1960s. Whereas the judiciary played a major role in the changes occurring in Missouri, in California the state legislature was to assume the lead in transforming the incorporation and annexation process. In Orange County and in the Saint Louis area, however, the arguments for change were similar. Government splintering had to be checked and some order imposed on the boundary adjustment process.

In 1960 the California legislature conducted a series of hearings to investigate the balkanization of suburbia and to consider how it could be halted. Meanwhile, the Governor's Commission on Metropolitan Problems was studying the same question. At a final hearing of the legislature's Interim Committee on Municipal and County Government, this commission, the League of California Cities, and the County Supervisors Association of California each presented its proposals for dealing with the seeming governmental chaos along the metropolitan fringe.

The three groups differed markedly on the issue of centralization versus local authority. Urging central control of incorporation and annexation, the governor's commission suggested the creation of "a State Board to review local boundary changes." This state board would "consider all proposals for annexation and incorporation, as well as for the consolidation and the formation of special districts" and would "be given power to approve or disapprove the proposals brought before it."[66] In other words, state officials in Sacramento would have the power to determine whether a community could become a municipality and whether territory could be added to a city. Understandably, this proposition did not please municipal or county officials. The County Supervisors Association strongly asserted that "the California tradition of local home rule and self-determination as applied to county government . . . be continued and strengthened" and contended that any state boundary commission should have only "advisory" powers.[67] The localities should retain the final decision-making authority. The League of California Cities was less definite in its proposals, but its associate counsel reminded the legislators that "the idea of a State agency having any degree of control over local boundary changes [was] abhorrent to those in local government." Moreover, he indicated that a "large number of city officials . . . recommended a county agency as the proper agency for decision-making in connection with annexations."[68]

Ultimately, the legislature opted for such a county agency. In a compromise bill enacted in 1963, California's lawmakers mandated the creation of a Local Agency Formation Commission (LAFCO) in each of the state's counties. These commissions had the power "to review and approve or disapprove with or without amendment, wholly, partially, or conditionally, proposals for the incorporation of cities, creation of special districts and the annexation of territory to cities or special districts."[69] If the commission disapproved of a boundary change, that would end the incorporation or annexation procedure, though petitioners could resubmit proposals after a year's interval. The commission was to be composed of two county officers, two representatives of the cities within the county, and a fifth member chosen by the other four.[70] Specifically, in Orange County the board of supervisors chose the county representatives and the Orange County League of Cities named the two members who spoke for the municipalities. Thus the commission supposedly balanced county and municipal interests, and its composition was intended to ensure that neither the supervisors nor the mayors would be able to dominate the annexation or incorporation process.

Through the creation of LAFCOs the California legislature clearly intended to achieve greater countywide coordination of annexation and incorporation initiatives. Rather than allow the helter-skelter carving up of the county into myriad municipalities, the state's lawmakers sought to impose a guiding hand on the boundary adjustment process. In Orange and other California counties, coordination would purportedly replace selfish fragmentation, and defensive dairy farmers would no longer be able to create protected municipal enclaves such as Dairyland and Cypress. With LAFCO monitoring local government organization in Orange County, rationality would supposedly supplant the unseemly race to the courthouse as the norm.

But reality differed somewhat from the reform ideal. In Orange County and elsewhere the creation of LAFCOs did not eliminate all border wars or result in a coordinated scheme of government organization. During the first decade of its existence, Orange County's LAFCO reviewed petitions for incorporation or annexation, but it did not create any plans for future government development. It responded rather than guided. It acted as a quasi-judicial body, hearing petitions and deciding on specific cases presented. Orange County's commission did not regard itself as a regulatory body charged with formulating guidelines and policies for prospective boundary adjustments. Moreover, the Orange County body as well as other LAFCOs were generally permissive rather than restrictive. Referring to petitions for incorporation and annexation, one account from 1970 noted that the LAFCOs "ordinarily ha[d] a poor record of resisting such requests."[71]

The shortcomings of the Orange County LAFCO were evident in the struggle over the incorporation of Irvine at the beginning of the 1970s. Like so many previous incorporation fights, the Irvine struggle was an old-fashioned battle to defend valuable turf from land-hungry municipal neighbors. Moreover, despite urgings to assume command of the situation, the Orange County LAFCO played a relatively passive role in the conflict, providing little guidance or direction.

By 1970 approximately seventy-six hundred persons already lived in the Irvine subdivisions and the Irvine Industrial Complex was attracting an increasing number of industrial taxpayers. Concerned about the future governmental status of the fast-growing area, in June 1970 about thirty community associations united to form the Council of the Communities of Irvine (CCI). These community associations enjoyed the backing of the powerful Irvine Company, which shared their concern about predatory municipalities eager to gobble up the ranch lands. John Burton, chair of the CCI, expressed the fears he shared with others when he told the *Irvine World News*, "Newport Beach has its eye on the Irvine Industrial Complex, Costa Mesa wants some of the County Airport area, Santa Ana can grow only one way—east into Irvine, and Tustin wants the Lighter Than Air station site. . . . We can consider studying incorporation now or we can do nothing at all, or we can incorporate later whatever is left to incorporate," Burton explained, "and if we try to do it later, we'll run the increased risk of our borders being annexed." Closing on an ominous note, he predicted, "We'll be forced to fight border wars."[72]

His worst fears were soon realized, for the city of Newport Beach applied to

LAFCO for the annexation of the 177-acre site of the Collins Radio plant in the Irvine Industrial Complex and that commission was to approve the boundary adjustment.[73] Burton said he was "shocked at the imprudent action" of Newport Beach, calling it "unjust, unfair, selfish, and short-sighted." Moreover, the Newport Beach city council proposed a "summit conference" with the cities of Santa Ana, Costa Mesa, and Tustin, to consider boundary changes and the future status of Irvine, an action viewed with suspicion by Irvine leaders fearful of further land grabs.[74] To thwart such raids by aggressive neighbors, in September 1970 the CCI petitioned LAFCO for incorporation of the city of Irvine.

Earlier that year the Irvine Company had submitted a large-scale plan for the development of the central section of the ranch, and that together with the incorporation petition aroused consternation through much of the county. Many observers believed that the Irvine Company was pushing incorporation so that it would no longer be subject to the interference of the county planning department or the veto power of the board of supervisors but would be able to do whatever it liked, operating through a rubber-stamp city planning agency. One planning firm summed up the prevailing fears of surrounding communities when it observed: "Action on this [incorporation] request will determine whether future planning and development activities of the Irvine Company will be subject to approval by representatives of the 1.4 million residents of Orange County or by representatives of the 7,000 residents of Irvine."[75]

The adjoining city of Santa Ana was especially fearful of the consequences of the incorporation scheme and hired a Chicago consulting firm to recommend a proper course of action. Included in the planning consultants' report was an appeal to LAFCO to take charge and deal forcefully with the problem. The report noted that LAFCO would play "*the key role* in the incorporation of the Irvine property and in the future governmental organization of the entire county" and urged the commission to deny the petition and undertake "a positive program . . . to recommend a system of government, including boundaries for the Irvine property." According to the consultants, "the commission must act as an *initiator* of policy rather than in response to implicit policies resulting from petitions such as the Irvine petition."[76]

A county planning department staff report likewise urged LAFCO to stand up to the Irvine Company and lead rather than follow. It recommended that the commission reject incorporation and annexation applications relating to the Irvine Ranch property until the community was more fully developed. Moreover, LAFCO's own executive director, Richard Turner, recommended that the commission deny the incorporation bid until it determined the ultimate boundaries of the cities adjacent to Irvine. Like other planners, Turner urged

LAFCO to guide governmental development rather than defer passively to the petitions for self-determination submitted by Irvine residents.[77]

Those residents, however, were to triumph, for in February 1971 Orange County's LAFCO rejected the advice of its executive director and endorsed the petitioners' request for incorporation. Two of the five LAFCO members opposed the incorporation petition, but even they were motivated more by political opposition to the Irvine Company than by concern for long-range governmental planning.[78] LAFCO's chair expressed the prevailing sentiment when he said, "I believe it should be up to the people of the area if they want to assume the problems and responsibilities of establishing a city of their own."[79] In a clash between county oversight and local self-determination, the latter still prevailed. Despite the creation of LAFCO, many Orange County leaders felt local residents should continue to have control over the carving up of the county.

In the Irvine incorporation battle, the Orange County LAFCO fell short of the dreams of those favoring central coordination of local government organization. Yet in 1971 California's legislature forced LAFCOs throughout the state to play a more dynamic role in charting the future course of government. The state lawmakers directed each LAFCO to formulate a plan for the prospective development of local governments and to specify the spheres of influence of cities and special districts to ensure a more orderly and predictable pattern of annexation. The LAFCO would determine what unincorporated territory lay within the sphere of influence of each county municipality, thus defining the zone appropriate for annexation to each city.[80] Henceforth, Tustin was not to annex land within the Irvine sphere of influence and Irvine similarly was not to invade Tustin's growing space.

In the future, then, Orange's LAFCO would be required to draft a countywide plan for governmental development, but during the first decade of its existence it did not revolutionize local government organization in the county. It did not assume dictatorial sway or overturn traditional suburban practice. In California as in Missouri, lawmakers curbed the tendency toward fragmentation without substituting heavy-handed central control. County and municipal officials convinced California's legislature to reject proposals for a state agency to determine boundary questions. Boundary adjustment would remain a local issue. Moreover, the Orange County LAFCO did not allow county planners to draw the boundaries of municipalities. The initiative remained with the municipalities and community residents. They petitioned for incorporation or annexation, and LAFCO responded to their petitions rather than issue dictates about future boundary changes or incorporation schemes. California lawmakers provided for review of grass-roots proposals; they did not stamp out such initiatives.

Elsewhere, as well, legislators were concerned about imposing order on the process of boundary adjustment. For example, in 1968 the Michigan legislature authorized creation of the State Boundary Commission to review proposals for incorporation and consolidation, and two years later the state's solons extended the commission's authority to annexation petitions as well. This commission included three gubernatorial appointees and two members chosen by the presiding probate judge of the county in which the petitions under consideration arose.[81] Thus Michigan, unlike California, opted for a measure of statewide control, but still retained a local voice in the deciding of boundary questions. Moreover, if the boundary commission approved the petitions, then the annexation or incorporation requests would be submitted to local voters, who would ultimately determine boundary adjustments.

During the 1960s Michigan, California, and Missouri were, then, retreating from the chaotic first-come, first-serve pattern of boundary change and incorporation that had prevailed during the decade and a half following World War II. Fragmentation was a dirty word and coordination and cooperation were the emerging fashion. Even in states where there was no dramatic change in the boundary adjustment process, many public officials were lambasting suburbia's legacy of divisiveness. For example, on Long Island Suffolk County executive H. Lee Dennison was expressing an opinion heard in an increasing number of state capitals and county courthouses. "Unquestionably, better public service could be provided at less cost by fewer agencies," he wrote in 1962, and throughout the decade he continued to decry "an inherited tradition of isolated, self-sufficient, independence, nurtured over the years for local political advantage under a slogan of local home rule."[82]

Yet devotion to this slogan remained strong, and a Suffolk County newspaper columnist responded to Dennison's cries for centralization by attacking "the starry-eyed county executive" who sought "to eliminate the safeguards of grass-roots town government."[83] Given such attitudes, in neither Suffolk nor any of the other emerging post-suburban counties was consolidation proceeding at a rapid rate. Fragmentation was being kept in check, but that did not mean that post-suburban areas were opting for the opposite extreme of centralization. Saint Louis County remained divided and Orange County's LAFCO refused to devise an authoritative plan for future incorporations and annexations. As they fashioned a government structure suitable for a world partially suburban and partially urban, post-suburban residents were eschewing the worst of the suburban past without abandoning the perceived advantages of small-scale government.

DISCARDING THE METROPOLITAN VISION

Accompanying the assault on fragmentation was a push toward metropolitanism. In the minds of many urban planners, business leaders, and academics of the 1960s, the solution to metropolitan ills was increased ties between the suburbs and the central city so that they could together tackle the problems plaguing urban areas. Proponents of metropolitan unity repeatedly claimed that the city and the suburbs were part of one social and economic whole and only artificial political boundaries separated them. What was needed was a new metropolitan vision to overcome barriers inherited from the past. For many reform-minded citizens a curb on fragmentation was not sufficient. What was needed was to reunite the city of Saint Louis and Saint Louis County, to strengthen ties between Oakland County and Detroit, and to establish an authority to coordinate government on Long Island and in New York City. Rather than think of themselves as suburbanites, residents of the fringe areas had to conceive of themselves as citizens of a single metropolis of interrelated governmental units.

A smattering of victories buoyed the hopes of metropolitan reformers. Nashville combined with surrounding Davidson County, and Jacksonville likewise absorbed the previously unincorporated areas of Duval County. But perhaps the most notable example of metropolitan consolidation was the union of Indianapolis and Marion County. In 1969 Indianapolis Republican leaders fashioned a scheme known as Unigov that extended the city's jurisdiction to virtually the entire county, boosting the city's population by 60 percent and adding thousands of suburban Republicans to the Indianapolis electorate, thereby ensuring the perpetuation of GOP rule. A cooperative Republican state legislature authorized this reform without referring it to the local voters. By avoiding a popular referendum, sponsors of Unigov were able to impose their scheme on a skeptical citizenry.

Elsewhere, however, metropolitan reformers were less successful in bypassing the popular will, and their campaigns for metropolitan unity faltered when confronted with the realities of the emerging post-suburban world. Despite repeated efforts to weave links between city and suburb, at the close of the 1960s Oakland, Nassau, and Saint Louis Counties were socially and economically more self-sufficient than they had ever been and as dedicated as ever to their governmental independence from the central city. Metropolitanism was not to triumph in the post-suburban world. Basic to that world was the desire to preserve the best of suburbia while accepting necessary compromises in the face of growing urbanization. Balance was essential. Metropolitanism, however, required acceptance of the notion that the post-suburban counties were, in fact, part of a big city and responsible for dealing with its problems. This vision was unacceptable, for it tipped the scales too far toward the side of centralization and threatened the traditional suburban ideal.

Nowhere did the battle over metropolitanism rage so loudly or long as in Saint Louis County. Since the early twentieth century the division between the city of Saint Louis and the county had been the subject of heated debate. Business leaders in the city had long argued that the city-county split slowed economic growth in Saint Louis, causing the city to fall behind its urban rivals throughout the nation. As early as 1926 a proposal to consolidate city and county under one city government was decisively rejected by county voters, and four years later the county's electorate also defeated a plan for a federative metropolis combining city and county under a single supergovernment but allowing existing municipalities to maintain control over certain local functions.[84]

Following World War II the all-too-evident decay of the central city stirred renewed demands for metropolitan reform. The city of Saint Louis was losing population and blight was seriously eroding property values in the urban core. Concerned leaders identified various causes for this decline, one being the governmental fragmentation of the metropolitan area. Surrounded by hostile suburbs and unable to extend its boundaries, Saint Louis could not embrace the new taxable wealth of the metropolitan fringe. Instead, its tax base shrank as money moved to the suburbs. Not only did governmental fragmentation sap the strength of the central city, it also supposedly slowed growth in the seemingly vital county. According to some business leaders, the ninety-eight municipalities in the county were unable to work together to promote economic development but instead competed for tax dollars to the detriment of the area's business growth. Saint Louis was on the skids and metropolitan reform seemed to be one means for turning the city around.

In 1954 voters in the city and county had approved the creation of the Metropolitan Saint Louis Sewer District to assume responsibility for constructing, maintaining, and operating sewer facilities for both the city and county.[85] But by the close of the 1950s advocates of metropolitan reform wanted a more far-reaching change in the governmental structure. Consequently, they proposed the creation of the multipurpose Greater Saint Louis City-County District with areawide responsibility for seven functions: formulation of a comprehensive master plan; traffic control on major thoroughfares; regulation of mass transit; promotion of the local economy; supervision of police training and communications; civil defense; and sewerage.[86] Existing municipalities would survive and continue to regulate local streets and provide such services as police and fire protection and garbage collection. The multipurpose district was intended to act as a metropolitan government, drawing the city and county together in an experiment in areawide rule.

Before the district plan could go into effect, it had to win the approval of a majority of the voters in the county as well as a majority of the city's electorate. To garner these concurrent majorities, supporters of the plan organized a vigorous referendum campaign. Supporting the reform proposal was an elite corps of business and civic leaders. The campaign committee included the president of the Southwestern Bell Telephone Company, the presidents of both the city and county chambers of commerce, and a past president of the League of Women Voters, an organization that consistently rallied behind reform crusades in the Saint Louis area. Moreover, Civic Progress, Incorporated, a group of downtown big-business moguls dedicated to urban revitalization, also backed the plan as did both the metropolitan daily newspapers.[87] Many of the most powerful people in the Saint Louis area thus sided with the metropolitan cause.

Yet prior to the November 1959 referendum on the plan, hostile county residents launched a counterattack. The district plan smacked too much of big government and offended the village ideal of traditional suburbia. Moreover, the proposed strengthening of ties with the city of Saint Louis stirred fears that the suburban municipalities were about to be sacrificed on the altar of downtown interests. The whole scheme smelled of the big city, and that was an odor that thousands of county residents could not tolerate. The Citizens Committee for Self-Government, led by Brentwood mayor A. Ray Parker, responded by urging "leaders of all of the County's 98 communities . . . to set up their own town meeting . . . so that everyone [would] have the opportunity to gather and express their disapproval of the proposal in the old-fashioned town meeting manner." Each town meeting would also appoint block workers to be known as town criers. "The town criers will move up and down their respective blocks ringing a bell, which we will furnish, to alert the people against the evils of the District Plan," Parker explained.[88] Like their colonial ancestors, Saint Louis Countians were, then, to take to the streets and warn of the forces of tyranny threatening their communities. According to Mayor Parker, warnings were necessary, for the district plan would result in "exorbitant taxation, duplication of services, and concentration of power in big government." He and his colleagues were prepared to fight against these evils and to ensure "popular and democratic self-government in St. Louis County."[89]

Within the individual cities and villages, opposition groups also developed to battle those who seemingly threatened suburban autonomy. For example, the president of the Webster Groves Task Force for Self-Government reminded voters: "Our local government is tailored to fit the needs of the citizens in our own locality and we believe has been doing quite an efficient job." Moreover, he urged Webster Groves residents to "read the fine print in the District Plan," which purportedly gave "extraordinary power to another group of politicians far removed from local communities."[90] Similarly, the Gravois Township Republican Men's Organization warned: "We do not want to lose sight of the very great advantage we county residents have in the services of our local citizens in governing our own communities. We also have the right to speak out, be heard and be governed by our own neighbors who are well acquainted with our problems. This participation and citizen action is discouraged by . . . the present District Plan."[91]

County newspapers joined in the assault on metropolitanism, printing one editorial after another exhorting voters to repel the big-city forces of amalgamation. The *Brentwood Scope* accused proponents of the district plan of attempting "to destroy the system of American democracy and local self-government . . . in the County. . . . They want us to give up our right to govern ourselves[,] to place the County in the hands of the St. Louis political machine." The *Claytonian-University City Tribune* warned: "When a super governmental structure is established it will be only a decade until a monster may be created." Meanwhile, the *Webster Groves News-Times* labeled the plan a "sugar-coated merger." "A vote for the District Plan on November 3 will be a little like taking castor oil from a honey jar: By the time you find out what's really there, it's too late," argued the Webster Groves editor. "And," he warned his readers, "the Metro medicine is forever."[92] Likewise, the *Watchman-Advocate* of Clayton claimed that the metropolitan district was not "just another layer of government" but "a complete superstructure." It predicted that voters would reject the proposal, leaving "professional do-gooders" to lick "their wounds, while feasting on crow and at the same time casting their eyes about for another cause to espouse." It was clear by election day that the weekly newspapers of the Saint Louis area had, in the words of one reporter, "formed a Rock of Gibraltar against the Metropolitan District Plan."[93]

Joining in the denunciations were the county's most important governmental groups and figures. The Saint Louis County League of Municipalities, representing sixty-seven government units in the county, voted without dissent to "condemn" the district plan, adopting a resolution that warned of the "endless confusion between the various governmental agencies" that would result from implementation of the reform scheme. County supervisor James McNary added his voice to those of the nay-sayers, claiming that the plan was "a mere foothold to establish the means of effecting eventual all-out city-county merger! . . . Vote

No—to protect your county's progress from strangulation by this costly added layer of government which is an all-powerful, potential octopus," the county chieftain told his constituents.[94] A few county leaders did support the plan. The mayor of University City was a backer of the district scheme, though his municipality officially sided with the opposition.[95] Three members of the Clayton Board of Aldermen also endorsed the reform, noting that it had been recommended "by unbiased experts in the fields of government and economics." "We must stop looking at local problems with a magnifying glass and survey the area as a whole," argued one of the Clayton officials.[96]

These metro-minded Claytonians, however, were in the minority, and on election day the scheme suffered defeat in the county by a three-to-one margin. Only 39 of the county's 353 precincts backed the plan, and it carried none of the county's 16 townships. Brentwood's Mayor Parker claimed that the election returns "pointedly reflect[ed] an inherent dislike by [the] American voter of large, centralized government," and his judgment seemed to correctly sum up the feelings of county residents.[97] Throughout the referendum campaign, county leaders had appealed to the suburban devotion to grass-roots rule by friends and neighbors. They had dredged up all the standard arguments that had appealed to suburbanites for decades, and the election returns demonstrated that those arguments were as attractive to the electorate in 1959 as in 1929. By the beginning of the 1960s Saint Louis Countians were willing to compromise the suburban ideal to allow some degree of county coordination and to permit the creation of a single-purpose metropolitan sewer district. But more radical experiments in government centralization were taboo.

In the early 1960s county voters were to make this clear once again when metropolitan reformers presented yet another scheme for governmental reorganization. Immediately following the defeat of the district plan, proponents of an alternative blueprint for the consolidation of the city and county launched their campaign for change. Labeled the "borough plan," this scheme would place the city and county under a single unit of government known as the Municipal County of Saint Louis. This municipal county was to be divided into twenty-two boroughs, each with a borough council exercising very limited powers. These councils would be able to advise the central government about local questions, submit bills to the central legislative council, and wield a veto power over some zoning changes.[98] Beyond that, power was vested in the mayor and legislative council of the municipal county. The borough proposal thus provided for a much more centralized structure of rule than the defeated district plan. This new scheme would destroy all existing municipalities and substitute one consolidated government ruling over both city and county.

Advocates of the scheme organized the Committee for the Borough Plan to Reunite Saint Louis and sought to achieve their goal through an amendment to Missouri's state constitution. Such an amendment, however, required the approval of Missouri voters, and prior to the 1962 referendum on the issue, both friends and foes of the plan engaged in a heated campaign that repeated much of the rhetoric of the 1959 struggle. Backers of the reform plan faced an uphill fight, for this scheme enjoyed less support from the civic and economic elite than did the district proposal. The *St. Louis Globe-Democrat* gave the borough plan token endorsement but the *Post-Dispatch* denounced the scheme, claiming it was "not at all necessary to abolish all the governments in city and county— the good and the strong along with the weak and the ineffective—in order to create a device for handling metropolitan problems."[99] Likewise, the League of Women Voters did not rally behind the plan nor did the city chamber of commerce nor any powerful business or political leaders.[100]

In contrast, the opposition was loud and vigorous. Led by a group known as Citizens for Home Rule and Opposed to the Borough Plan, foes of the scheme blitzed the county with dire warnings. Mayor F. William Human of Clayton headed this citizens group and it had the strong backing of the county chamber of commerce. Human argued that the plan "would completely erase forever many communities such as Clayton, Webster Groves, Kirkwood, and University City" and in their stead would create "an impersonal unwieldy governmental setup that would be far removed from the wishes and feelings of [the county's] citizens." Many criticized the attempt to foist this plan on the people of the city and county through a constitutional amendment. By doing so, the backers of the scheme were allowing voters throughout Missouri to determine the governmental fate of metropolitan Saint Louis rather than reserving that prerogative to the city and county electorate. "I do not believe any proposal has ever been placed before the people of this state more objectionable than this one," cried the president of the county chamber of commerce, who further denounced the plan's "flagrant disregard for the rights of more than 1,500,000 citizens and taxpayers who reside in the City and County." Similarly, a past president of the Missouri League of Municipalities denounced the proposal as "contrary to the principles of local self-government, self-determination and Home Rule."[101]

County municipalities and periodicals also lambasted the supposedly tyrannical scheme. The city of Shrewsbury's board of aldermen denounced the plan and urged local citizens "to protect the principles of home rule and self-government."[102] By the end of October 1962, just a week before the referendum, the governing bodies of more than sixty Saint Louis County municipalities had adopted similar resolutions.[103] The *Saint Louis County Observer,* published in

Maplewood, concurred with the plan's foes, referring to the proposed municipal county as "a governmental monstrosity." Repeating a cliche of traditional suburban ideology, the *Observer* editorialized, "The people in St. Louis County approved incorporation of present municipal governments because . . . they wanted to keep close watch on the kind of administrative functioning they expected and for that matter, they were promised." The borough plan would violate this article of suburban faith and create a government absolutely contradictory to suburban beliefs. Meanwhile, the *Watchman-Advocate* of Clayton rejected the notion that city and county residents should "abrogate their right of self-determination or that they should embrace the first and worst thing that [came] along simply for the sake of doing something."[104] The *St. Louis County Medical Society Bulletin* added its influence to the attack on the metro monster when it diagnosed the borough plan as infected with "the chronic and acute illness of bigness." "We have always held that governmental units can be so big that they easily become unwieldy, expensive, inefficient, slow and ineffective," announced the bulletin.[105]

With such angry denunciations of the scheme appearing in editorial columns and city council minutes, it was not surprising that on November 6, 1962, the borough plan went down to devastating defeat. County voters opposed it by a four-to-one margin, and statewide, the vote was three to one against the plan.[106] Again as in 1959, metropolitan reform failed to win a majority in any of the county's townships. "We feel the vote demonstrates once again the feeling of our citizens that they believe in free choice of government through the free expression of the citizens to be governed," observed the triumphant Mayor Human. And in its postmortem, the *St. Louis County Observer* concluded: "It is our conviction that people in the County . . . want to retain the identities of the communities in which they live [and] want to retain close contacts with their respective governmental officials."[107]

Following the borough plan's defeat, county leaders did not, however, embrace a policy of total isolation. Instead, they indicated their desire to cooperate with the city of Saint Louis and with one another without opting for the extreme of consolidation or merger. Mayor Human explained that he did not "intend to take this victory as a mandate for the status quo" but pledged "to support those proposals which offer[ed] a realistic, acceptable answer to metropolitan needs." John Dowling, the chair of the county council, likewise proposed cooperation among the county government, the city of Saint Louis, and the county's municipalities to solve joint problems. In a letter to Normandy mayor Walter Lundholm, president of the St. Louis County Municipal League, Dowling urged the county and municipal league to "collaborate with officials

of the City of St. Louis on all matters . . . of metropolitan-wide importance."
Mayor Lundholm responded by assuring Dowling of the league's willingness to
cooperate "in any program designed to provide the people of [the] metropolitan area with better areawide services." Similarly, the newly elected county
supervisor Lawrence Roos promised "to work out with Mayor Tucker (of St.
Louis) and officials of municipalities of the County a program of coordination
and cooperation in connection with certain area-wide functions in which all of
the local governments [had] a common interest."[108]

By the close of 1962, then, cooperation, not consolidation, was the watch-
word. In both the 1959 and 1962 contests, foes of reform had spouted the
standard suburban ideological slogans of home rule, small-scale government,
and administration by friends and neighbors, and the election returns had
proved that this rhetoric still swayed voters. Despite mounting criticisms of
fragmentation and a gradual increase in county authority, the suburban faith remained strong, and adherents to that faith would not tolerate the heresy of metropolitanism. In fact, talk of metropolitan government in the Saint Louis area
waned after 1962. Never again would anyone be foolish enough to seriously
propose the consolidation of the city and county under a single government.
The county and its municipalities had reaffirmed once and for all their independence. They were willing to cooperate if it would result in some demon-
strable improvement in services, but they would cooperate as equals, not as
subordinate offspring. The county supervisor, president of the County League
of Municipalities, and mayor of Saint Louis were seeking links with one another, but none was willing to defer to the superior position of the others.

Elsewhere friends of metropolitan reform were placing their hopes on councils of governments. The typical council of government included representatives of counties and municipalities from throughout the metropolitan area and
was dedicated to a cooperative and consolidated attack on metropolitan problems. It was a voluntary association with only advisory powers, a United Nations of local units of government. Yet devotees of the metropolitan vision believed that such councils might lay the foundation for more thoroughgoing
metropolitan reforms of the type proposed in the Saint Louis area. They might
be the first step in a process of metropolitan reorganization. In 1968 the federal government bolstered these emerging councils of governments by giving
them authority to review all federal grant proposals submitted by local governments within the metropolitan area. Known as A-95 reviews, this procedure
made the councils clearinghouses for federal funding and was intended to encourage metropolitan-wide planning.

Yet councils of governments faced often insuperable opposition from foes of metropolitanism. In emerging post-suburban areas, local officials viewed them with suspicion and were willing to back them only if the councils could produce concrete benefits. If metropolitan cooperation paid off in better services, it was an acceptable compromise of traditional suburban ideology. Unity for the sake of unity, however, was unappealing to most mayors and county officials. In the end, the rocky career of most councils of governments only proved that suburban devotion to small-scale, intimate rule remained much more powerful than belief in regional government or metropolitan union.

This was evident in the conflict over the Metropolitan Regional Council. Created in 1956 at the behest of New York City's mayor Robert Wagner, the council attempted to build bridges between public officials in the New York metropolitan area to enable them to work together to tackle problems affecting them all. As Mayor Wagner told the assembled representatives of local governments at the initial meeting, "We can identify and define more clearly the nature of our mutual problem[, and] if we should seek the assistance of the Federal government in certain cases, the combined action of all our communities will give us a power that no one of us could wield individually."[109]

This group, however, was not to be a unit of government with any coercive powers. The council's original steering committee specified, "The organization is voluntary in character, both in composition and in binding policy determination." Moreover, it was to respect "the principle of home rule and the integrity of the communities in the region."[110] It offered, then, government leaders from throughout the metropolitan region an opportunity to talk together about problems and use their combined clout to wrench money from Washington. But its members discussed rather than dictated, and throughout its history, the council was primarily dedicated to researching metropolitan problems, disseminating information to metropolitan counties and municipalities, and establishing contact among the region's public officials.

In 1958, however, Mayor Wagner initiated an effort to achieve legal status for the Metropolitan Regional Council. He and like-minded leaders wanted the New Jersey, New York, and Connecticut legislatures to formally recognize the council as a federation of county and municipal governments with authority to engage in research and foster cooperation among the governments of the metropolitan area. Moreover, the council would have a full-time staff and be authorized to levy a tax on each member government proportionate to the population of that governmental unit.[111]

Though it provided for a seemingly modest change in the status of the council, the proposal aroused a furor among Long Island leaders who felt it was the first step by a predatory New York City to swallow them alive. Nassau County executive A. Holly Patterson refused to support the move, and in 1959 he told other metropolitan leaders that his county would never participate in a council that enjoyed such legal status. He stated point blank that Nassau would never join "any junior United Nations or super-duper government." "Nassau County will cooperate with one and all but will surrender its autonomy to no one," Patterson announced. Moreover, he declared his opposition to "putting another overcoat of government on an already smothering taxpayer . . . [which might lead to] an obliteration of county boundaries."[112] Nassau County continued to participate in the council, but it also persisted in opposing any legal status for the body.

The debate over legal status for the Metropolitan Regional Council continued through the early 1960s. Long Island leaders believed that New York City was seeking to create a regional planning body that would gradually acquire authority to override the decisions of local planning agencies. Mayor Wagner, the council's chief sponsor, fueled these fears when in 1962 he wrote in the *New York Times Magazine* of the New York of the future as a "super-city," requiring a "supergovernment to which all local government in the area—along with the three state governments of New York, New Jersey, and Connecticut—will have to yield some of their present authority."[113] Moreover, false reports and exaggerated rumors reinforced the mounting opposition among Long Islanders. In October 1960 the *Long Island Press* incorrectly claimed that if the council were granted legal status, then membership by Nassau, Suffolk, and other area counties would be "compulsory" and that New York City would "hold the balance of power in the Council."[114] The threat of a metro monster seemed to be looming large, and a fervent band of Long Island citizens was ready to rally to the defense of local autonomy.

The fight over the Metropolitan Regional Council reached its climax in Suffolk County in May 1962. County Executive H. Lee Dennison, a Democrat in a predominantly Republican county, had asked the Republican-controlled board of supervisors to endorse an agreement among the metropolitan-area counties and municipalities calling for legal status for the Metropolitan Regional Council. At the board meeting to consider the endorsement, Dennison faced a barrage of protest. The Committee to Protect Suffolk County from Metropolitan Regional Government was perhaps the most vehement in its denunciations, but its arguments were supported by the Citizens Planning Council of Huntington, the Long Island Federation of Women's Clubs, and the right-wing Young Americans for Freedom.[115] Foes of the metropolitan body also read a letter from Robert Moses, chair of the Long Island State Park Commission, which denounced the creation of "any more super agencies." In a telegram to the board, State senator Elisha Barrett urged Suffolk to "avoid any entangling alliances with [the county's] all but bankrupt city neighbor" but to opt instead for "cooperation without affiliation."[116] At the hearing Arthur Cromarty, chair of both the board of supervisors and the county Republican party, recited the suburban credo, asserting his belief in "home rule and in grass-roots government." Moreover, he linked Dennison with his fellow Democrat Mayor Wagner in a plot to foist metropolitan rule on Suffolk Countians. Cromarty charged that the metropolitan council was "the first step toward total centralization of all government under a huge bureaucracy directed by political appointees" and argued that New York City wanted "to take over control of Suffolk County . . . and make the Eastern seaboard one unit of government with appointed bosses responsible to no one."[117]

The county planning director, a former president of the Suffolk County League of Women Voters, and Bernard Hillenbrand, executive director of the National Association of County Officials, spoke on behalf of the metropolitan council, but their arguments were pallid compared to the fervent warnings of the council's foes. Hillenbrand later recalled, "I never had witnessed such wild, irrational, yet apparently well planned outbursts."[118]

At the close of the hearing, the board of supervisors voted unanimously to sever ties with the council, claiming that "the best interests of the County [would] be served and promoted by not participating."[119] Following the defeat in Suffolk, the executive secretary of the Metropolitan Regional Council lamented that the council's opponents were "dealing with something out of Fairyland, not reality." But Cromarty and his allies remained firm in their beliefs, fantasy or not. When testifying before Congress in 1963, Cromarty repeated his charges against the council, attacking New York City politicians who sought to "annex . . . Suffolk and saddle [it] . . . with the city's vice, corruption and welfare problems." The Suffolk County leader told the members of Congress, "Only the local official can accurately gauge the importance of a project and only a watchful eye can ferret out waste and corruption."[120]

Though Long Island's most widely read newspaper, *Newsday*, dismissed the nay-saying Suffolk County supervisors as "rural reactionaries," other local newspapers supported Cromarty's stance. "Perhaps it is stuff and nonsense to believe that the regional council envisions setting itself up as a super-government," the *Port Jefferson Times* editorialized, "but the straws in the wind indicate that the city constantly wishes to exercise greater influence on its neighbors." Moreover, it claimed the "sprawling regional council . . . would have New York City dominating the entire area to the benefit of New York City." Likewise, the *Smithtown Messenger* suggested that legal status for the regional council "would be a step in the direction of setting up a super-government. . . . It would be only the opening wedge in ultimately making our county an appendage to New York City and all that metropolitan control involves."[121]

After the 1962 debacle, the Metropolitan Regional Council remained in existence but acted only as a relatively weak clearinghouse for the exchange of information among regional public officials. No supercity or supergovernment was to assume control of the New York City area and threaten the authority of Nassau or Suffolk. The boundary between the city and Nassau remained unbreachable, and the two Long Island counties were not to become subordinate units in a grand metropolitan scheme. Instead, on Long Island as in Saint Louis County, leaders of the emerging post-suburban domain were jealously defending their prerogatives and repelling the central city's overtures for closer links. The rhetoric of grass-roots rule survived in Suffolk and Nassau as well as Saint Louis County, and what some deemed a fairyland ideology of autonomy thwarted the metropolitan vision of Mayor Wagner and his ilk.

During the late 1960s a similar clash between local officials and supporters of a metropolitan council of governments occurred in Oakland County. As early as 1954 supervisors from the various counties of southeastern Michigan had met to discuss the water supply problems that plagued the area. Recognizing the need for a permanent forum for the exchange of information and opinions, they formed the Supervisors Inter-County Committee (SICC), which was granted legal status by the state legislature in 1957. The committee consisted of forty-two representatives, seven from each of the region's six counties, who met once a month. The group lobbied for the passage of state legislation favorable to the region and sponsored research studies on sewerage and water supply in southeastern Michigan.[122] It was, then, a voluntary association of officials dedicated to furthering the common goals of the six area counties without infringing on the powers of those counties.

By the mid 1960s, however, some metropolitan leaders believed a new umbrella agency for the region was needed. Municipalities, including the city of Detroit, had no direct representation on the SICC and that body had no authority to coordinate the efforts of special-purpose districts. Moreover, many Detroit-area leaders complained that the SICC and the separate Detroit Metropolitan Area Regional Commission needed to combine their efforts to avoid wasteful duplication. A joint initiative by the two regional groups seemed more sensible than each pursuing a parallel, or possibly overlapping, course of action.[123]

Consequently, in 1965 a Committee of One Hundred, consisting of public officials from throughout the region, suggested the creation of "a voluntary association of local governments" to supplant the SICC and "assume the functions and projects of the existing Detroit Metropolitan Area Regional Planning Commission." In its report on the proposed association, the Committee of One Hundred observed "that the more than four hundred local governments, . . . in Southeast Michigan form[ed] one regional community" with a citizenry "bound together physically, economically, and socially." But given the existence of "many separate, yet interrelated, local governments," the committee faced the dilemma of how "to retain local home rule while combining [the area's] total resources for regional challenges. . . . We believe that the expansion of effective voluntary cooperation among our local governments is the best solution for dealing with this dilemma," concluded the Committee of One Hundred.[124]

By 1967 a number of the region's governments had agreed to membership in the new association, and on January 1, 1968, the Southeast Michigan Council of Governments (SEMCOG) was formally established, superseding the SICC. At the same time, the Detroit Metropolitan Area Regional Planning Commission became SEMCOG's planning division. Each governmental unit, no matter its population, sent one voting representative to SEMCOG's general assembly, with the exception of the city of Detroit and Oakland and Macomb Counties, which had two votes each, and Wayne County, the most populous unit, which had four votes.[125] Like the SICC, SEMCOG was intended to serve as a lobbying and research group that could further the mutual goals of the region's many governments. Moreover, it conducted the A-95 reviews of federal grant proposals submitted by area governments. It did not, however, have any authority to dictate policy.

Despite its limited powers, SEMCOG aroused the same fears that metropolitan proposals had stirred on Long Island and in Saint Louis County. Some Oakland Countians viewed it as the first step in a metro takeover of local government and were not reluctant to express their misgivings. In the Royal Oak municipal election of November 1967, membership in SEMCOG, according to a local newspaper, "produced, by far, the widest split among the 15 contesting for city commission seats and the mayor post." Some candidates favored the regional group, others opposed it, and a few expressed mixed feelings, but virtually all made it clear that they did not want to proceed too far down the path of metropolitanism. "I think getting into the council of governments set up . . . is the worst thing Royal Oak ever did," announced one mayoral candidate. With a typically suburban aversion for large-scale government, he explained, "You don't need a great big agency." A commission candidate likewise observed, "[SEM]COG's so big it looks like a scary monster. It looks like 'big brother' to me." "In things like [SEM]COG you're bypassing local autonomy," warned a winning contestant for a commission seat, and a fellow victor expressed mixed feelings when he noted, "On a voluntary basis, it's great. But we have to be awful careful of it growing, without realizing it."[126]

Royal Oak's mayor L. Curtis Potter took a favorable stance on SEMCOG, attacking the "isolationism" of the association's opponents. But even he placated his constituents by assuring them that SEMCOG would "only be a coordinating agency, not a controlling one. . . . Control will be in the general assembly where every unit will have a vote," Potter explained. "This will defend against a big city ruling the roost."[127]

In part, the antagonism to SEMCOG arose from fears that it might encourage social programs fostering the migration of low-income Detroit blacks to the suburbs. The Detroit riot of 1967 heightened the already tense race relations in southeastern Michigan, leaving white suburbanites suspicious and fearful of any additional links with the seemingly threatening big city. A Royal Oak mayoral candidate warned that SEMCOG could "be used as a big club to beat local cities into submission," and as evidence he cited a recent threat from Detroit's mayor that if the suburbs did not provide more low-cost housing, Detroit might cut off Oakland's water supply and sewage treatment services. Moreover, in 1967 the *Detroit News* noted that foes of SEMCOG had equated the regional association "with a vast conspiracy to eliminate local government, to racially integrate every hamlet and to stifle individual freedom." The *News* assured its readers that those who claimed that SEMCOG was "a tool to force integration, higher taxes and school district changes" were "either totally misinformed or deliberately dishonest."[128]

During the following few years, however, criticisms of SEMCOG mounted, with some attacking the agency as a malevolent centralizer and others contending it nurtured a do-nothing bureaucracy. In fact, a number of Oakland communities rejected affiliation with the organization. Pontiac, the county seat and largest city, never joined SEMCOG and booming Southfield likewise did not opt to participate. In 1969 Southfield's mayor Norman Feder said he favored joining but suspected the city council opposed membership. "Frankly our council hasn't talked about it for nearly three years," admitted Mayor Feder. Other Oakland cities talked a great deal about the metropolitan association. In 1969 Troy angrily withdrew from SEMCOG, indicting it as a "monolithic extra layer of government seeking to usurp the powers of local governments." Troy mayor Jules R. Famularo claimed, "SEMCOG usurps home rule powers." But he also expressed an increasingly familiar complaint about the seeming inactivity of the organization, when he concluded, "All they do is piddle around."[129] By 1970 Hazel Park and Clawson had withdrawn as well. Hazel

Park's mayor explained his city's departure, noting, "There was the general feeling we just weren't getting that much out of it, that it's too big and too diversified."[130] A Hazel Park city council member complained, "Our dues go toward paying figureheads who do nothing." But he also raised the standard complaint that SEMCOG was "a stepping-stone to supergovernment." And in 1970 Clawson's chief executive explained his city's withdrawal: "We had hoped for a solution to our refuse disposal problems with SEMCOG's help. It never came. We couldn't give a reasonable explanation to our taxpayers for staying in."[131]

That same year Royal Oak also abandoned the metropolitan association. One member of the city commission labeled SEMCOG "a dynasty of empire builders" and said he voted in favor of withdrawing from the organization "because of my lasting distrust of bureaucracy." He further contended that the people in charge of SEMCOG were "extremely liberal in social orientation." "I just don't believe in a lot of vast social programs where everything is run by a director," he confessed. Royal Oak's mayor attacked SEMCOG as "another layer of government which perform[ed] lengthy studies costing millions of dollars." Like their colleagues in Hazel Park, Clawson, and Troy, Royal Oak's leaders could find nothing good to say about the regional association. In their minds it threatened autonomy, spent money, and did nothing constructive for Oakland County's communities. In any case, by the beginning of the 1970s few Oakland County municipal officials had been converted to the ranks of metropolitan reform. In 1970 the *Detroit Free Press* observed, "Royal Oak's imminent departure virtually wipes out Oakland County participation in SEMCOG."[132]

Throughout the late 1960s and early 1970s supporters of SEMCOG were on the defensive. The organization's director, E. Robert Turner, repeatedly denied that he and his staff were "metropolitanists" and claimed that if SEMCOG failed, the federal government might well impose regional government on the Detroit area. According to Turner, "SEMCOG, rather than being the first step toward metro or 'super' government, may actually be the last chance for preventing it." "Our major role is the maintenance of strong, local government," Turner insisted, and this could best be achieved through regional cooperation that ensured optimum services in each of the area municipalities.[133] Yet Turner's protestations won relatively few converts to the SEMCOG camp, and by August 1971 the number of members in the council of governments had dropped to 91, down from a high of 114 members in 1969. Oakland County's government continued to participate, and William Richards, the chair of the Oakland County Board of Supervisors, was a supporter who believed in the necessity "for all communities to work together to benefit everyone." But in 1971 even he lamented, "What kind of a lobby can you have with only 25 percent of the possible membership belonging. With only 91 of 346 government units represented, SEMCOG loses its credibility."[134]

Both Richards and Turner were being made aware of the persistent strength of the traditional suburban ideal of small-scale government. Repeating rhetoric heard for decades along the metropolitan fringe, Oakland municipal officials complained of the bigness and bureaucracy of the metropolitan association. Moreover, they feared the big-city influence of Detroit over SEMCOG. Though the metropolitan vision may have prevailed in academic and planning circles, it made little headway in the city halls of Troy or Royal Oak. True to the emerging post-suburban compromise, municipal officials would accept regional cooperation if it paid off in more efficient or effective services. Yet when SEMCOG did not deliver benefits as quickly as desired, municipal leaders balked. Clawson would deviate from suburban isolationism for the sake of improved refuse disposal, but if metropolitan coordination did not solve the garbage problem, it would withdraw. In post-suburban Oakland as on Long Island and in Saint Louis County, village rule remained the ideal; regional cooperation was an acceptable compromise of the ideal if it produced the desired results.

Given this attitude among municipal officials, SEMCOG had little chance to fulfill the vision of its supporters. It survived, in part because of the federal government's policy favoring regional agencies. But it was not a major force in the government of southeastern Michigan during the late 1960s or 1970s.

Underlying its weakness was the fallacious assumption of its founders. Despite the beliefs of the Committee of One Hundred, southeastern Michigan was not one community bound by common social and economic ties. Post-suburban Oakland County was increasingly removed from the central city of Detroit. As the municipal officials of Troy, Royal Oak, Clawson, and Southfield made clear, the dominant ideal of small-scale government in Oakland deviated markedly from the model of centralized administration that prevailed in the big city. Not only did views on government differ, so did social and economic interests. Southfield was not a bedroom community dependent on Detroit; it was a competitor of downtown Detroit. Race riots in the heart of the Motor City were a boon to commercial developers in Southfield as tenants of downtown offices fled the violence and bad reputation of the central city. Detroit's loss was Southfield's gain. Moreover, the increasingly black city of Detroit was socially alien to the predominantly white cities of Oakland. In the minds of many Oakland Countians, Detroit meant low-cost public housing, declining property values, and an abysmal school system, everything that was anathema to the residents of Oakland.

SEMCOG was, then, attempting to impose cooperation among government units that had diminishing grounds for cooperation. The communities of the six-county region shared water supply and sewerage problems, and Oakland Countians were willing to cooperate in the provision of such services. But beyond sharing the same watershed, Oakland municipalities had relatively little in common with the central city. Increasingly, Oakland and Detroit were socially, economically, and governmentally incompatible.

DuPage and Orange Counties found metropolitan ties equally uncomfortable. Orange County joined the Southern California Association of Governments (SCAG) but was cool toward the Los Angeles-based group, suspecting that it served the interests of Los Angeles first and those of Orange second.[135] During the 1970s twelve Orange cities dropped out of SCAG. Some rejoined, but by the late 1980s twelve of the county's twenty-eight cities remained outside of the association.[136] Likewise, DuPage Countians maintained an arm's length relationship with metropolitan agencies in northeastern Illinois. An Orange County supervisor summed up a truth applicable to post-suburban areas throughout the country: "Let's face it. Local governments in Orange County have voted with their feet. They've walked away from SCAG."[137] In Illinois and California as in Missouri, New York, and Michigan, the metropolitan vision did not conform to the emerging post-suburban vision and municipalities did not hesitate to opt out of metropolitan schemes.

This post-suburban vision glorified traditional suburban values while appreciating the practical benefits of commercial development and governmental cooperation. The metropolitan vision, however, regarded suburbia as an intrinsic, involved part of the big city and its problems, not as a haven where one could enjoy the good life. Supporters of metropolitanism believed regional cooperation was a natural outgrowth of the common bonds that linked the entire metropolitan area. Yet among leaders of the emerging post-suburban areas, intergovernmental cooperation was unnatural, an artificial creation that could prove useful but could also threaten the small-scale community governments they valued. By 1970 this post-suburban vision had proven to be a powerful molder of future government. In Suffolk, Nassau, Oakland, DuPage, Saint Louis, and Orange Counties it had eclipsed its metropolitan rival.

5

Post-Suburban Imperialists

Referring to Oakland County's planning activities, a municipal official of the early 1970s exclaimed, "That's the kind of regional planning I can understand, and the kind of planning I think I have some control over."[1] In this sentence, the Oakland Countian summed up an attitude basic to the development of post-suburban government in the 1970s and early 1980s. SEMCOG and other metropolitan agencies had proven unacceptable; they threatened the post-suburban way of life and ideal of government. But in the mind of this municipal official and many of his ilk along the urban fringe, the metropolitan debacle of the 1960s did not doom all regional cooperation or coordination. Such regional efforts were necessary, but henceforth the region should be defined as including only the post-suburban county. Though the community of interest linking Detroit and Oakland was diminishing, Southfield and Royal Oak still had much in common, and countywide planning and coordination could prove beneficial to their residents. The forces of fragmentation were at bay and metropolitanism was in retreat; now, in the 1970s and early 1980s, it was time for county governments to further define the middle way of post-suburbia and ensure coordination without too seriously bruising the ideal of grass-roots rule.

A number of dynamic county leaders readily accepted this challenge. During the 1970s and early 1980s they sought to expand the role of county government and draw together the disparate municipalities and special districts within their domains. Rather than focusing on metropolitan-wide coordination and cooperation, these leaders concentrated on creating a more unified county, one in which the county government provided central guidance for the many small cities and villages. Like their suburban predecessors, these post-suburban county chieftains viewed the big city with suspicion and distrust. Moreover, they were well aware of the persistent devotion to small-scale units of government. Yet unlike so many village devotees, they did not fear big government but instead sought to transform their counties into post-suburban empires, giant regimes that would rival the nation's great cities. Oakland, DuPage, and

Saint Louis Counties were already rivaling older central cities as hubs of commerce, attracting Fortune 500 companies to new office towers and campuslike corporate parks. Now the governments of these counties needed to assume an unprecedented dynamism suitable for their emerging post-suburban regions.

The change in county government was least noteworthy on Long Island. Nassau County's Republican machine continued the Russel Sprague tradition of central dictation accompanied by soothing rhetoric extolling grass-roots rule. And clashes between the townships and county government kept Suffolk's rulers in a state of upheaval. But in Oakland, DuPage, and Saint Louis, as well as to a lesser extent in Orange, county leaders were attempting to fashion a new pattern of government. Building on the example of Nassau County, they sought to revise the traditional structure of county rule and create a focus of authority in the office of the county executive. This mayorlike figure would supposedly provide the unified leadership necessary to cope with the problems of the post-suburban world and would substitute professional, efficient administration for rule by courthouse political hacks. Moreover, during the 1970s and early 1980s county governments assumed a broader vision of their responsibilities. Economic development, airport construction and management, and the creation of recreational and cultural facilities attracted increasing attention from county lawmakers and planners alike.

Attempts at empire-building did not always succeed. Like the advocates of metropolitanism, the post-suburban imperialists sometimes faced stubborn resistance from those dedicated to the traditional suburban ideal of village government. But there were victories for the imperial forces as well as defeats, and devotees of countywide coordination succeeded in nudging their counties further toward centralization of authority. During the 1970s and early 1980s, then, county imperialism was shifting the balance of post-suburban government. To the consternation of some and the pleasure of others, the scale was tipping toward the side of centralization. Given the persistent belief in small-scale government, however, it was not to tip too far.

RE-CREATING SAINT LOUIS COUNTY

The chief spokesperson for post-suburban imperialism in Saint Louis County during the late 1960s and early 1970s was County Supervisor Lawrence Roos. After graduating from Yale University, Roos had settled in the posh suburb of Ladue and pursued a career in banking with a sideline in Republican party politics. No common ward heeler, he was a businessman with a devotion to efficient, businesslike government. When in 1975 he retired after twelve years as county supervisor, the *St. Louis Post-Dispatch* said "the most noteworthy feature" of his administration had been "efficiency" and commended the "smoothly-run system" instituted under Roos's leadership.[2]

Given his predilection for efficiency and orderly management, Roos naturally cringed when confronted with the multitude of municipalities and the divided authority in Saint Louis County. Throughout the late 1960s he was not reluctant to express his concern over the administrative mess he faced, and during his twelve years in power he argued repeatedly for countywide coordination and administrative reorganization. As early as 1963 in a meeting with the county's state legislators, he emphasized the "urgency" of broadening the county government's authority to provide certain services countywide, in both incorporated and unincorporated areas.[3] A year later in his State of the County message, he claimed that the county and municipalities had to "cooperate in the development of a clear definition of proper municipal responsibilities, those services which [could] be most effectively undertaken by county government, and the means of accomplishing necessary governmental reorganization without sacrificing the values of [the] municipal form of organization."[4] Then in 1965 he spoke of "the objective of full county-municipal partnership" and the need "to fashion municipalities large enough to provide municipal services efficiently, yet small enough to remain responsive to the wishes of the citizen." And in 1968 he urged the state legislature to "give St. Louis county the authority and financial means to implement [a] police reorganization plan," which would transfer all police support services, such as training and crime laboratories, to the county with the municipalities retaining responsibility primarily for patrol duty.[5]

Year after year, Roos argued for a reallocation of power, with the county assuming responsibility for all functions best handled on an areawide basis and the municipalities charged with strictly local tasks. He recognized the devotion to small-scale governments that were responsive to the wishes of the citizenry. But he also believed that the county and municipalities had to work together to eliminate incompetent units of government and clearly define the respective spheres of county and municipal authority, thereby avoiding wasteful duplication of effort and needless conflict. Basic to his beliefs was that the county government must be capable of leading the municipalities so that all area governments would rationally respond to changing conditions. The county had to be an effective engine of change to guide the modernization and streamlining of the governmental structure.

Before the county could guide the creation of a new coordinated system of rule, however, county government itself had to be reformed. The county charter of 1950 had created a legislative body, the county council, and an executive branch headed by the supervisor. But it had allowed a long list of elected county offices to survive and operate largely independent of the council and supervisor. With Roos's support, in 1967 a charter commission was created to rectify this shortcoming and further enhance the authority of the county executive and legislature. This commission drafted a new charter that eliminated virtually all elected administrative officers, including the county treasurer, recorder of deeds, clerk, coroner, and sheriff, and replaced them with appointed officials. Those exercising executive branch responsibilities would become appointees of the supervisor or his subordinate department heads, whereas those performing functions related to the courts were to be appointed by the judicial branch.[6] The result was a form of government that bore very little resemblance to the traditional county framework. Instead, it conformed to the structure of big-city government, with an executive charged with appointing the chief administrators who would operate under that executive's supervision.

Officeholders from both parties protested the prospective loss of their jobs and organized "Republicans and Democrats United for the Rights of Voters" to oppose adoption of the new charter. The county central committee of Roos's own Republican party voted unanimously not to endorse the charter, and the committee chair charged that under the new framework the supervisor would be "all powerful with little control of government in the hands of the electorate."[7] Another foe spoke of "the almost unlimited power given to the office of supervisor," and still another attacked the charter commission's argument that a "strong central county government would be more efficient. Bureaucracy is no substitute for democracy."[8]

These disgruntled politicians, however, failed to convince most county residents. The *Florissant Valley Reporter* summed up the feelings of many voters in an editorial headed, "Politicians Wail, But Fail to Make Case." "The urbanization of St. Louis county makes government reform mandatory," the county newspaper explained. "For better or worse, the county is in reality the 'City of St. Louis County' and we're stuck with the necessity for creating a machine with wheels directed in unison by a compact machine."[9] No matter how much county residents might yearn for the cracker-barrel regimes of a rural past, the post-suburban age had arrived, and the Florissant newspaper was reminding its readers that this new age required a degree of centralized command. For years, reformers along the metropolitan fringe had made the same point. Urbanization demanded a compromise of the village ideal. Saint Louis County residents had to empower Supervisor Roos to cope with the problems of an urbanizing region.

A majority of the county's electorate agreed with this prognosis, and in April 1968 they approved adoption of the new charter by a vote of 76,833 to 65,705. The charter carried ten of the eighteen townships and proved most popular in the wealthy central county area of Clayton, Ladue, and Creve Coeur.[10] Supervisor Roos lauded the victory, characteristically commenting that the new charter, together with other recent reforms, would enable "the officials of St. Louis county to provide a more efficient, economical and modern local government."[11]

The revised charter, however, did not broaden the county's authority over the ninety-five municipalities within its boundaries. The goal of reallocating government responsibilities thus remained unrealized. But Roos and like-minded reformers launched an attack on this problem as well, sponsoring a "home rule" amendment to Missouri's constitution. The state constitution of 1945 permitted the county to legislate on questions of traffic and police, public health, building construction, and planning and zoning in unincorporated areas and to provide such services in incorporated areas by negotiating a separate agreement with each municipality wishing to avail itself of the service. To assume countywide responsibility for a municipal function, the county had to fashion a deal with each of the myriad municipalities, including such miniscule units as the village of Champ. In contrast, the Roos-sponsored home rule amendment "would allow citizens of a charter county to determine what services" would be "supplied to their incorporated and unincorporated areas by local and county governments."[12] In other words, Saint Louis County voters would have free rein to specify in their county charter which functions the county should exercise and which would be reserved to the municipalities. Through a charter amendment a simple majority of county voters would be able to transfer a function from the municipalities to the county. Negotiations with each city and village would no longer be necessary.

In 1970 Roos and his allies in the state legislature succeeded in placing this constitutional amendment on the ballot and thereby stirred another debate over centralization of authority. Municipal leaders in the county were sharply divided on the subject, with the mayors of most of the larger municipalities, such as University City, Ferguson, Florissant, and Webster Groves, favoring the county home rule amendment, whereas officials in the smaller units opposed it.[13] Mayors of these smaller units believed that the amendment would allow county voters to destroy miniature municipalities by transferring their functions to the county. "We'll be reduced to 10 or 12 big cities and then someone will say 'why not just one big one?'" warned Mayor Ray T. Dreher of the small community of Warson Woods.[14]

Supervisor Roos responded by repeating his standard arguments for governmental reorganization. "Home rule would enable our citizens to fashion a more workable assignment of county and municipal responsibilities," Roos argued, "and would provide the key to more effective and more efficient government."[15] Moreover, Roos and others claimed that unless voters adopted the home rule amendment, devotees of metropolitanism would forcibly impose more drastic schemes of government reorganization, such as the district plan of 1959 or the borough plan of 1962. "If due to inflexibility and unwillingness to change we have a breakdown in service or other chaotic circumstances, those conditions will provide a basis for advocates of single over-all government to destroy the county-municipality arrangement," Roos contended. A state representative from University City who backed the amendment expressed a similar view when he claimed that home rule would allow the county to adjust to arising problems one by one and thus save Saint Louis County from a wholesale scheme of "big government." According to this lawmaker, "[home rule] is going to be held up as the strongest argument against the larger government—since it provides the tool to isolate a problem as it comes and deal with it on an area-wide basis if that's the only way it can be effectively handled."[16]

Roos and his allies were, then, employing the standard arguments of centralizers in the emerging post-suburban counties. In the past, voters had been willing to deviate from the ideal of small-scale government for the sake of more efficient and effective services, and this is what Roos was promising. Moreover, he was arguing that a compromise of the ideal was necessary to thwart the forces of truly big government. If county residents did not bend a bit in response to changing conditions, they might later be forced to kowtow to a unitary scheme of government that would wipe out the villages and small cities so sacred to them. According to the supervisor, the choice was between the mild palliative of county coordination or the harsh regimen of metropolitanism.

Saint Louis County residents bought the argument. On November 3, 1970, the amendment garnered the support of 63 percent of those casting ballots in Saint Louis County, and statewide it won 57 percent of the votes. Home rule carried fifteen of the eighteen townships in the county and, like the 1968 charter, received its strongest support in the wealthy central county.[17] Roos was jubilant, having now won the chance to reorganize government to ensure efficiency and streamlined rule. "November 3, 1970 is a date that will go down in the annals of St. Louis County in giant letters. . . . Passage of the home rule amendment has been hailed as the greatest step forward for local government in Missouri in nearly one hundred years," the 1970 annual report for Saint Louis County announced, for this reform provided "the key to improving the effectiveness and efficiency of local government everywhere."[18] Moreover, in the wake of his victory, Supervisor Roos was not reluctant to promote county government as the answer to the problems of the post-suburban future. "County government has the broad tax base, the area-wide jurisdiction, the economy of scale, the close ties with other governmental units and the political account-ability to perform a valuable function in dealing with the challenges facing us," Roos argued.[19] The county was, then, purportedly the government of the fu-ture, a government large enough to ensure effective and efficient service but sensitive enough to the concerns of the small-scale municipalities to be ac-ceptable to the mass of suburban voters.

Soon after the adoption of the home rule amendment, Roos set to work to realize the great promise of county government. In December 1970 Roos and Shrewsbury mayor Robert C. Wehner, president of the County Municipal League, announced the creation of the fifteen-member Intergovernmental Relations Commission, composed of citizens and public officials and headed by Mayor Robert Bess of Crestwood.[20] During the ensuing weeks, this commission for-mulated three proposed county charter amendments that reallocated respon-sibility for services. Bess and his colleagues first proposed an amendment providing for minimum countywide standards for police training and perfor-mance, applicable to all municipal forces as well as to the county police de-partment. A second amendment would authorize the county to establish a uni-form countywide building and construction code, and the third proposal would impose a uniform minimum housing code on all incorporated and un-incorporated areas. If these changes were approved by voters in a referendum scheduled for November 1971, the county government would assume control of standards for policing countywide, and the municipalities would be forced to relinquish to the county responsibility for building codes and to meet the county's minimal requirements for housing.

Predictably, in the months prior to the referendum some county residents once again raised the frightening specter of big government. Mayor Dreher of Warson Woods remained the chief spokesperson for the small municipalities, which generally opposed the proposals. Dreher characterized the charter amend-ments as a "giant step toward establishing one super-county government" which "could mean the demise of municipal government" as Saint Louis Countians knew it.[21] In fact, the feisty mayor claimed that the battle over the amendment was between "those advocates of one super-county government who believe[d] that somehow big government automatically mean[t] efficient government, and, on the other hand, those who believe[d] in a decentralization of govern-ment and an identity with individual municipalities." The cochair of the Citi-zens Committee for the Preservation of Local Government likewise labeled the proposal a "glaring power grab" and warned voters that "passage of these three amendments would in fact mean two things—BIG BROTHER and HIGHER TAXES."[22]

The smaller municipalities had good reason to fear the proposed centralization of authority, for it would affect them more than most of the larger communities. Specifically, the police standards amendment could have been the death knell for police forces in many of the miniature polities. In January 1971, Supervisor Roos proposed eliminating municipal police departments that could not provide "24-hour-a-day, round-the-clock service, including preliminary investigative service, by fully trained professional officers."[23] Such sentiments lent credence to the frightening rhetoric of Dreher. In the minds of many village mayors and council members, Roos was planning to replace their small-town guardians of the law with members of the bureaucratized county police force.

Meanwhile, the building and housing code amendments offended many wealthy residents of the central county who had formerly rallied behind the "good-government" reforms of Roos. If the amendments were adopted, the county would probably impose lower minimum standards than those then existing in such elite communities as Clayton and Ladue. Rigorous building and housing codes had helped make Clayton the ideal executive city and had contributed to Ladue's success as a residential preserve for plutocrats. Uniform county codes would weaken the defenses deemed necessary to protect the high status of these communities. Consequently, Clayton's board of aldermen resolved to oppose the amendments authorizing uniform building and housing codes, claiming that such countywide standards would not be suitable "to the individual local needs, problems and situations existent in all the various communities involved." Since the amendments "could restrict the enforcement by a community of more stringent codes" for the maintenance of "high standards," the Clayton board deemed the propositions not "in the best interests of the Clayton community."[24] Ladue's governing board adopted a similar resolution, rejecting a homogenization of building and housing standards that could threaten the special character of the gilded community.[25]

In response, Roos discounted charges that the amendments would weaken local rule. "The best way to strengthen local government is for strong and viable municipalities to work as full partners with County government," he argued. Roos believed that "unwillingness by local government officials to modify and improve" delivery of services would result in the "collapse of local government and a take-over by the Federal Government." "To keep local government fragmented and completely fouled up just invites intervention by the Federal Government."[26] A group called Mayors of the Larger Cities in St. Louis

County sided with Roos, unanimously endorsing the police standards amendment and backing the housing and building code proposals with only a few dissents. This organization, representing nineteen municipalities, was headed by Mayor Nathan Kaufman of University City, who remarked, "All three service areas, police protection, uniform building code administration, and minimum housing code enforcement involved many economic and social problems which often ignore municipal boundaries."[27] In the minds of Roos and Kaufman, the county had to take charge of those problems that transcended municipal boundaries. If it did not, then the biggest brother of them all, the federal government, would send in its bureaucrats to subvert the administrations of Mayor Dreher and all his colleagues.

Such warnings, however, failed to convince a majority of the electorate. On November 2, 1971, all three amendments suffered defeat; the police standards proposal won approval from only 46 percent of the voters whereas the building code and housing code amendments were supported by only 40 percent and 39 percent, respectively. Adopting the position of the Clayton and Ladue governing boards, voters in the wealthy central county area defected from the reform camp and cast ballots against the imposition of countywide building and housing standards. In the less affluent north and south county areas, voters opposed all three propositions.[28] It was a stunning blow to the plans of Supervisor Roos; the *St. Louis Post-Dispatch* was later to refer to the defeat as "the single largest blot on the Supervisor's . . . years in office."[29]

Moreover, many blamed Roos personally for the defeat. In postmortems on the referendum he was repeatedly attacked for failing to communicate with the county's mayors and for his unwillingness to admit them as full partners in the governing of the region. Criticizing Roos for not consulting more fully with the electorate and officials, the *St. Louis County Observer* referred to the seemingly aloof supervisor as "the 'great white father' in the government center in Clayton." Following the referendum, Mayor James Eagan of Florissant remarked: "I hope that the supervisor and the county council have learned that they cannot 'jam down the throats of the voters' only their views. The partnership that the Supervisor keeps talking about must be on a 50–50 basis, and not his usual 90–10 partnership, with the County getting the 90% and the Cities, the 10%."[30] According to Eagan and others, Roos was assuming the airs of county emperor before having secured his empire. In November 1971, however, the mayors and their constituents had reminded Roos of his true place in the scheme of government.

They had also reminded the supervisor of the political facts of life in the post-suburban world. County residents would endorse the abstract concept of county coordination to achieve efficiency and more effective services. They had demonstrated that through their strong support for the home rule constitutional amendment of 1970. But when faced with concrete proposals that contradicted the suburban ideal of small-scale government tailored to the needs of the individual community, they would rise in revolt and cast a no vote. Roos's proposals seemingly had threatened to replace the village cop with an impersonal police bureaucracy and had endangered the privileged status of Clayton and Ladue through homogenizing the building standards of the county. Residents had created the city of Ladue to establish and enforce higher standards than existed elsewhere, and now Roos was challenging this basic premise of the community's existence. In his desire to shift authority to the county, Roos had proceeded without sufficient caution and violated the still-prevalent suburban ideal of government. He had touched some sensitive nerves and a pained electorate had commanded him to stop.

Following the defeat, Roos did not abandon his belief in broadening county authority. Two days after the election he urged the County Municipal League and County Mayors Association to submit charter amendments that both organizations could support. "It is easier to criticize than to be constructive," Roos commented, "and it is time for these municipal officials in Saint Louis County to take the initiative and make recommendations as to how best to use the county's home rule authority to solve the problems confronting our citizens."[31] The county's municipal officials, however, were not to achieve Roos's dream of government reorganization. In his 1972 State of the County address, the supervisor was still complaining of the "fragmented service delivery system" in the county and "the waste and inefficiency inherent in our confusing structure of local government." While insisting that he was "totally opposed to a large, monolithic metropolitan government," Roos did promise to foster a new "spirit of county-municipal partnership." Toward this end, he initiated regular Saturday morning meetings with municipal officials but discontinued the practice after six or seven such sessions. Roos claimed that the meetings had proven to municipal officials "that the county [didn't] have horns," but others continued to comment on the "mutual finger-pointing" between Roos and the mayors, as each side blamed the other for county problems.[32] When Roos stepped down as supervisor at the beginning of 1975, he left a legacy of mutual distrust that remained an obstacle to realization of his plans for a bigger, bolder county government.

Roos's successor, Gene McNary, however, carried on the effort to strengthen the county's role as regional coordinator. McNary, like Roos, was a Republican who, according to the *St. Louis Post-Dispatch*, centered his initial campaign for supervisor around "the theme of the outgoing Roos administration—honesty and efficiency, a business-like government."[33] Thus McNary reiterated many of his predecessor's criticisms of fragmented rule and shared Roos's exasperation with the parochialism of most municipal officials. From 1975 to 1989 McNary served as the county's executive, perpetuating the Roos tradition and facing some of the same problems as his predecessor.

In 1979 the role of county government again became a subject for debate. That year the supervisor and county council appointed a charter review commission, headed by Lawrence Roos, to consider reforms in county rule.[34] Appearing before the commission, Supervisor McNary suggested that the county assume responsibility for a broader range of municipal services in unincorporated territory and specifically take charge of fire protection in those areas. In other words, he urged the abolition of the special district governments charged with fire protection and the substitution of a county firefighting force. McNary also proposed charter amendments authorizing the county government to assume countywide responsibility for solid waste disposal, to operate a mass transit system, to create a countywide emergency communications system to handle 911 telephone calls, to fix minimum countywide standards for firefighters, and to establish a county fire academy.[35]

It was an ambitious agenda, but some wanted even further centralization, with one county council member calling for a county takeover of such services as fire and police protection in both unincorporated and incorporated areas.[36] Municipal police officials, however, reacted vigorously to suggestions for consolidating law enforcement agencies. The police chief of the tiny municipality of St. George told the charter commission that municipal forces had "a personal touch. Everybody knows everybody. We aren't called 'pigs.' The people love their police department."[37] Likewise, the police chief of Sunset Hills testified that residents in his community liked "the personalized service and the friendliness" of that municipality's officers.[38]

Faced with such enduring arguments in favor of small-scale rule and remembering the debacle of 1971, the charter commission opted to submit less far-reaching amendments to the electorate. Most notably it proposed that the county assume countywide control of waste disposal and exercise authority "to establish minimum training and educational standards for all firefighters employed by any public agency in the County."[39] Moreover, the commission members suggested some minor cosmetic revisions, such as changing the title of the county supervisor to county executive so that it would conform to the nomenclature for county chieftains elsewhere in the nation.

Unlike the amendments of 1971, these proposals won the support of most municipalities and the endorsement of the County Municipal League.[40] Trash and garbage disposal was an increasingly troublesome environmental problem for area municipalities, and they were generally willing to transfer responsibility for this undesirable task to the county just as they had earlier shifted control of the equally difficult function of sewage disposal to a special metropolitan district. Landfills were reaching capacity, waste disposal experts were calling for expensive trash-burning plants, and the threat of hazardous wastes was making the headlines in newspapers across the country. This was a policy problem many municipal officials gladly handed over to the county. Private waste-haulers did oppose the amendment, claiming it would increase the costs of trash collection.[41] But pragmatic municipal leaders, for the most part, deemed it a desirable compromise of local autonomy.

County-imposed standards for firefighters also were not considered particularly threatening. With the long history of mutual assistance agreements in Saint Louis County, firefighters from one fire protection district or municipality were frequently called upon to aid in extinguishing major blazes in other cities, villages, or districts. Uniform standards and training would simply facilitate the implementation of these long-standing assistance pacts and make joint firefighting efforts more effective. Moreover, Saint Louis County's existing fire departments generally serviced a larger area with a more substantial tax base than did the typical municipal police force. Consequently, the fire departments were already relatively well equipped and professional. Only twenty of the most populous municipalities maintained their own fire departments, the other cities and villages relying instead on protection contracted from larger neighbors or from the twenty-five fire protection districts that comprised both incorporated and unincorporated territory.[42] By comparison, sixty-four municipalities, as well as Saint Louis County, maintained full-time police departments and an additional six supported part-time patrols.[43]

On November 6, 1979, most county residents accepted these relatively minor changes in county authority. The training standards proposal passed by a vote of 162,516 to 63,513; the waste disposal amendment won, 140,950 to 78,005; and the minor revisions also were approved by a substantial margin.[44] Under Supervisor McNary voters were, then, willing to endorse modest transfers of authority that bolstered the county's role as coordinator of governmental services. The charter commission's caution in submitting amendments, however, reflected the realistic approach of county leaders during the late 1970s. Roos, McNary, and others realized that they should not act too hastily and upset the traditional balance of power in their post-suburban domain. For the time being, an equilibrium between the fragment and the whole had to be maintained.

Yet Saint Louis County's government was becoming more significant not simply because of modest transfers of authority. Perhaps more important was the expansion of existing county services. Each year millions of additional dollars were spent on the county's traditional responsibilities and the ranks of county employees grew ever larger. County highway, park, and police programs were large-scale operations and expanding at a rapid rate. Big government was, then, developing along the metropolitan fringe as the county grew increasingly remote from its rural roots.

The expansion of the county's police force and parklands was indicative of the changes occurring in post-suburbia. Between 1970 and 1976 the number of commissioned officers in the county police department rose 36 percent, from 422 to 573. By the latter date, the county force had seven times the number of officers of the county's largest municipal force.[45] From 1970 to 1980 the number of county parks rose from thirty-seven to sixty-three and the area of county-owned parklands more than doubled, from 5,052 acres to 11,950 acres. During this decade the county's park and recreation budget quintupled. At the close of the 1970s the acreage of Saint Louis County parks was more than three times the combined total for all municipal parks within the county.[46]

County government's role in transportation also expanded. During the 1970s the county purchased the Spirit of St. Louis Airport to accommodate the growing number of private aircraft, and it established a port authority to boost industrial development in riverfront areas. The mileage in the county road system rose from 1,071 to 1,510. Moreover, in 1971 the state legislature authorized the county to designate arterial roads in both incorporated and unincorporated areas and to assume full responsibility for the maintenance of these principal thoroughfares and for traffic regulation on them. The extent of this arterial system increased from 209 miles in 1972 to 356 miles in 1980.[47]

The *Graeler* decisions of the 1960s further enhanced the county's role as a provider of services. As a result of these state supreme court rulings, municipalities found it difficult to annex new territory, and consequently the percentage of county residents living in unincorporated areas increased rapidly. Whereas in 1970 only 33.6 percent of the county's population lived beyond municipal boundaries, by 1980 42.4 percent did so.[48] Since the county was the principal provider of municipal services for these unincorporated zones, its government grew accordingly. At the beginning of the 1980s Gene McNary was, in effect, the mayor of the more than 400,000 people residing in unincorporated regions, and he headed a large-scale government to service those residents.

Thus despite resistance, big government was establishing itself in post-suburban Saint Louis County. In contrast to the much-vaunted personalized service of the village patrol, the county police department offered protection by a large bureaucratized force. Similarly, county recreation facilities were not controlled by friends or neighbors but by seven county council members, each representing a constituency of 140,000 people. Moreover, this big government was in a position to assume an increasing number of functions. A simple majority vote of county residents could transfer any municipal responsibility to the county. As yet the electorate had not acceded to the wishes of leaders such as Lawrence Roos and approved a significant reallocation of authority. But county rule seemed to be the wave of the future, and this wave was poised to engulf the small-scale village governments inherited from the suburban past.

MODERNIZING DuPAGE

In DuPage County the forces of post-suburban imperialism also wielded power in the county courthouse. Until the beginning of the 1970s the structure of county government in DuPage had remained relatively unchanged. A board, consisting of the supervisors from each township, exercised legislative and administrative powers, and a long list of elected officers, such as sheriff, clerk, and treasurer, operated largely independent of the board. In the 1960s, however, the United States Supreme Court determined that legislative bodies had to be apportioned on the basis of population, and this was to force a change in the antiquated structure of county rule. No longer could township status entitle an area to representation on the county board, no matter the area's population. Consequently, the Illinois Constitution of 1970 mandated the restructuring of county boards and election of board members from districts of equal population.[49]

This constitution further disrupted the status quo by providing for county home rule. Any county that elected a chief executive officer could enjoy home rule and wield any power and perform any function not specifically denied counties by the state constitution or by act of the state legislature. If a county opted for an executive form of government, it could, then, exercise a broad, but rather vague, range of powers. Through this provision, the members of the Local Government Committee of the Illinois Constitutional Convention expressed their desire to enhance county authority, especially in urbanizing regions. According to one student of Illinois county government, "a strengthened county government was . . . seen by the Local Government Committee . . . as a device for providing basic services to unincorporated suburban areas, for stemming the growth of unnecessary local governments and perhaps eliminating some units that already exist, and for providing coordination of services in metropolitan areas."[50] Thus the Constitution of 1970 forced a change in the composition of the DuPage County Board, and the framers of the document also gave DuPage leaders a green light to proceed with an expansion of county authority.

One figure who sought to take advantage of the new home rule provision was DuPage County board chair Gerald Weeks. Weeks, a native of Chicago's South Side, moved to Glen Ellyn as a young man, became involved in Republican politics, and was elected supervisor of Milton Township. As such he held a seat on the county board of supervisors, where he grew restive with the unwillingness of other supervisors to confront the emerging urban problems facing DuPage. In 1969 Weeks unsuccessfully sought to oust the incumbent board chair, and later that year, following the death of this incumbent, he became the board's presiding officer. In the words of one local columnist, during his nine years as chair, Weeks "brought DuPage County government into the modern era and equipped it to deal with problems and opportunities as they [were]. . . . Weeks realized that . . . the price of corn and the building of farm to market roads were no longer the paramount concerns of the people of DuPage County." Instead, the board chair had a new vision of what the county should and could do. In 1972 Weeks commented, "The County's drainage, transportation and environmental matters are top priority items, and I believe restructuring County Government and giving it broad jurisdiction in regional matters is basic to the solution of these problems."[51] Like Lawrence Roos in Saint Louis County, Weeks believed that county government could serve a vital function in handling regional problems that transcended municipal boundaries. In Weeks's opinion, DuPage County leaders needed to shift their focus from cornfields to airports, sewers, and urban highways. From 1969 through 1978 he was instrumental in forcing this altered vision.

Sharing Weeks's enthusiasm for the empowerment of county government was state senator Jack Knuepfer of the DuPage community of Elmhurst. Knuepfer was a Republican businessman who, like Weeks and Roos, was dedicated to honest, efficient, businesslike government. "Don't waste your time with Knuepfer," commented one corrupt lobbyist, "he's one of those goddamned do-gooders."[52] Hardworking and intelligent, Knuepfer had little tolerance for the petty courthouse politicians who had traditionally governed DuPage. He believed that DuPage was developing into a post-suburban empire and it deserved and required a government that could tackle the regional problems resulting from this grand destiny. In the state legislature and later as Weeks's successor as chair of the DuPage County board, Knuepfer endeavored to create such a government.

In the late 1960s Knuepfer served as cochair of the Illinois Commission on Local Government, and the commission's report expressed views basic to Knuepfer's thinking during the following two decades of his public career. The report announced in a straightforward manner that it was "the Commission's desire to expand the power and discretion of county government." In words that Lawrence Roos would have seconded, Knuepfer's commission concluded, "There are many functions—law enforcement, public health, pollution, etc.— where the county must not only serve the unincorporated portions of its area but also give support to the governments of the incorporated municipalities through providing more comprehensive and technical equipment, personnel and services than individual municipalities are able to provide by themselves." Moreover, among the commission's "guidelines for a strong local governmental structure" was the goal of empowering "urban county government so that it [could] perform those services which [could] more economically be provided by large units or which require[d] a large and diverse tax base."[53] Throughout the pages of the Knuepfer commission report, the message was the same. Metropolitan counties in Illinois had to be transformed into effective regional coordinators to overcome the limitations imposed by municipal fragmentation.

During the 1970s, as both state senator and county board chair, Knuepfer remained dedicated to this stance. Repeatedly he argued that some necessary services could not "be performed by a host of small municipalities." Instead, "the county would be the logical government to provide many services such as . . . sanitary waste disposal."[54] "The county is constricted, and has not had the chance to grow[;] . . . it will never mature until given the opportunity," Knuepfer insisted.[55] Together with Gerald Weeks, Knuepfer would, then, lead the forces calling for the maturation and modernization of county government, and by modernization both men meant county control over regional questions and recognition of the county as the natural guide and coordinator of the many municipalities within its boundaries.

In 1972 Weeks and Knuepfer sought to win a vital victory in their campaign to create a county empire. For that year the ballot included a proposal to make DuPage a home rule county with an elected executive of the type existing in Nassau, Suffolk, and Saint Louis Counties. As yet no county had taken advantage of the home rule provision in the Illinois constitution, so it was unclear what exactly the new status would entail for DuPage Countians. But the consensus was that home rule would enhance county authority and open doors for creative reforms in local government.

In DuPage as in Saint Louis County, the possibility of centralized authority raised fears of creeping metropolitanism, and prior to the 1972 referendum many reform opponents offered heated defenses of local self-rule. Perhaps the most outspoken foe of the home rule proposal was Thomas Kelleghan, the only delegate to the state constitutional convention who refused to sign the resulting constitution. Kelleghan viewed the county executive-home rule form of government "as leading in a direct line to a metropolitan-type government." "Regional government is what they want," Kelleghan warned, "and I hope they won't get away with it." A columnist for the *Downers Grove Reporter* reiterated these fears when she claimed that home rule and the constitutional reforms of 1970 would produce "centralized bureaucracies and county metro-regional government." Another DuPage Countian concurred, warning her fellow residents, "County Executive government is requisite to, and could be a first step toward, 'Metro' government!"[56]

Foes of home rule not only raised the bogy of regional government but also emphasized the prospect of power concentrated in the hands of an omnipotent executive. Thomas Kelleghan charged that the reform would create a "dictatorship."[57] Similarly, a candidate for the county board attacked the proposal as an attempt to impose "one-man rule." Another candidate explained, "I object to [the] County Executive form of government because it is [a] highly restrictive, inflexible form of centralized government [that] destroys the time-tested concept of governmental checks and balances by placing too much power in the hands of one man."[58] A local columnist said much the same thing when she insisted, "Giving a county executive such awesome power and control can result only in further loss of representative government at the county level."[59]

The most frequent argument against home rule was that it would produce new and higher taxes. The home rule provision had no limit on the county tax rate nor any county debt ceiling. Consequently, many DuPage Countians viewed the reform as an invitation to a Bacchanalia of government taxing and spending. The principal group formed to oppose home rule was Stop Taxing Our People (STOP), which distributed handbills claiming that the reform would legalize "unlimited taxes, unlimited public debt[, and] unlimited licensing fees on services and products."[60] "As proposed, home rule would open the door wide for unlimited property taxes, taxes on rents, gasoline, and virtually any product or service available," commented STOP's chairman. The *Naperville Sun* warned of "unlimited buying sprees" and "unleashed spending." "A bottomless, undefined budget would tempt the best of us to spendthrift habits," editorialized the *Sun*, "and any government with unlimited debt, and no ceiling on taxation or licensing, could be expected to build political monuments in the name of 'increasing demands for services.'" Likewise, the *Downers Grove Reporter* told its readers, "County home rule is an open invitation to new taxes and to higher rates on existing taxes." One DuPage Countian summed up the feelings of many of her neighbors when she wrote, "The 'benefits' of Home Rule are largely additional revenue for taxing bodies!"[61]

Many influential DuPage Countians accepted these arguments and announced their opposition to the home rule proposal. By a vote of fourteen to eight, the DuPage County board formally expressed its disapproval of the reform.[62] Similarly, the County Press Association, representing DuPage newspapers, voted nine to four against home rule, and one newspaper after another ran articles and editorials criticizing the proposal.[63] Some municipal leaders also spoke out against the threat of centralized authority. For example, the Downers Grove village council adopted a resolution urging a rejection of home rule in the upcoming election. The council complained that the proposal incorporated "no means of limiting the powers" that home rule would bestow.[64]

Village councils, newspapers, the county board, and irate citizens were making much the same comments. Repeatedly, criticisms of the home rule proposal focused on unlimited government power and bureaucratic or executive authority irresponsible to the people. Whether complaining of incipient regional rule, executive dictatorship, or unrestrained taxing and spending, opponents of home rule were all contending that the reform would impair the suburban ideal of small-scale government checked by the surveillance of friends and neighbors. "We will be up to our ears in government," one DuPage state representative complained about the proposed reform.[65] In the minds of many DuPage Countians, home rule was a misnomer. The reform would not enhance the power of DuPage residents over their local government. Instead, it would foster big government, big spending, and big-headed politicians with little regard for the welfare of residents in Hinsdale, Glen Ellyn, or Oak Brook.

Weeks, Knuepfer, and like-minded allies attempted to answer these criticisms and allay the fears of county residents. Repeatedly they argued that home rule would preserve local power, for in the absence of a strong county government, state or federal authorities would intervene and impose true metropolitan rule. "It is absolutely essential that the County have the power and authority to solve its problems," Weeks contended. "If not, some higher echelon of government is ready and willing to fill the void."[66] Appealing to DuPage Countians' devotion to local rule, Weeks reiterated this point, saying, "We have to meet the challenge of our urban county, and I would rather have the priorities set at the local level rather than at the state or federal level."[67] Knuepfer also claimed that adoption of the home rule proposal would create a bulwark against "metro-government." "Home rule means taking a look at the problems right here and solving them where they ought to be solved," Knuepfer insisted.

"I think local government can make better decisions for you than state and federal governments have in the past," he told DuPage voters.[68] Making the same argument, a state representative from Hinsdale commented, "I believe that power should go directly from the voters up rather than from 'big brother' down."[69]

Like Lawrence Roos in Saint Louis County, the defenders of home rule for DuPage were claiming that a strong county government was the best defense against the ultimate big brother in Washington. Metropolitan government, encouraged by federal bureaucrats, loomed as a threat to the political ideals of suburbia, and to thwart that threat, DuPage Countians needed to compromise their devotion to the small-scale polity and rally behind the county. Leaders in Illinois and Missouri attempted to sell county coordination and control as a pragmatic alternative to the worst case—metropolitan rule by big-city politicians and federal social planners.

These arguments, however, failed to sway most DuPage Countians. On March 21, 1972, they rejected the home rule proposal by a vote of 59,738 to 23,542.[70] That same day voters rejected similar proposals in eight other Illinois counties. In none of the nine counties considering home rule did reformers come close to victory.[71] The 1972 referendum thus represented an overwhelming defeat for the forces favoring the restructuring of local rule. Basic to the defeat in DuPage and the other counties was the fear of too much government and too many taxes. Analyzing the defeat, John Pankhurst, who had chaired the Local Government Committee at the 1970 Constitutional Convention, observed, "It represented a combination of fear of taxes and fear of government people." Moreover, the fears were not momentary. Strong opposition to home rule persisted in counties throughout the state, leading the field administrator for the Urban Counties Council of Illinois to author a 1976 article titled, "County Home Rule: Doesn't Anybody Want It?"[72]

One person who did continue to want it was Jack Knuepfer. As chair of the county board during the late 1970s and 1980s, Knuepfer acted as if he was indeed county executive and did not mask his belief in the need for expanded county authority. In 1982 at the close of his first term as county chair, the suburban edition of the *Chicago Tribune* commended Knuepfer's "commitment to such countywide problems as waste disposal, flooding, highways, planning and water supply," which he sought to deal with "through an expanded role for county government that also preserve[d] municipal independence." Like Roos and McNary in Saint Louis County, Knuepfer was attempting to fashion the county as a coordinative middle level of government between the municipality and the state. He did not seek to destroy municipalities, but he endeavored to establish the county as the guide and counselor for the corps of cities and villages within the boundaries of DuPage. Given his broad vision of the role of county government, Knuepfer did not tolerate the parochialism of some county board members. "Knuepfer thinks of them as too local," commented one veteran of the board.[73] If the county was to realize its proper place in the hierarchy of governments, such localism had to be eliminated. In the mind of Knuepfer, board members had to recognize the countywide interests that bound residents of Glen Ellyn, Elmhurst, and Naperville together.

Moreover, basic to Knuepfer's vision of modernized county rule was a strong executive. As county board chair he did not simply preside at board meetings, he exercised an unprecedented command over county affairs. To enhance his control, in 1980 Knuepfer successfully sponsored the creation of a board finance committee consisting of his key allies in the county legislature and headed by himself. The chair routed many of the most important measures through this finance committee which followed Knuepfer's lead in approving or disapproving them. In 1983 one journalist summed up the situation when he reported, "Ultimately, Knuepfer gets his way."[74] By the late 1980s Knuepfer's control of DuPage County government led some to label him the "Mayor Daley of the suburbs." One critic expressed the feelings of many of the chair's foes when she said of Knuepfer, "He is making all the decisions out of his office. The committee system has become ineffective."[75]

Despite the defeat of the home rule-executive form of government in 1972, Jack Knuepfer was, then, establishing a strong county executive role and urging an expansion of county government. What the people had rejected at the polls, Knuepfer was gradually attempting to impose upon them. During the 1970s and early 1980s DuPage County's government was not as big as those of Nassau, Suffolk, or Saint Louis Counties; it retained many of the traditional elected county offices, and no urban-style police department had replaced the county sheriff and his deputies. But under both Weeks and Knuepfer, DuPage County was becoming a more significant unit of government. For example, by the mid-1980s the DuPage County Forest Preserve District, governed by Knuepfer and the county board, maintained thirty-six parks with a combined area of 17,500 acres. Twelve of these preserves had been acquired by the district since 1970.[76]

Advancing the county's role as coordinator of local services and development during the Weeks-Knuepfer years was the DuPage County Regional Planning Commission. Created in September 1969 by the county board of supervisors, the eleven-person commission consisted of three members of the county board, three officials representing municipalities within the county, and five members from the general public selected by the chair of the county board with that board's approval.[77] This body was charged with preparing and updating a comprehensive plan for the county which would supposedly guide the development of DuPage. Moreover, it was to encourage cooperative planning efforts among the county government, the municipalities, and the special districts. Coordination and cooperation were basic to its efforts. The commission was intended to draw all the governments of DuPage County together in a common endeavor to chart future development.

To realize this goal of coordinated planning, the county commission worked closely with the DuPage Mayors and Managers Conference, a group founded in 1962 to facilitate mutually beneficial communication among the county's municipalities. According to the commission's "progress report" from 1976, "the Planning Commission coordinates with the DuPage Mayors and Managers Conference on an almost daily basis . . . [and] bases much of its program on coordination and cooperation with the many municipalities of DuPage county. All County plans are presented to the officials and planning directors of each municipality for their comment, and appropriate revisions are made to insure that the County plan reflects the needs and policies of the municipalities."[78] Moreover, the county agency provided expert help to municipalities unable to maintain adequate planning staffs. For example, in 1976 Winfield, Itasca, Bensenville, and Wood Dale had all contracted for assistance from the commission. The county planning body also reviewed federal grant proposals from county municipalities and ensured that the proposals did not "conflict with existing or proposed county-wide planning programs and policies."[79]

Overall, the intent of the commission was to transfer to a countywide body responsibility for overseeing the growth and development of DuPage. Rather than allowing each fragment to pursue its own goals irrespective of those of its neighbors, the commission sought "to develop a unified, mutually agreed upon, land use plan for the entire County."[80] In 1972 DuPage voters had expressed their fears of big government with unrestrained taxing and spending powers. Yet city and village leaders were willing to expand the county's authority to coordinate municipal efforts. Traditional suburban misgivings about large-scale centralized authority had scuttled the plans of Weeks and Knuepfer in 1972, but in DuPage as in Saint Louis County, county government was assuming new tasks that ensured a desirable pattern of development without robbing the municipalities of too much of their power.

QUIET CHANGE IN OAKLAND COUNTY

During the 1970s and early 1980s Oakland Countians were less divided over changes in local government than were their counterparts in Missouri or

Illinois. Municipal officials expressed fewer fears about the growth of county authority and alarmists issued fewer warnings about the onset of big government and executive leadership. The rhetoric in Oakland was relatively subdued and the few battle wounds inflicted seemed to heal more readily. There was no Ray Dreher charging a Lawrence Roos with designs to destroy municipalities. Nor was there any Jack Knuepfer aggressively pursuing county aggrandizement no matter what the people might think.

Yet change did occur in Oakland County's government. As in Saint Louis and DuPage Counties, local leaders sought to modernize the structure of county rule and create a more efficient government. And as in the other counties, modernization meant creation of a strong executive to oversee the varied county operations and, in effect, serve as county mayor. Modernization also meant expanding the county's role in providing regional services and in coordinating the efforts of the scores of governments within its boundaries.

The man who presided over the change in Oakland County government was Daniel Murphy. As chair of the board of auditors, Murphy had served as the county's chief administrator from 1964 through 1974 and then occupied the newly created post of county executive from 1975 onward. After serving in World War II, he had returned to Oakland County, joined the Young Republicans, and become a courthouse fixture as deputy county clerk. When the incumbent register of deeds died, Murphy was appointed to the post, and from 1958 through 1963 he also held the position of county clerk. In 1963 he announced his candidacy for Congress but withdrew from that race when he was appointed by the county board of supervisors as chair of the board of auditors. He explained: "My heart has always been in county government. That's why I sought the Auditors post instead of running for Congress."[81] Given his virtually perpetual tenure at the helm of county government over the next thirty years, this remark proved something of an understatement.

Possibly the key to Murphy's political longevity was his low-profile, nonconfrontational style. During his early years in politics, he was known as an aggressive opponent, but when appointed chair of the board of auditors he assured Oakland Countians, "I'm not going to move too quickly."[82] He kept that promise, earning a reputation as a conservative, competent administrator. He did not push an agenda of rapid change nor did he crave publicity or strive to get his name in the headlines. In fact, in 1980 one poll found that only 25 percent of all Oakland voters knew who he was.[83] After a quarter century in major county offices, Murphy remained unknown to three-fourths of his constituents. By comparison, a 1968 survey of Saint Louis Countians reported that 91 percent could identify Lawrence Roos as county supervisor.[84] Murphy was a man who governed quietly but governed long.

The most significant change in Oakland County's government during Murphy's long career was the adoption of the unified form of government in 1974. Authorized by the Michigan legislature in 1973, this plan abolished the three-person board of auditors and replaced it with a county executive. Under the plan, the county boards of health and public works would also be eliminated as would the planning commission. The responsibilities of these boards would be transferred to the county's legislative body, the board of commissioners.[85] This scheme thus concentrated authority in the hands of a single executive and legislature rather than dispersing it among independent boards and commissions. The unified plan, however, bestowed no additional powers upon the county. It was a plan for the reorganization, not the empowerment, of government. County voters had the option of selecting this reform scheme, which more closely resembled the standard structure of city government, or retaining the traditional framework.

Long excluded from power in the predominantly Republican county, Oakland Democrats were especially eager to adopt this optional plan, and in 1974 it was placed on the ballot. Perhaps because it did not assign any new taxing or spending authority to the county, the unified plan aroused much less controversy than did reorganization schemes in DuPage or Saint Louis Counties. Not only did the local Democratic party officially endorse it, so did the reform-minded League of Women Voters. The Republican party took no formal action on the proposal, but most prominent Republicans seemed agreeable to the change, and the GOP's county chair announced that he would vote in favor of the plan.[86] The *Observer and Eccentric* chain of suburban newspapers editorialized: "Oakland County is too large to remain in the administrative backwoods. . . . A yes vote on the unified county government will result in the administrative efficiency and effectiveness needed today." Moreover, the reform plan would "provide a focal point for leadership and a single office to coordinate county functions," a "place where the buck stops."[87] Some Oakland Countians seem to have feared that the plan might produce higher taxes and larger, irresponsible government. But there was no significant organized opposition to the reform. Modern, streamlined rule was a notion that appealed to most Oakland residents.

Controversy did arise over the role of the proposed county chieftain. Michigan law permitted county voters to determine whether they wanted an elected executive with veto power over the legislative board or an appointed manager with no veto who, like a city manager, would act as the administrative servant of the board and implement its policy decisions. Democrats favored the more powerful elected chieftain but most Republicans, including Daniel Murphy, and the League of Women Voters opted for an appointed manager. The chair of the league's county government study committee explained her group's support for a nonpartisan professional administrator when she observed, "The county has the capacity to deliver needed services to urban areas, but we need a topnotch professional running the government." Elizabeth Howe, chair of the county Democratic party, however, emphasized the need for a strong political figure to lead Oakland out of the morass of Republican misrule. Attacking "the county courthouse clique," Howe promised, "we're going to clean this place up."[88] Moreover, Howe pointed to the need for a powerful elected official to speak for Oakland interests in Lansing and Washington. "[Mayor] Coleman Young clearly speaks for the City of Detroit," she reminded Oakland Countians. "It is likely that there will be a county executive for [Detroit's] Wayne County. Who will have the stature to answer them and speak out for Oakland County?"[89] A strong elected chieftain was needed to bolster the county government's role as guide and guardian of its post-suburban domain. An administrative appointee would prove too weak to fulfill this function.

On election day in August 1974 Oakland voters approved both the elected executive option and the unified plan of government. The unified plan triumphed by almost a two-to-one margin, winning in all parts of the county. Voters were almost equally favorable toward an elected executive, with more than 60 percent of those casting ballots supporting that option.[90] County Democrats were jubilant and repeated their promises of cleaning out the courthouse and ushering in a new era of government.

As their candidate for the first county executive the Democrats selected Eugene Kuthy, a former member of the county planning commission, whereas the Republicans backed the longtime chair of the board of auditors Daniel Murphy. In the ensuing campaign for executive, the Democrats continued to favor a more radical change in county government whereas Murphy characteristically assumed a more conservative stance. Kuthy vowed to work for the abolition of any remaining "autonomous, anonymous boards" in county government and to transfer their authority to the office of the county executive. "The county executive must regard himself as a leader and a policy maker, not as an administrative functionary," argued Kuthy.[91] Murphy, however, said of the executive, "He is a strong administrator and a policy advisor."[92] For Kuthy the new figure would be a strong county mayor; Murphy viewed the position as similar to his old job as chair of the board of auditors but with enhanced appointive powers and veto authority. Kuthy was the voice of change, Murphy that of continuity.

In November 1974 continuity won, for Murphy captured the executive post with a narrow victory over Kuthy. Following his victory Murphy admitted that he would have to become more visible politically but assured Oakland Countians, "I can be both an administrator and a politician."[93] During the next decade, he realized this goal, and in 1984 the *Detroit Free Press* was still able to describe him as "a low-key, efficient administrator." Moreover, this was the image Murphy sought to present. When running successfully for reelection in 1976, Murphy repeatedly referred to himself as "an amateur politician," even though he had spent virtually his entire adult life in political office.[94] Democratic opponents attacked Murphy's low-key approach, with his foe in the 1980 election criticizing the county executive for his lack of leadership.[95] As late as the 1984 election the Republicans had to invest in a media blitz to boost Murphy's name recognition among Oakland voters.[96] That same year the *Detroit Free Press* commented on Murphy's image "as a man who ha[d] done his job quietly and without controversy. . . . Murphy is the sort of man you might not remember if you saw him on the street again," reported the *Free Press*.[97]

Yet in 1976, 1980, 1984, and 1988 Murphy won reelection, remaining at the helm of county government. Moreover, his low-key, efficient image contributed to his success. A more flamboyant, aggressive executive with openly imperial dreams for county government could have stirred a revolt among the many foes of big government in Oakland. Newspapers repeatedly commented that the post of Oakland County executive was the third most powerful in the state, behind only the governor and the mayor of Detroit.[98] But Murphy exercised that power in a way that quelled the fears of the many true believers in small-scale rule. The unobstrusive county executive provided the efficient, effective government admired along the metropolitan fringe without arousing undue apprehension about centralized authority. A 1984 Murphy campaign advertisement stated: "Many people in Oakland County don't worry about their county government. They don't have to."[99] Murphy was appealing because he did his job and disturbed a minimum number of people. Voters could sit back and allow him to steer the county government, safe in the knowledge that he would not proceed too fast or too recklessly.

Other, less cautious, county officials did occasionally raise a furor with their proposals of aggrandized county authority. For example, in 1977 the Democratic county sheriff Johannes Spreen, a former Detroit police commissioner, sparked a chorus of protests when he suggested a consolidation of some police services in Oakland. Spreen had long criticized the "fragmentation" of law enforcement in the county, and local newspaper accounts of his comments on consolidation implied that he favored a countywide police department. Spreen responded to these accounts, claiming that he favored county control only of "support services," such as crime laboratories and major crime investigation units. He insisted that under his plan for consolidation, citizens would continue to "have a local chief under their control that they could go to for a redress of grievances." Moreover, before assembled representatives of the press he did "solemnly swear, affirm and attest": "I don't believe in a county police force. . . . I do believe in local government and local rule."[100]

Local police chiefs, however, were suspicious of the overreaching sheriff with a big-city background. Royal Oak's chief expressed the views of many when he said of Spreen, "He's just trying to build his own little empire . . . or nightmare."[101] Devotion to small-scale local rule remained strong in Oakland County, and any county official who proposed changes in the pattern of government had to proceed carefully. A blundering aggressor such as Spreen would make little progress, but a quiet devotee of efficient, effective administration such as Murphy could survive and succeed.

During Murphy's long tenure the role of county government did expand without arousing too much resistance from municipal officials. In Oakland, as in DuPage and Saint Louis Counties, the county was broadening its coordinative duties, attempting to overcome the adverse consequences of municipal fragmentation. Moreover, it was assuming new countywide responsibilities to supplement the services offered by the cities, villages, and townships. Though the county executive was maintaining a low profile, the county's government was assuming unprecedented significance and compensating for the shortcomings inherent in the traditional suburban pattern of fragmented small-scale rule.

For example, the county government was undertaking new regional services inappropriate for the individual municipalities to handle. In 1966 it followed the lead of DuPage and Saint Louis Counties and created a county park system intended to complement the municipal systems. By the early 1980s this county network included nine parks with a combined area of 3,700 acres. These were larger than the typical municipal preserves, three of the nine having more than 750 acres, and they offered camping, boating, and nature study, services usually not found in the city and village parks. Meanwhile, the county also assumed responsibility for local airports that served a countywide clientele. In 1967 it purchased an airport from the city of Pontiac, and by the early 1980s this field was the busiest in the state with over eight hundred landings and takeoffs daily.[102] In fact, it boasted of being the second busiest in the entire Midwest. To supplement this field, in 1977 the county purchased a second airport, located in Troy.[103] Both the county parks and airports serviced a public from throughout the county and thus appropriately were the responsibility of Daniel Murphy and his appointees rather than any individual city or town.

In 1980 the county government took the lead in promoting economic growth as well by forming the Oakland County Economic Development Corporation with a board of directors appointed by the county executive. This corporation was responsible for marketing and promoting Oakland County in an effort to attract new business to the area. It also offered assistance to local businesses, providing them with needed data and steering them to government agencies that could provide financing for expansion. The corporation itself provided loans and loan guarantees to aid local firms whose growth would benefit the county's economy.[104] Rather than leaving it up to each little community to battle for commercial development in a free-for-all for tax-rich businesses, Daniel Murphy's administration was pooling the county's resources in a large-scale initiative for growth and was adding economic promotion to the list of county functions.

During the 1970s and early 1980s the county was also expanding its role as coordinator of the local services offered by the many units of government within its boundaries. In 1973 the board of commissioners created the Oakland County Library Board, which established a regional reference service with a "hotline" linking local public libraries to the reference desk of the Oakland University library. It also compiled a union list of serials, so that librarians would know what periodicals were available at all the libraries in Oakland County. Just as the county library board enhanced coordination among the various public libraries in the county, the Division of Emergency Medical Services and Disaster Control sought to coordinate emergency and disaster relief programs available in the county's various communities. Created in 1977, this division endeavored to ensure that the various providers of emergency services in the county knew how one another was operating and that each maintained equally high standards.[105] In times of disaster or medical emergency, conflicting procedures and jurisdictional obstacles could prove fatal, and the county sought to guarantee that victims of tornado or flood would not have to suffer additional misery owing to the multitude of jealous cities and villages governing Oakland.

By the early 1980s, then, Oakland County had clearly emerged as a regional government, occupying an intermediate position between the municipality and state. Functions that the villages and cities would not or could not handle, the county assumed, maintaining regional parks, airports, and economic development programs as well as the regional public works networks initiated in the 1950s. Moreover, Oakland was building necessary bridges between the many local units, thereby mitigating some of the adverse effects of balkanization. In Oakland County, post-suburbanites were continuing to negotiate the pragmatic compromise that would ensure efficient and effective administration without sacrificing the village ideal of government by friends and neighbors. Under Daniel Murphy they were negotiating this compromise with less diatribe and debate than in Saint Louis or DuPage Counties. Quietly and unobtrusively, Murphy and his colleagues in county government were building a post-suburban empire, moving in the same direction as the more aggressive Lawrence Roos and the more dictatorial Jack Knuepfer.

THE MATURATION OF ORANGE

Orange Countians were to join their midwestern counterparts in adapting their government to the new post-suburban era. Like the residents of Saint Louis, DuPage, and Oakland Counties, they did not opt for a sweeping consolidation of local units. Instead, they, too, sought greater efficiency and effectiveness while endeavoring to avoid the burdens of big government and a centralizing bureaucracy. They recognized the need for change, yet they were reluctant to deviate too far from the patterns of the past.

In both 1966 and 1980 the board of supervisors considered the option of becoming a home rule county and thereby enjoying the authority to restructure county government. But both years the board rejected the alternative of drafting a home rule charter, believing that home rule status would not solve the problems confronting Orange.[106] In 1980 a San Francisco-based consultant hired by the board to consider home rule recommended against adoption of a charter, claiming that under California's constitution, home rule status did not enhance the authority of the county sufficiently to warrant the change.[107] For the time being, it seemed preferable to remain a "general law" county, with a structure determined by the state legislature.

Though Orange's leaders refused to attempt a wholesale reorganization of county government, they did recognize the shortcomings of the traditional scheme and the need for concentration of administrative authority in the hands of a single officer. In Orange as in the other counties, modernization meant in part creation of an executive officer to ensure a focus for the expanding county government. The post-suburban counties were no longer mere agents of the state charged with imposing state law and administering justice. They had assumed functions traditionally associated with cities as well as regional coordinating responsibilities of the type exercised by metropolitan authorities. In Orange as in the other counties, this change seemed to demand some sort of executive responsible for administration while the board of supervisors restricted itself to legislative duties.

Consequently, in 1967 the Orange County Board of Supervisors created the position of chief administrative officer (CAO). Prior to that date, the five-member board itself had supervised administration of county government through board committees charged with the oversight of the county departments. Now, however, a CAO appointed by the board would act as administrator, seemingly occupying a position similar to that of city manager. In other words, the CAO was to remain a nonpolitical, nonpolicymaking post; this new official was to carry out the policies determined by the board and ensure that county government operated with the utmost efficiency.

Supporters of the reform repeated the argument that an emerging giant such as Orange County required such a chief administrator. In 1967 the board's chair observed that since 1955 the county's population had doubled, but the number of county employees had soared 391 percent. Skyrocketing budget figures demanded "centralization of authority in the hands of a qualified professional."[108] Another supervisor seconded this view, claiming, "No business could operate as we do with department heads reporting to five executives." Administration by the board's committees was obsolete, according to this devotee of modernization. "In business the committee system would be ridiculed."[109]

Not all Orange Countians were as enthusiastic about this attempt to achieve effective, efficient rule. The arch-conservative *Santa Ana Register* opposed any measure that could possibly shrink the prerogatives of the private sector, and in the mind of this county newspaper the CAO smelled of big government. "The CAO and staff will be only another layer on top of the present level of bureaucracy," surmised the *Register.*[110] This new official appeared to be just one more costly bureaucrat who would inevitably bloat the public sector and squeeze the taxpayer. For the right-wing *Register,* "modernization" meant more government, further removed from the control of the taxpaying public.

In fact, in Orange County no one was quite sure what the exact role of the CAO was supposed to be. Some seemed to view this official as a county manager, others as a powerful, distant bureaucrat, and still others as a weak administrator performing routine chores for the board of supervisors. In 1967 one supervisor took the latter position when he argued that without a home rule charter the CAO would be able to effect little change in the operation of county government. According to this skeptic, creation of the post of CAO would be "only gilding the present lily" of county government.[111] The CAO seemingly offered a glittering facade of modernization but little substance.

The man who would have to attempt to define this ambiguous position was the county's first CAO Robert Thomas. A retired navy officer, Thomas, for the most part, obediently followed the commands of the board of supervisors and dutifully sought to keep the county government shipshape. Yet, in the words of one newspaper, during his eighteen years in office Thomas walked a "political tightrope," attempting to maintain a delicate balance satisfactory to both friends and foes of centralized governmental authority.[112] Big government was anathema along the metropolitan fringe, and especially in conservative Orange County, yet many voters valued modern, efficient rule by a firm, professional administrator. Thomas's dilemma, and the dilemma of many of his colleagues in post-suburban government, was how to achieve effective, efficient government without appearing to be a heavy-handed bureaucrat who violated the traditional suburban ideal of small-scale rule.

In 1971 the tightrope proved especially slippery for Thomas as he came under sharp attack from the chair of the board of supervisors Robert Battin. Battin urged the dismissal of Thomas, claiming that the administrator had "tended to assume . . . a dictatorial rule" and had "thereby made this government less responsive to the public." According to Battin, the ordinance creating the post of CAO made "the county administrative officer an agent of [the] board, an administrator and coordinator of its decisions and policies." It did not create "a non-elected super-manager of county business," a role that Thomas supposedly had usurped. Moreover, Battin claimed that under Thomas there had been "an alarming increase in the county bureaucracy," and the county had been led "to the brink of fiscal disaster." In fact, Battin attacked not only Thomas but the very office of CAO. "It costs county taxpayers too much money for what they get, is fraught with inefficiencies and enhances the tentacle-like clutch of bureaucracy on elected officials."[113]

Others concurred with this analysis. A local newspaper columnist labeled Thomas an "empire builder" and the *Santa Ana Register* renewed its appeals for the abolition of the position of CAO.[114] "The idea of inserting an extra layer of government in the county's machinery was a mistake in the first place," the *Register* editorialized, "[and] the supervisors should start paring back the extra layers of bureaucracy by this action." Moreover, when the rival *Los Angeles Times* expressed its support for Thomas, the *Register* responded by blasting the *Times* for wanting "bigger and bigger government."[115] The president of the Orange County Taxpayers Association added his voice to the complaints, blaming Thomas for the doubling of the county budget during the administrator's four years in office. "He gave you a $200 million budget in four years while it took 77 years to reach $100 million," protested the outraged fiscal watchdog.[116]

Many Orange Countians, however, rallied to the defense of Thomas. The

Fullerton News Tribune claimed Battin's attack had "all the earmarks of a political vendetta" and described Thomas as "an exceptionally capable administrator."[117] Moreover, three former supervisors commended Thomas for "establishing an efficient operating system for Orange County government" and labeled Battin's accusations as "tissue paper charges with little background to substantiate them." Thomas himself said of Battin's assault, "It was like going ashore with a wartime landing party in the Pacific; you had no idea what was waiting for you behind the trees."[118]

But as a naval officer Thomas had survived the war in the Pacific, and in 1971 he would survive the sniping of Robert Battin. A majority of the board of supervisors voted to study the operations of the CAO and postpone any action to dismiss him.[119] For the time being, Thomas remained upright on his tightrope and continued to proceed precariously toward the goal of concentrating administrative authority in the hands of the CAO.

In the mid 1980s, however, Thomas would finally suffer a fatal slip. In 1984 a critical board of supervisors refused to grant him a salary raise, signaling their dissatisfaction with his performance, and Thomas elected to retire the following year rather than face further conflict. Ironically, this new board criticized the supposedly dictatorial empire builder for not being forceful or aggressive enough as an executive figure. "I wish he was a stronger manager," commented board chair Harriett Wieder. The Orange County edition of the *Los Angeles Times* said of Thomas, "He lacks the flash and political savvy the supervisors are looking for as they seek to establish Orange County as a force to be reckoned with in the state arena." Responding to these criticisms, Thomas said of his office's relationship to other county officials: "We work behind the scenes to make these guys successful. So what happens? I get the egg all over my face, apparently."[120]

Working behind the scenes was not sufficient by the early 1980s, for by this time the board of supervisors had accepted the imperial proportions of Orange County's government and wanted an administrative commander who could handle the sweeping challenges of big government. In 1984 the *Los Angeles Times* wrote of Orange County government and its supervisors, "Today the four men and a woman who meet in the five-story, $10-million Hall of Administration preside over a $1-billion budget and a 12,000-member bureaucratic empire that covers six major courthouses, a state-of-the-art road and flood control agency and a host of welfare, counseling, health care, legal and recreational programs." According to the *Times,* "the board has evolved from a panel charged with regulating essentially agricultural interests into the most powerful political entity in California's second largest county."[121] The supervisors operated in a world of "big-time, big-money politics" that was a far cry from the traditional courthouse milieu. Thomas's office alone had a staff of 417 persons to help in the preparation of the county's billion-dollar budget.[122] As the *Times* noted, Orange County had developed into a governmental empire and its supervisors were well aware of the fact.

Many Orange County citizens were also aware of the emerging governmental giantism and unhappy with the consequences. The five county supervisors were accused of being increasingly remote from their constituents and indifferent to their wishes. Describing the supervisors' perfunctory public hearings, one leader of a Huntington Beach environmental group complained, "We have to make an entire presentation on an enormously complex issue . . . in 15 or 20 minutes. That's when quality of access becomes an problem. Big money can hire lobbyists that can go in and take them [the supervisors] to lunch or dinner and meet them in a private, relaxed setting with time to explain their problems and their needs. We as constituents seem to be constrained to the appointment calendar demands in a daily business day situation."[123] Residents of the Santa Ana Heights subdivision agreed. Targeted by county planners to become the site of commercial development, this residential subdivision appeared doomed, and embattled homeowners expressed their sense of helplessness when confronting the nabobs on the board of supervisors. "Politically, we don't have any clout," insisted the president of the subdivision association. "We're just homeowners they expect to make a certain level of protest. . . . Then they ignore it."[124]

Exacerbating the growing sense of distance between the ordinary voter and the imperial supervisors was the belief that the county chieftains were easily bought off by giant county developers who could purchase whatever they wanted from the board. From 1971 to 1987 no new municipalities were incorporated in Orange County; thus during the 1970s and early 1980s much of the new development was taking place in unincorporated areas directly subject to the authority of the board of supervisors. Whereas less than one-eighth of the county's residents lived in unincorporated areas in 1970, by 1984 an estimated one-sixth did so. The supervisors collected hundreds of thousands of dollars in campaign contributions from developers eager to enjoy a free rein in the booming unincorporated areas, but this practice further alienated many county residents. Explaining her inability to influence county policy, the president of the Santa Ana Heights homeowners association said of the supervisors, "I can't drop $10,000 or $5,000 into their political campaigns."[125]

The supervisors were, then, perceived as big-time operators. Each represented a supervisoral district of approximately four hundred thousand people, and they did not seem to conform to the ideal of government by friends and neighbors. Third district supervisor Bruce Nestande was a former aide to President Ronald Reagan and enjoyed close connections with power brokers in both Sacramento and Washington. In 1983 he served on two presidential advisory panels, a state commission, and a gubernatorial task force.[126] Second district supervisor Harriett Wieder was a veteran of Los Angeles politics, having served for several years as an aide to the Los Angeles mayor and as his representative on the region's metropolitan planning agency, the Southern California Association of Governments.[127] Each of the supervisors had a staff of powerful aides who were wined and dined by lobbyists. One supervisor candidly admitted that the aides were "a force to be reckoned with in their own right."[128]

With large and powerful staffs, bulging campaign treasuries, connections in Washington, and experience in big-city politics, the Orange County supervisors of the early 1980s were far different from the stereotypical suburban officials of the past. Though Orange Countians had not opted for a structural reorganization of their government through the creation of an elected executive as had their counterparts on Long Island and in Saint Louis County, they had witnessed a marked change in county rule. By the early 1980s Orange County government was big government.

Moreover, the supervisors were increasingly absorbed with big-city problems. For example, throughout the late 1970s and early 1980s, the county's John Wayne Airport was the crux of controversy and concern. It developed into a major commercial field, supplementing Los Angeles's facility in servicing the millions of air travelers in Southern California. Yet increasing jet traffic at the busy airport disturbed Newport Beach residents living in the flight path. A classic post-suburban clash developed between those seeking to exploit the commercial potential of John Wayne Airport and those dedicated to the more traditional ideal of Orange County as a residential refuge for upper-middle-class homeowners.[129] In the middle were the supervisors who found themselves in command of a busy airfield worthy of an expanding metropolis yet representing a constituency reluctant to see their county transformed into a clone of Los Angeles.

Meanwhile, countywide coordination of services was becoming increasingly significant and was tempering the tradition of fragmentation and local autonomy. This was especially evident in the field of transportation. For example, the Orange County Transit District (OCTD) assumed responsibility for transit operations throughout the county and by 1981/82 was operating 362 buses at peak hours on weekdays and employing 1,328 people.[130] The county supervisors appointed two of the district's directors, the county's mayors selected an additional two, and these four jointly chose the fifth member from the general public.[131] Chairing the board of directors from the time of its creation in 1972 through the early 1980s was county supervisor Ralph Gray, nicknamed "Mr. OCDT" and described by the *Los Angeles Times* as an "unabashed proponent of a sophisticated mass transit system linking the tourist and business centers of Anaheim, Costa Mesa, and John Wayne Airport."[132] Because of his devotion to mass transit, a fellow supervisor labeled Gray a "single-issue supervisor" who wanted to turn Orange County into something resembling Los Angeles's San Fernando Valley.[133]

Orange Countians remained cool to Gray's mass transit dreams, but, like John Wayne Airport, the transportation proposals and countywide bus system indicated the degree to which Orange was deviating from the suburban past.[134] Jet traffic and mass transit were not part of the suburban dream; they were nightmares for those seeking a semirural home along the metropolitan fringe.

The forces of big government did not, however, obliterate the institutions inherited from the past. Though Supervisor Bruce Nestande had the audacity to question the wisdom of the continued existence of some municipalities in the fragmented region, no Orange County cities disappeared nor did the county supervisors ever seriously attempt to eliminate these units of government. Repeatedly during the 1970s and early 1980s grand jury investigations of local government recommended elimination of many of Orange County's special districts, and county officials vowed to merge or abolish these supposedly obsolete miniature domains. "They've kind of become dinosaurs," contended one functionary in the county administrator's office. Yet between 1974 and 1984 only two independent special districts were eliminated, and during the early 1980s Orange Countians were still willing to defend these small governments by employing the oft-repeated rhetoric of local self-determination.[135] For example, the director of the Yorba Linda Water District argued: "The best way to run something is by getting local people to run a local issue. The larger you get in trying to run something, the more inefficient you get."[136]

Melvin Hilgenfeld, president of the three-member board of the Orange County Cemetery District Two in Anaheim, likewise expressed the credo of small-scale government. "I'm against big government, to be truthful," confessed Hilgenfeld. "Maybe they can operate it [the cemetery] better in having a computer do it or something, but I think there's a value to having local people." "If we consolidate, . . . I'll resign," admitted Hilgenfeld. "I'm not interested in the whole county; I'm interested in Anaheim. The only reason I even do it is civic pride—you want to do something for your community, and when you put something countywide, you lose that." According to this devotee of localism, "you have to light your own little candle in your own community, and keep it going."[137]

In Orange as well as Saint Louis, DuPage, and Oakland Counties many such little candles were still burning, but county imperialists like Lawrence Roos, Jack Knuepfer, and the California supervisors seemed all too willing to snuff them out. Though the imperialists of the 1970s and the early 1980s had faced almost as many defeats as victories, countywide services and coordination appeared to be the trend of the future. Whether the Melvin Hilgenfelds had any chance of surviving in the post-suburban future remained to be decided. They spoke the language of the suburban past and now seemed called upon to translate that language for a more urbanized world. So far they had generally held their own in the face of cries for centralization and consolidation. Roos, Knuepfer, and their ilk had made limited headway, but if the Orange County supervisors were any indication of coming events, big government appeared to enjoy a historical momentum that would be difficult to check.

6

Recognition and Rebellion

During the 1980s America discovered post-suburbia. By the close of the decade journalists and scholars were churning out articles and books on this remarkable and supposedly new phenomenon. With its postmodern office towers, its high-tech industries, and its state-of-the-art shopping malls, it seemed the embodiment of American life in the 1980s. It was a region of material success on the cutting edge of American civilization; its sleek, new buildings and well-manicured landscape contrasted sharply with the shabby structures and seedy appearance of many of the older central cities that had dominated the first half of the twentieth century. Post-suburbia had arrived and finally forced its way into the American consciousness. Now it was recognized as a central element of American life and the incarnation of the American future.

Yet during this hour of recognition, many residents along the metropolitan fringe expressed strong doubts about the new world surrounding them. Authors like Joel Garreau and Robert Fishman were proclaiming the onset of a new life style in post-suburbia, but many of the residents of these areas remained devoted to the suburban mindset of the past and bridled at the changes that were engulfing their communities. Since the 1950s residents of Suffolk, Nassau, Oakland, DuPage, Saint Louis, and Orange Counties had sought a balance between the treasured suburban ideal of residential refuge and the necessity for luring jobs, retailers, and industrial taxpayers. They had generally welcomed some degree of commercial development but had remained devoted to preserving the purported advantages of suburban life. Now in the 1980s the high rises, traffic jams, and wall-to-wall humanity appeared to be destroying these advantages and tipping the balance too far in the direction of urbanization. From Long Island to Orange County diehard suburbanites awoke to the fact that they lived in a post-suburban world, and they did not like what they saw.

Rallying around the fashionable slogans of environmentalism, these disgruntled residents of post-suburbia launched controlled-growth or slow-growth campaigns. In their minds, profit-hungry developers were the villains, and gridlock on the freeways was prime proof of the entrepreneurs' villainy. If left unchecked, the rapacious developers would ravish the small-town havens that had drawn city dwellers to the suburban fringe. At the very moment that the world was finally recognizing the advent of post-suburbia, opponents of breakneck development were, then, reasserting suburban values and repeating standard suburban rhetoric in the hope of halting the drift away from the village life style. The 1980s was a decade not only of recognition but also of rebellion, when angry citizens perceived the pitfalls inherent in post-suburban changes and sought to check those changes.

Moreover, many citizens rose up against the threat of centralized government authority so antithetical to the traditional village ideal. Just as the high rises were monuments to excessive commercial development, the schemes of such post-suburban imperialists as Jack Knuepfer and Gene McNary were manifestations of the governmental giantism so threatening to small-scale suburban rule. And in the 1980s residents of post-suburbia were no more willing to kowtow to big government than to big developers. Reasserting the balance between the county and the smaller local units, residents in DuPage and Saint Louis Counties put Knuepfer and McNary in their place, just as Orange County's citizenry pulled the reins on their empire-building supervisors.

Thus during the 1980s an increasing number of observers recognized that post-suburbia existed, but at the same time an increasing number of residents in post-suburban areas reasserted the ideals of suburbia. Despite booming businesses, bloated populations, and the other omnipresent signs of urbanization, residents from Suffolk to Orange reaffirmed their suburban identity and rebelled against those who threatened that identity. The balance deemed so desirable in the past was not to be destroyed. Instead, inhabitants of post-suburbia clung to suburban ideals and fought bigness, in the forms of both commercial development and government centralization.

THE POST-SUBURBAN ASCENDANCY

By the 1980s post-suburban development was so pronounced that even the most obtuse observer could see that Suffolk, Nassau, Oakland, DuPage, Saint Louis, and Orange Counties no longer conformed to the suburban stereotype. As seen in table 8, by 1990 four of the six counties had populations over one million, and one fell just short of that mark. Moreover, three had a population density of more than two thousand people per square mile, with one other approaching that figure. The census data demonstrated quite plainly that these counties were populous and increasingly crowded.

TABLE 8. Population and Density of Population, 1980 and 1990

	Population		Population per Square Mile	
County	1980	1990	1980	1990
Suffolk	1,284,231	1,321,864	1,409	1,451
Nassau	1,321,582	1,287,348	4,609	4,489
Oakland	1,011,793	1,083,592	1,159	1,242
DuPage	658,858	781,666	1,970	2,337
Saint Louis	974,180	993,529	1,919	1,957
Orange	1,932,921	2,410,556	2,448	3,053

Source: Bureau of the Census, *State and Metropolitan Area Data Book, 1991* (Washington, D.C.: U.S. Government Printing Office, 1991).

Yet the data also demonstrated that four of the six counties were no longer experiencing rapid population growth. Nassau was fully developed and its population had peaked in 1970. The number of residents in Suffolk, Oakland, and Saint Louis Counties rose only slowly after 1970, and even in relatively fast-growing DuPage and Orange Counties the rate of increase was far smaller than in the 1950s and 1960s. Older suburbs in each of these counties were losing population or only inching upward, and in new outlying communities the amount of vacant space available for residential construction was diminishing.

Commercial development continued, however, as each of these counties lured a growing number of office buildings, malls, and factories. In fact, these counties won recognition during the 1980s not because of booming populations but because of their magnetic attraction for business. They were emerging even more clearly than before as business hubs, with the facilities, functions, and services once reserved to central cities. It was this continuing commercial development that earned communities from Suffolk to Orange the titles of *edge city* and *technoburb.*

Further distinguishing these counties was their wealth. Though residential neighborhoods were aging and commerce and industry were engulfing thousands of once-sylvan acres, each of these counties remained far above the average in per capita income. In 1987 Oakland ranked first in per capita money income among the seven counties in the Detroit area; DuPage likewise was number one of the eleven counties in the Chicago-Gary region; Saint Louis County was first among the ten counties in metropolitan Saint Louis; and the per capita income of Orange exceeded that of the four other counties in the Los Angeles area. Though not first in wealth in the New York area, the Nassau-Suffolk region was well above the metropolitan average. Moreover, for the period 1979 to 1987 the rate of per capita income growth in these counties generally exceeded that of their neighbors. Oakland, Saint Louis, and Orange each ranked first in their respective regions in rate of per capita income growth, DuPage held second place, and the Nassau-Suffolk area again surpassed the regional average.[1] In other words, these post-suburban counties were still wealthy, and they were growing even wealthier relative to their neighbors. The figures demonstrated that they were indeed achieving the ideal fashioned earlier in Clayton and Oak Brook. They were luring office blocks without losing mansion dwellers. They were continuing to foster a lucrative amalgam of polo fields and corporate headquarters. These counties were realizing the post-suburban dream—a land of affluent corporations and affluent residents.

Exemplifying this material triumph was the commercial growth of Long Island during the 1980s. In 1982 *Business Week* summed up an emerging consensus in the business world when it concluded, "Long Island's economic success story may be one of the best kept secrets in the U.S."[2] Traditionally stereotyped as a wealthy bedroom community, Long Island was now emerging as a recognized business dynamo. Though the population of the Nassau-Suffolk region only inched upward in the early 1980s, the number of jobs rose 16.5 percent from 1980 to 1985. By the latter date over one million people were employed in the two counties, and *Newsday* concluded that "Long Island's economic forecast [was] still hot."[3] Year after year Long Island's unemployment rate was far below that of New York State or the United States as a whole, with Nassau's rate dropping from 6.0 percent in 1982 to 2.8 percent in 1988.[4] In fact, during the economic recession of the early 1980s, unemployment figures for Long Island held relatively steady while the number of jobless in the nation rose markedly. Such economic resilience led one business journal to feature an article titled, "How Long Island Beats the Slump."[5]

Long Island political leaders were not reluctant to boast of their region's success. In 1985 Nassau County executive Francis Purcell bragged of the county's "booming" economy and described his domain as a "growing, thriving, bustling center of commerce and industry."[6] In 1988 the county comptroller reported that "the economy of Nassau County continue[d] to flourish," and the following year he observed that "vacancies among the County's 310 shopping centers and fifty million square feet of industrially zoned buildings [were] at all time lows."[7] By 1987 Suffolk County executive Michael LoGrande feared too much of a good thing and urged appointment of an advisory panel to recommend how to "ease off" economic growth. Private-sector jobs in Suffolk had risen 33 percent between 1979 and 1985, fueling LoGrande's concern. "The county's economy is operating on a rubber band that is stretched very tautly," the executive warned. "We must ease off or the economy may break."[8]

Meanwhile, an ever-increasing inventory of office space further testified to the commercial triumph of Long Island. By the close of 1984 Nassau-Suffolk already could boast of over 34 million square feet of prime office space, approximately equal that of downtown Los Angeles. Thirty buildings with almost 5 million square feet had been constructed in the previous two years, including the fifteen-story EAB Plaza at the Mitchel Field complex, one of the major office hubs in Nassau County. Approximately 2.5 million square feet were under construction and an additional forty-four buildings with almost 8 million square feet were proposed or projected.[9]

Employment in the office sector, and in manufacturing and retailing as well, was expanding so rapidly that Nassau and Suffolk leaders worried about a labor shortage. Housing costs on Long Island were skyrocketing, leaving many workers priced out of the market, and exclusionary zoning placed obstacles in the path of builders of moderate-priced homes. Thus Long Island was failing to attract as many additional residents as it needed for its future commercial growth. One expert predicted, "The relatively small increase in Long Island's population will not be sufficient to provide the labor force necessary to sustain the demands of the growing economy." Economists projected that by the year 2000 there would be forty-six jobs for every one hundred Long Island residents as compared to the 1982 ratio of forty-one to one hundred. To solve the problem, "non-resident workers from other adjacent areas of the New York region [would] have to be relied upon "[10] Already in 1985 a local newspaper reported that "some labor shortages [had] begun to appear at both ends of the wage scale" and it was difficult "to find either engineers or fast-food restaurant workers."[11]

In other words, Long Island seemed to be on the threshold of becoming a net importer of labor, a direct reversal of the traditional image of Nassau and Suffolk as bedrooms for New York City. Moreover, the same prospect faced other post-suburban areas. The post-suburban formula of residential wealth mixed with a desirable number of well-endowed commercial taxpayers did not leave much room for lesser-paid employees of businesses establishing themselves along the fringe. Clerks and secretaries could ill afford the rising housing costs of Nassau and Suffolk Counties or comparable post-suburban areas elsewhere in the country. Consequently, an increasing number of these essential workers were having to commute from beyond the counties' boundaries. During the first two-thirds of the twentieth century, the less affluent lived closer to their jobs while the wealthy commuted from distant suburbs. In post-suburbia this pattern was being turned on its head, with executives enjoying a short drive to their offices while their underlings footed the bill for a longer commute.

Fueling Long Island's demand for labor was its development as a hub of high technology. "High-tech" business was the symbol of success in the 1980s, and every region sought to attract a share of this post-modern bonanza. Nassau-Suffolk, as well as the other post-suburban counties, was especially successful in luring such business, and this added further luster to the reputation of the newly recognized areas. In 1982 *Business Week* reported that Long Island was "fast becoming a thriving high-technology center with hundreds of small companies serving the defense industry and other rapidly growing markets such as telecommunications and computers."[12] "We could be the new Silicon Valley," predicted the chief economist for the Long Island Regional Planning Board, and advertisements in a 1982 issue of *Barron's* proclaimed, "Long Island is Tech Island, where it's at in high technology!" The head of a local consulting firm reiterated this view when he boasted, "Name a high technology and you will find it on Long Island."[13]

Long Islanders offered ample data to support their claims of technological triumph. In 1985 a boosterish publication stated that Nassau ranked third among the nation's counties in the manufacture of electronic equipment and fifth in aircraft production. Moreover, Suffolk held sixth place in output of radio and television communication equipment and tenth rank in aircraft manufacturing.[14] Over forty thousand engineers and scientists purportedly lived and worked in the two counties, providing the know-how necessary for its high-tech greatness. In 1988 one student of the island's economy summed up the prevailing belief when he wrote, "The story of Long Island's lasting economic health is specifically attributable to the proliferation and success of its high technology industries."[15]

The economic success of the 1980s seemed to prove once again that Long Island was no longer simply a satellite of New York City but a commercial and industrial hub with a density of its own. In a poll conducted during the second half of the 1980s, 71 percent of Long Islanders disagreed with the statement, "Long Island is merely a bedroom community of New York City," whereas only 16 percent agreed with this claim.[16] A representative of the local electric company was one who would have disputed this statement. "We have evolved from a bedroom community to a more independent economic community," he contended. And with an optimism typical of the decade, he added, "We're all bullish."[17]

In Oakland County local boosters were expressing the same upbeat spirit. With its traditional dependence on the automobile industry, Oakland had suffered greatly from the economic recession of the early 1980s; in 1982 the local unemployment rate had reached a dire 16.3 percent. The county quickly rebounded, however, and became an economic bright spot in Michigan's otherwise gloomy business picture. By 1989 County Executive Daniel Murphy was reporting on "a bright and prosperous present" following "seven years of unprecedented growth."[18] From 1982 to 1989 the number of people employed in Oakland soared 49 percent, and that county alone accounted for almost 25 percent of all new jobs created in Michigan during the 1980s.[19] "People outside Oakland County often say, 'Gee, what kind of magic do you have?'" observed the county's economic development director at the close of the decade. "The answer is, there is no magic . . . we just happen to have the best product around."[20]

Southfield continued to reign as the edge city par excellence of Oakland County. In 1984 for the first time in the city's history, the value of new construction topped the $100-million mark. During that year ground was broken for a 28-story office structure that joined existing 32- and 20-story office towers and a 33-story apartment building in the Prudential Insurance Company's Town Center Development.[21] Moreover, the boom continued. In 1986 the local newspaper reported optimistically, "Southfield's vibrant office market . . . is destined to keep expanding until all land is gone." The figures from 1988 proved the accuracy of this prediction, for in the single month of April that year, Southfield approved a record $70.2 million of new construction.[22] With twenty million square feet of office space, the city had meanwhile surpassed downtown Detroit as the office center of southeastern Michigan. Southfield called itself the "office capital of the Midwest" and the 250,000 people who worked in the city far outnumbered the 75,000 residents.[23] "As the hub of southeastern Michigan and the heart of the metropolitan area," Mayor Donald Fracassi proudly proclaimed, "Southfield has it all."[24]

Yet in standard suburban fashion, Southfield's leaders did not see their community as a place primarily to make money. Instead, in their eyes, it retained the suburban virtues of home and family. "Ultimately, Southfield is about families," Mayor Fracassi insisted. "We are dedicated to families, neighborhoods, shared values, and a wholesome quality of life." According to the mayor, "We're a community in the truest and warmest sense of the word." Southfield planner Tod Kilroy agreed. "Fly over the city and all you see is a sea of greenery," Kilroy noted. "When you drive through, you tend to see the highrise buildings and retail complexes. But what we really have here are hundreds of fine neighborhoods."[25] Thus even in Michigan's office capital, officials repeated the traditional suburban rhetoric. Southfield was at heart a community of homeowners who benefited from the fact that the city's many businesses paid 60 percent of the local tax burden.[26]

By the mid 1980s, however, Southfield's western neighbor Farmington Hills and the city of Troy to the northeast were assuming the lead in new business development. With eleven million square feet of office space in 1988, Troy boasted of the Golden Corridor, a tax-rich zone of office buildings lining Big Beaver Road. As early as the late 1960s Kmart had located its corporate headquarters along this corridor, and in the 1980s it was to be joined by many others, including the offices of General Motors's Saturn Corporation. So many auto-related businesses located their headquarters in Troy that one executive labeled the city "the nerve center of the automotive industry, worldwide."[27] Describing the extraordinary demand for office space, a vice president of a leading real estate firm remarked, "If someone came in my office right now and asked for 2,000 square feet in Troy, I'd have to tell them 'no.'"[28] Moreover, the *Wall Street Journal* pronounced Troy "one of the hottest corporate boomtowns in America."[29] Meanwhile, Farmington Hills was also developing at a rate sufficient to stir the admiration of any profit-hungry investor. Between 1986 and 1988 the value of its commercial real estate soared 40 percent and the value of industrial property rose 30 percent. By the latter date both Troy and Farmington Hills had surpassed Southfield in assessed value of real estate.[30]

In Oakland as on Long Island, many local boosters bragged of the county's leadership in high technology. At the heart of the region dubbed "Automation Alley," Oakland County claimed to be the home of 40 percent of America's robotics industry. Shedding its image as the source of hulking Pontiacs, Oakland was now selling itself as a maker of industrial robots and as an area on the very cutting edge of technology. The county's economic development director boasted, "Whereas across the country everybody wanted to become big tech-centers, this place succeeded at it."[31]

The crown jewel of the county's high-tech initiative was the Oakland Technology Park, an eleven-hundred-acre tract in the newly created municipality of Auburn Hills, east of Pontiac. It was to become the site of a number of high-tech concerns, including the Chrysler Technology Center which was expected to employ six thousand people by the early 1990s.[32] The technology park was visible proof that Oakland had an eye on the future, and the enthusiastic Auburn Hills mayor described some of the park's facilities as being "beyond *Star Wars.*" "It will be a center of technology which I don't think is going to be repeated in the Midwest," a county official observed. "It firmly establishes Oakland County as being the technology center of this region."[33]

With high technology, booming office construction, and fine upper-middle-class neighborhoods, Oakland was the embodiment of the post-suburban dream of the 1980s. It was assuming a higher profile in the business world and becoming a dominant player in Michigan, shattering Detroit's pretensions as the state's preeminent economic hub. By the late 1980s Oakland County had surpassed the Motor City in population and surpassed Detroit's Wayne County in assessed valuation of property. With some justice a county official could conclude that Oakland was "the business center of southeastern Michigan."[34]

DuPage Countians, however, would have challenged Oakland's claim to be the technology center of the Midwest. For like other post-suburban areas, the Illinois county was riding a wave of high-tech euphoria. "The aspirations of DuPage County to become the base for a major high-technology complex seem well along toward realization," announced the *Chicago Sun-Times* in 1982.[35] In 1986 the state officially dubbed the chain of research facilities along the East-West Tollway as the Illinois Research and Development Corridor, while others christened the area "Silicon Prairie."[36] Naperville proved especially attractive to companies seeking to create research and development laboratories in campuslike settings. Referring to the nation's two preeminent high-tech areas, that city's mayor Margaret Price asserted without hesitation, "Naperville is in the class with Silicon Valley and Boston."[37]

Though knowledgeable observers might have accused her honor of hyperbole, there was no denying that DuPage was experiencing a business boom, both high-tech and otherwise. From 1980 to 1988 the number of jobs in the county soared 59.5 percent whereas the population rose only 18.6 percent. By comparison, the number of jobs in Chicago's Cook County fell 1.5 percent and employment in Illinois as a whole increased only 1.5 percent.[38] The influx of jobs meant that communities once deemed Chicago's bedrooms were becoming business centers to be reckoned with. "Downers Grove is basically to the point where if you dropped it down in the middle of Kansas it would function as an independent community," insisted that municipality's village manager. The boom also sent housing prices soaring, to the consternation of employees seeking a residence near their work. Both Mayor Price and her counterpart in Wheaton said that if they were newcomers, they would not be able to afford a house in the communities they governed.[39]

Yet another index of the boom was the rise in office space. In 1979 there was 6.8 million square feet of such space along the research corridor; nine years later the figure was almost 22 million square feet.[40] In the Lisle-Naperville area the inventory of office space increased almost tenfold between 1980 and 1985.[41] The chief monument to office growth was the thirty-one-story Oakbrook Terrace Tower in the village of Oakbrook Terrace. The tallest building in northeastern Illinois outside of Chicago's central business district, this tower stood at the eastern gateway of DuPage County, reminding all who passed on the adjacent tollway that DuPage had entered the post-suburban era.[42]

Oakbrook Terrace Tower also marked the beginning of a new phenomenon in DuPage County—the selling of entire residential neighborhoods to commercial developers for a handsome profit. In 1988 forty-six homeowners in the seventeen-acre Ernie Pyle subdivision immediately south of the tower jointly sold their properties to Chicago developers for $16 million.[43] Moreover, in a more ambitious scheme, homeowners sought to cash in on the commercial boom by proposing to sell about 99 percent of the single-family housing in Oakbrook Terrace to developers. Supposedly, they would be able to sell their homes for a price two to four times greater than they could receive on the residential market. The mayor of Oakbrook Terrace extolled the "Mayberry-like" community he governed, but he also recognized that the area was changing. "We're small, but we walk among the giants now," he observed. A real estate consultant summed up the situation best when he noted, "When you have a county as attractive as DuPage is for living and working and where the amount of available commercially zoned land has been dwindling, it simply comes down to a matter of reuse and highest and best use of existing land."[44] In DuPage as elsewhere, the Mayberrys of the suburban past thus seemed to be yielding to the highest and best use of the post-suburban present.

To the south Saint Louis County was also feeling the pressures of change and boasted of the standard indices of the post-suburban boom. Though its population remained steady between 1980 and 1990, the county's employment figure soared 46 percent. By the beginning of the 1990s, the county accounted for 49 percent of the jobs in the Saint Louis metropolitan area and approximately one-fourth of all employment in the state of Missouri.[45] In 1986 County Executive Gene McNary expressed the prevailing optimism. "St. Louis County is young, strong, prosperous, growing up in the '80s," he remarked in his State of the County address. "St. Louis County is on the move with a burst of construction that is reshaping the local landscape."[46]

As in Nassau, Suffolk, Oakland, and DuPage Counties, much of this new construction was in the form of office buildings. From 1980 to 1985 office space in the county rose almost 30 percent, from 18 million square feet to over 23 million square feet. By 1992 it was up to 45 million square feet.[47] Some growth occurred in the Clayton business district, but the increase was more dramatic in other areas, especially in the West County. Chesterfield in that region and Earth City in the northwest sector witnessed much of the commercial construction. As a result of this building boom, the county could boast of almost 70 percent more occupied rentable office space than existed in downtown Saint Louis.[48]

Meanwhile, the story was much the same in Orange County. Between 1980 and 1986 the inventory of office space in Orange County grew from 16.1 million square feet to 36.6 million square feet, and in 1987 a real estate expert was still able to say that the county was "in the midst of an unprecedented boom in office construction."[49] Much of the building took place in the vicinity of John Wayne Airport and the giant South Coast Plaza shopping mall, but other office hubs were also developing. For example, the area adjacent to Anaheim Stadium sprouted four eighteen-story office towers as phase one of Stadium Center, which was described by one newspaper as an "integrated business center in a park-like setting."[50]

Anaheim was not simply attracting office space, it was also acquiring other big-city adornments. In 1980 the Los Angeles Rams professional football team began playing in Anaheim Stadium, joining the California Angels baseball team, which had been based in the city since the early 1970s. Moreover, Anaheim played in the big leagues of the convention business. "Anaheim competes head-on with Los Angeles for the big convention trade," the *Los Angeles Times* reported in 1982, "and has meetings scheduled through 1993." By 1988 annual convention attendance reached 1,026,728, a figure that placed Anaheim among the top convention cities in the nation.[51]

Yet in Anaheim, as in other successful post-suburban boomtowns, the leaders and residents did not embrace big city status without reservation, for they remained devoted to the advantages of suburbia. "As a city, Anaheim can be as small-town and suburban as any of its neighbors," the *Times* observed. "And that dual standing has resulted in an ambivalent—some call it schizophrenic—civic posture." Like Southfield it was, then, a town with a "big-little-city personality," proud of its supposed neighborliness but the home of two major-league teams and a leading convention center.[52]

As elsewhere in post-suburbia, an additional element of Orange County's emergence in the 1980s was its self-proclaimed status as a high-tech hub. Whereas DuPage had pretensions of being "Silicon Prairie," Orange adopted the sobriquet of "Silicon Valley South."[53] The county had long been known as a center of the aerospace industry, but in the 1980s Orange's new economic frontier was biomedical technology. In 1984 Orange was reported to have the nation's largest concentration of cardiovascular product manufacturers, and, according to the *Los Angeles Times,* the county had "undertaken an ambitious, multimillion-dollar project designed to . . . build a high-technology center of national prominence with a focus on medical technology."[54] A leading manufacturer of medical instruments predicted that "in 15 years (Orange County) will be a national, probably an international, center for bioscience." A research director at a local university likewise observed, "Orange County is racing to be the capital of biotechnology research and, given the available resources, it would have to work awful hard to screw things up."[55] The developers of Irvine seconded these prognostications when they included in their plans an Irvine Bioscience Center, with seven million square feet of building space for biomedical pursuits.[56]

Biomedical research and big-league sports were certainly prominent manifestations of Orange County's post-suburban ascendancy. But another sign of change was the construction of cultural facilities such as the $72.8 million Orange County Performing Arts Center, which opened in 1986. In 1973 the *Los Angeles Times* had reported disparagingly: "An accepted barometer of an area's cultural status is its commitment to the live performing arts. . . . In Orange County, the reading is definitely low." Fourteen years later, however, according to one national magazine, "the stunning new Orange County Performing Arts Center in Costa Mesa dramatically symbolize[d] Orange County's coming of age."[57] One observer after another said much the same thing, referring to the opening of the center as a "civic rite of passage" or a declaration of "cultural independence" for Orange County.[58] "In population, commerce, education and technological creativity, Orange County shed its role as a suburb of Los Angeles years ago," editorialized the newly respectful *Times*. Now the county had "shed its role as a cultural suburb as well."[59] With big-time culture, sports, and convention business, Orange County had everything any aspiring American metropolis could desire. All this announced to the world that Orange was indeed no longer a child of Los Angeles but had grown up.

The performing arts center was, then, not only a monument to the arts but a granite-clad landmark of post-suburban ascendancy. At its opening, former U.S. Attorney General William French Smith remarked, "I think [this] could really be classified as an historic occasion."[60] Smith was more accurate in his judgment than he perhaps realized. For this opening concert marked the final recognition of an independent Orange County. The principal newspaper in the nearby metropolis of Los Angeles recognized the end of suburbia, and few could fail to second the *Times'* observation. Orange, as well as Saint Louis, DuPage, Oakland, Nassau, and Suffolk Counties, had won acknowledgment as a post-suburban powerhouse. In Anaheim, as in Naperville and Southfield, the suburban age most definitely appeared to have come to an end.

Rebelling against Post-Suburbia

Not everyone applauded as the curtain descended on the suburban age. For many who embraced the traditional village ideal, Oakbrook Center Tower and the Golden Corridor of Troy were hardly happy finales. In fact, during the 1980s these malcontents joined together to rewrite the plot. They believed that the promise of suburbia could be fulfilled if disenchanted citizens rose up to halt the forces of growth and development. Through concerted effort they could ensure that Oakbrook Center Tower was the last skyscraper to mar the DuPage horizon and that the flow of traffic through their once placid neighborhoods was stanched. For decades, suburbanites had welcomed a certain degree of commerce, which bolstered the local economic base and thereby reduced the tax bills of homeowners. But by the 1980s a growing number of residents were ready to call a halt. Urbanization had proceeded too far and it was time to rebel.

Nowhere were the forces of rebellion so active and fervent as in Southern California. Orange Countians had long been proud of their perfect climate, beautiful beaches, and fine residential communities. Their county was the embodiment of the good life. Yet breakneck development seemed to threaten the quality of living along this American Riviera, and with increasing frequency disillusioned residents described their county as paradise lost. When asked what he liked about Orange County, one wealthy homeowner responded: "The openness. The orange trees. The feeling that there is room for everybody. The quiet." But then he added, "All the things we like best are disappearing."[61] This was an attitude many Orange Countians shared. The best of Orange was being destroyed.

In the 1970s slow-growth advocates had exerted pressure on Orange County planners and politicians, but during the following decade growth limits became a local obsession and few communities were spared bitter battles over proposed commercial development. Exacerbating the situation were mounting traffic problems, which advocates of limited growth blamed on excessive development. In Tustin's municipal election of 1982, the principal issues were traffic and a projected office and retail complex that included two five-story buildings and one four-story structure. According to one newspaper account, this project was deemed "a threat to Tustin's low-key, hometown atmosphere" and "would bring traffic to a standstill" along an already congested thoroughfare.[62] That same year candidates were arguing over what height limits should be imposed on downtown buildings in Huntington Beach, and in Newport Beach the fight was over a proposal for industrial, commercial, and residential structures on a seventy-five-acre tract on the city's western edge. The chief foe of this project described the clash as "overgrowth versus regulated growth."[63]

Though often castigated as prodevelopment, the members of the county board of supervisors were catching the spirit of restrained growth as well. In his 1983 State of the County address, Supervisor Bruce Nestande urged Orange Countians to accept "sensible densities" and "avoid the fiction that high densities and high rises enhance a community's image." "What's wrong with quaintness?" the supervisor asked.[64]

Many Orange Countians would have answered, "Nothing." The quaint fake adobe of Orange County suburbia had attracted thousands of urban refugees, and Tustin was not the only community in the county that treasured its "low-key hometown atmosphere." Orange County was facing an increasingly common post-suburban dilemma—opt for the quaint suburban past or embrace slick, high-rise post-suburbia. This dilemma would lie at the heart of the decade's battles over growth.

During the following few years these battles became more frequent and more bitter. In the wealthy seaside community of Newport Beach slow-growth advocates were especially formidable, and in 1986 they clashed with the Irvine Company over its plans for three new office towers in the Newport Center complex. Acting through such grass-roots organizations as SPON (Stop Polluting Our Newport) and Gridlock, foes of the office towers claimed that the new structures would add forty thousand automobile trips each day to the clogged thoroughfares around Newport Center and "further transform picturesque Newport Beach into a crowded urban center." "The bay is polluted—the air is polluted. Forty thousand plus cars means 40,000 plus tailpipes," complained one irate Newport Beach resident. "This is the St. Tropez of the United States," he added. "There is no replacing it."[65]

In a November 1986 referendum Newport Beach residents voted on whether to permit the Irvine project and handed the giant developer a stunning defeat. Though the Irvine Company had spent half a million dollars to convince voters to accept the expansion scheme and Gridlock's campaign fund amounted to only about $10,000, 58 percent of those casting ballots sided with the slow-growth forces. "The developers who have been cleaning the place out will go look someplace else for their quick profits," commented one of the elated founders of Gridlock. And a slow-growth city councilman observed, "The fundamental message of Tuesday's election is that citizens want to slow down the pace of development and avoid overdevelopment."[66]

Encouraged by this and other victories, slow-growth forces laid plans for a countywide measure to curb development. In June 1987 Orange County Tomorrow, a citizens group dedicated to considering growth issues in the county, announced the Citizens' Sensible Growth and Traffic Control Initiative, which it intended to place before countywide voters in the June 1988 election. By February 1988 slow-growth advocates had collected petitions bearing 96,000 signatures, 30,000 more than were necessary to ensure a place on the June ballot.[67] The stage was set for a dramatic clash between the county's powerful developers and citizens who wanted to preserve what was supposedly most desirable about Orange County.

The initiative, known as Measure A, set "minimum acceptable standards" for traffic flow, parks, flood control, and county fire, paramedic, and sheriff services. If the measure passed, the county would not permit any new construction that might cause traffic conditions or county services to fall below these standards. For example, Measure A required that rush-hour delays at intersections not exceed forty seconds and that rush-hour traffic on new arterial highways move at an average of at least twenty-two miles per hour. Police, fire, and paramedic squads would have to respond to emergencies in no more than five minutes. If the Irvine Company or any other developer sought to construct high rises or housing that threatened to extend the response time to six minutes, then the county would deny the developer a building permit. Measure A's standards applied only to unincorporated areas of Orange County, but that was where most of the future construction would be taking place.[68]

The proponents of Measure A were a motley band, including figures from every part of the political spectrum. Leading the campaign was Tom Rogers, a former chairman of the Orange County Republican party who was described by one newspaper as a "craggy-faced . . . rancher." Rogers himself had profited from the transformation of his family's land into shopping centers, and he was certainly no foe of private enterprise.[69] Among Roger's allies, however, was Irvine mayor Larry Agran, an arch-liberal Democrat who was acquiring a national reputation for his radical stands on such issues as nuclear weaponry and Central American politics. Agran was the type of left-winger who would not hesitate to attack "a greedy development community, working in league with a county Board of Supervisors who act like lap dogs."[70] Somewhere between the right-wing rancher and the left-wing mayor were a large number of people who were simply fed up with the traffic and disturbed by the destruction of Orange County's suburban environment. For example, a Garden Grove councilman argued, "Without Measure A, we can expect to spend more and more time at a standstill on our roads."[71] Another Orange Countian remarked: "It's just too crowded. I returned from a trip to Ohio, and it took two weeks just to adjust to the roads again." And still another complained, "If things keep going the way they are, we'll all be locked in concrete."[72] An Anaheim attorney whose neighborhood was threatened by growth and "progress" deplored the demolition of "single-family homes, to allow the development of a multi-story, high density apartment project, in a residential neighborhood." "My wife's bugging me to move," explained another slow-growth advocate. "She says there's [already] too many people over here and that she can't get out of her driveway. She talks about Southern Utah. Southern Utah doesn't have any people."[73]

These complaints, however, did not go unanswered. During the campaign developers spent $1.6 million to defeat Measure A whereas Rogers and his allies could only scrape together $48,000.[74] In their sales pitch to Orange County voters, the developers presented themselves not as post-suburban devotees of commercial growth but as defenders of the suburban way of life, and more specifically the affordable single-family home. Repeatedly they claimed that the curbs on new construction would drive home prices even higher and destroy all hope of home ownership for many Orange Countians and their children. According to the Irvine Company and its ilk, Measure A would not undo the damage wreaked by post-suburban development but instead would endanger one essential element of the quality of life in suburbia.

The Santa Margarita Company, the developer of a large-scale community in southern Orange County, presented this argument in full-page advertisements. "Keep Housing in Orange County Available and Within Reach," exhorted the Santa Margarita ads in boldface lettering. The *Orange County Register* made this same point in its editorial columns when it contended that Measure A would "make new housing harder to find, and . . . all housing, new and old, more expensive." According to the *Register,* "just the anticipation of Measure A's approval ha[d] an effect on Orange County housing prices," driving the county's mean price up 18 percent in a single month. "The growth-control door first closes on new residents and first-time homebuyers," the newspaper explained. "But it also closes on current residents, who find they cannot afford to move up, and on their children, who find they cannot afford to live in the communities in which they were raised."[75]

Moreover, if Orange County workers could not afford housing within the county, then they would have to find shelter in nearby Riverside County and commute long distances each day on the freeways. The result would be even more traffic, as the arteries leading to Riverside County became clogged with the victims of Measure A. "In my opinion, more people will be forced to commute from outside the county, adding to the traffic problem," argued the Orange County sheriff.[76] Likewise, the *Register* observed, "The ironic thing is that the more people we force to live in Riverside County, the more overloaded becomes our own transportation system as they commute back here to work." Basic to these arguments was the proposition that Measure A would not preserve the good life of Orange County but only bar worthy people from enjoying that good life. "The middle classes of people, who want to grow and gather for the future, who want their children's lives to be more abundant than their own, have always found a welcome environment in Orange County," remarked one foe of Measure A. But according to this Orange Countian, if that measure passed, the environment would sour for homeseekers and their offspring.[77]

Indicative of the strength of the rebellion against post-suburbia was the fact that both sides of the debate wrapped themselves in the suburban ideal and presented themselves as saviors of the suburban way of life. Foes of Measure A portrayed developers of twenty-story high rises as providers of the traditional American home, and slow-growth advocates appealed to the voters' yearning for the semirural environment of the past, when concrete and asphalt had been the exception and not the rule. Orange County was home to 2.4 million people and could boast of the busiest shopping malls in California as well as booming office and industrial parks. But these realities of the post-suburban age were now anathema. The slow-growth rebellion of 1988 sought to correct the imbalance in development and reassert the suburban way of life. No one seeking to win a referendum was willing to buck this trend and forthrightly embrace post-suburbia.

During the months leading up to the June 1988 referendum, the campaign strategy of Measure A foes reaped the desired rewards. Whereas in December 1987 a poll showed that supporters of the measure outnumbered opponents by a four-to-one margin, by the end of May only 49 percent of those polled favored passage, with 26 percent undecided.[78] Especially in the largely developed northern half of the county, opponents made strong inroads. Rapid growth was not a problem in much of this area, and north county residents feared that attempts to bring county services up to the standards mandated by Measure A might inflate their already bloated tax bills. Recognizing this, the council of the north county city of Fullerton passed a resolution opposing Measure A, and Fullerton's mayor argued that "the county would be forced to spend between $300 million and $1 billion just in the unincorporated areas" to meet the initiative's requirements.[79] The mayor pro tem of the north county hub of Anaheim likewise opposed the reform, as did that city's daily newspaper. The *Anaheim Bulletin* contended that "Measure A promised to be all things to all people, while the only thing it really did was attempt to formalize the mentality of 'we got ours, the rest of you go somewhere else.'"[80]

By June the momentum of public opinion had clearly turned against Measure A, and on election day it won approval from only 44 percent of the voters. It carried the south county but a large north-county vote against the proposal doomed it to defeat.[81] Yet both friends and foes of Measure A realized that this was not the end of the slow-growth movement, for Tom Rogers and his allies had forced county officials and developers to proceed more carefully in the future. "Notwithstanding the failure of Measure A, the slow-growth message has been heard loud and clear," observed one county supervisor. The executive director of the local chapter of the Building Industry Association agreed: "The way the county views development and how it relates to public facilities is changed forever as a result of this initiative." And a slow-growth activist from Huntington Beach told reporters, "I think the Board of Supervisors, the city councils, are going to have to wake up and deal with the problems we brought up by beating the pavement."[82]

This slow-growth proponent had good reason to believe that her cause would not be ignored. The same day Measure A was defeated countywide, the south county city of San Clemente approved its own slow-growth initiative, and the north county city of Seal Beach defeated a similar local measure by only one vote, with 5,004 opposed and 5,003 in favor.[83] The following November the Orange County municipalities of Costa Mesa, San Juan Capistrano, Huntington Beach, and Newport Beach all had slow-growth initiatives on their ballots; in the first two cities voters approved the measures whereas in Huntington Beach the initiative failed by a small margin. Moreover, Costa Mesa voters refused to approve a 3.1-million-square-foot office development that would have included a twenty-story structure and the regional headquarters of IBM.[84]

Meanwhile, in Seal Beach residents battled over development plans for the last major parcel of vacant land in the city. According to one foe of the proposed development, if it were built, Seal Beach would "lose its charm." "It's going to lose its character," she argued. "It's going to be just like everything else along the coast. Just a big mess of condos." Similarly, in Cypress plans to develop a former golf course stirred opposition. One dissenting council member expressed a typical view when he observed: "I feel cheated at the fact that this place is now going commercial. I think we've lost a great deal of green space. Something has been taken away from me and the people of Cypress."[85] And in Laguna Beach the dominant bloc of council members was associated with Village Laguna, a citizens organization "dedicated to preserving and promoting the village atmosphere" of the community. In the election of November 1988 one of these council members listed first among his goals the desire "to preserve [the] small-scale village" and "to protect the rural nature of [the] neighborhoods."[86]

Moreover, the county board of supervisors also took action to placate slow-growth advocates. In March 1989 they approved a growth management plan intended to achieve the same ends as Measure A.[87] Later that year they promoted Ernie Schneider, the director of the county's Environmental Management Agency, to the post of county administrative officer. Because of his background in environmental regulation, Schneider seemed to offer new hope to slow-growth advocates, one of whom commented, "I hope he can teach the board to say no [to development]."[88] With large campaign funds handsomely endowed by major developers, the county supervisors were still objects of suspicion. But even they had felt the impact of Measure A and responded accordingly.

Thus at the same time commentators were finally recognizing that Orange County had come of age and declared its independence from Los Angeles, Orange Countians themselves were rebelling against what they deemed the adverse effects of post-suburban maturity. The village ideal remained powerful in Laguna Beach and the residents of San Juan Capistrano still wanted to pretend that they lived in a small mission town. Tustin also wished to preserve its supposed small-town atmosphere, and everywhere "charm," "character," and "quaintness" were valued but endangered commodities. The happy median between polo fields and corporate headquarters that post-suburbanites sought to maintain was being threatened as high rises and the traffic they generated seemed to be pushing post-suburbia too far toward the urban end of the spectrum and away from the suburban ideal. Retaining their devotion to the suburban dream and their abhorrence for the big city, Orange Countians were doing their best to reestablish a balanced environment.

Similar signs of rebellion were evident elsewhere in the country. For example, Long Islanders were also questioning the impact of continued growth on their quality of life. In New York, as in California, the benefits of suburban life and of green open spaces seemed endangered by the onslaught of development, and residents were rejecting the notion that bigger was better. "Many residents are fearful that encouraging others to work, settle or even visit their immediate area will strain existing resources, accelerate problems such as road congestion, and hamper their own good quality of life," wrote one observer of Long Island in the late 1980s.[89] As in Orange County, many in Nassau and Suffolk deemed further development antithetical to the good life.

Throughout Long Island communities attempted to apply the brakes to development through zoning changes that raised minimum lot size requirements, thereby precluding dense development. In the once-tranquil estate village of North Hills this was a major issue in the 1980s. During the 1970s developers began subdividing North Hills estates, causing the population to jump sixfold from 300 to 1,800 in a fifteen-year period. Reacting to fears of overbuilding, in 1980 the village council raised minimum lot requirements, and in 1985 another upzoning was proposed to deal with what one newspaper called "the onslaught of condominium developments in the area." The minimum lot size for several large tracts was to be raised from 1 acre to 2.5 acres.[90] The former estate community of Brookville was engaged in much the same fight. In 1989 the first contested mayoral election in more than twenty years divided the community, and at the heart of the conflict was the desire to increase the minimum lot size from two acres to at least three acres. Significantly, both candidates favored larger lot sizes, but the challenger to the mayoral incumbent argued that the upzoning should have occurred earlier. Moreover, horse owners in this Nassau County community were concerned that developers threatened to destroy the village's informal riding trails and endangered Brookville's status as an equestrian refuge. "When people come into our area, they should be allowed to ride on the horse trails we have in the village, and any future subdivisions that are allowed should have adequate provisions for the preservation of the horse trails," insisted the mayoral candidate endorsed by the Brookville Horseman's Association.[91] Meanwhile, the Suffolk County townships of Southhampton, East Hampton, Riverhead, and Brookhaven all joined in the movement to upzone vacant land, thereby ensuring that each new house would be surrounded by a mini-estate of two, five, or ten acres.[92]

Even in the largely built-up Nassau township of Hempstead, public officials were imposing limits to prevent excessive development. For example, in 1989 county Republican boss and presiding supervisor Joseph Mondello introduced a proposal to restrict the size and height of future buildings, arguing: "We are not going to be overdeveloped. . . . At this point, we're just saying, 'You're just not able to build as much on a piece of property as you were able to build before.'" "What we're talking about here is controlled growth, not no growth," observed the president of a Garden City property owners' association who supported the Mondello proposal. "Uncontrolled growth will put undue strain on traffic circulation, air and water quality and on solid-waste disposal." Moreover, according to this homeowner, "the overdevelopment would stymie and stagnate nearby residential areas."[93]

Foes of supposed overdevelopment also called for building moratoria to check the further erosion of the quality of life on Long Island. In 1985 the planning board of Huntington township in Suffolk County proposed such a moratorium on commercial construction along the booming Route 110 corridor. During the 1970s there was slightly more than one million square feet of office and industrial space along the corridor, but by 1985 this figure had risen to six million square feet. Moreover, between 1980 and 1985 the rush-hour traffic flow on Route 110 doubled. The chair of Huntington's planning board concluded: "The infrastructure cannot withstand that kind of development. Huntington has to stop and make some serious decisions about its future."[94] That same year another moratorium advocate engineered a successful revolution in the Nassau County municipality of Mineola. For fifty years the Citizens Party commanded a majority in Mineola, but in 1985 Ann Galante of the Hometown Party defeated the incumbent mayor, running on a platform that called for "a building moratorium and a study of the impact that development ha[d] had on traffic, air pollution, sewage disposal and the water supply." "It's time for a change," Galante announced, for she believed it was time to combat what *Newsday* referred to as the "erosion of the village's suburban character."[95]

On Long Island, as in Orange County, traffic congestion was among the curses of post-suburban life, and a local newspaper characterized the Long Island Expressway as "a metaphor for commuter gridlock." Designed to carry 85,000 vehicles past a given point each day, the expressway had reached the 135,000-mark by 1985. In August of that year a truck accident caused a fourteen-hour jam on the expressway, closing all six lanes. "There was no movement whatsoever," complained one Long Island motorist. "People were pulling to the side, fanning themselves and relieving themselves."[96]

In their arguments against further development, slow-growth advocates, however, most frequently cited the endangered water supply. Nassau and Suffolk residents depended on groundwater sources, but the paving over of large portions of the island, the construction of sewers to divert rainwater to the sea, and growing consumer demands threatened the existing underground aquifer. Moreover, further development might also pollute existing supplies, rendering them unusable. By 1987 the state had already mandated water consumption caps on forty-one suppliers in Nassau County, leading the *Newsday* voter's guide to identify water as "the biggest issue facing the next county executive."[97] In both counties, the Long Island aquifer had to be preserved and protected, and proponents of controlled growth claimed that limits on construction were the best means for achieving this end.

Controversy in Suffolk focused on the pine barrens, an expansive wooded tract in the center of the county under which lay the island's largest groundwater reservoir. To halt development of this area, Suffolk residents in 1987 overwhelmingly supported a $570 million county program to purchase more than thirty-one thousand acres of pine barrens. But by 1989 many were criticizing the cost and pace of the acquisitions.[98] Believing the program was inadequate, the Long Island Pine Barrens Society brought suit to halt construction on one hundred thousand acres of the central county, delaying development projects valued at $11.2 billion.[99]

Yet the clash over the pine barrens entailed more than a pragmatic concern for water supply. As in Southern California, slow-growth advocates lashed out at developers not only because of the danger they posed to water resources but also because of their impact on the general quality of life. One leader of an "environmental" group expressed a common sentiment when he claimed to be fighting for "a place where families [could] enjoy a high quality of life, including pure drinking water, magnificent vistas, splendid recreational opportunities—a chance to preserve a little of what Suffolk County once was." Developers and their allies appeared dedicated to vandalizing all that was good about the county. "They want to build and Long Islanders be damned," the director of the Pine Barrens Society said of the local construction industry. And the builders' supposed friends in county government were attacked as "a group . . . that want[ed] to blacktop Long Island."[100]

Farther west, in DuPage County, slow-growth sentiment was also widespread, though not of the magnitude of Measure A or the pine barrens conflict. Instead, in one community after another DuPage residents repeated the oft-heard complaint that new development was destroying the quality of life. For example, a group of Downers Grove residents organized START (Save Trees and Residents Today) to oppose plans for two office-hotel projects which would generate not only tax revenues but traffic and congestion as well.[101] Oak Brook residents likewise were irate about the traffic spawned by the construction of Oakbrook Terrace Tower just north of their municipal limits. In this case the municipality of Oakbrook Terrace reaped the tax benefits whereas neighboring Oak Brook was forced to absorb most of the flood of additional automobiles. Foes of the tower were so bitter that they spread a false rumor, printed in the *Chicago Tribune,* that the thirty-one-story behemoth was tilting.[102] Yet widened roads were not deemed a satisfactory solution to Oak Brook's problem. When the county proposed to broaden a thoroughfare in the congested community, the entire village board showed up at a hearing to protest the action and others carried signs saying "No Growth."[103] One commentator accurately concluded, "Oakbrook Terrace Tower symbolizes the mess that can happen, in planning and in politics, when neighboring suburbs look out for their pocketbooks—and don't play a regulatory role." Even in tax-rich Oakbrook Terrace some residents were unhappy with plans for further commercial development, organizing the Save Our City Committee. "We have always been a friendly neighborhood, where we worked together to get things done, but I don't want to see the whole city go commercial," explained one dissatisfied Oakbrook Terrace resident.[104]

In 1986 plans to build a new stadium for the White Sox baseball team brought the issue of growth control before the residents of the village of Addison. Faced with the prospect of a stadium in their backyard and thousands of additional automobiles on their streets, the homeowners in nearby residential subdivisions mobilized to halt the project. Tom Zver, president of the Kings Point Homeowners Association, explained that he moved to Addison so that he could "roll up the sidewalks at 6 o'clock and settle in for a quiet night in front of the VCR. I've always loved the suburban life, the quiet." Looking out his window, Zver continued: "And now I'm gonna look out at an 11-story monstrosity. It's gonna tear my heart out."[105] Other foes of the scheme claimed that the stadium site was an invaluable wetland that had to be preserved in its natural state.[106] The DuPage County board voted against spending any public funds for the stadium, and in a November referendum a slender majority of Addison voters sided with Zver and opposed construction of a new home for the White Sox in their community.[107] Though the owners of the baseball team had conducted a high-powered, well-financed campaign to convince Addison residents, the president of the homeowners association was vindicated, and by the close of the year the baseball team had abandoned plans for the DuPage County site. "All we have is our love of the land and our lifestyle. We don't want them," said Zver, speaking bitterly of the White Sox.[108]

As in other post-suburban areas, many DuPage leaders boasted of the county's economic success while they harbored doubts about excessive growth. Though a proponent of the White Sox stadium and virtually every other development that would bolster the DuPage economy, County Board Chairman Jack Knuepfer also mouthed concern about rapid growth and the dangers it posed. For example, in the 1990 election he listed "reduced growth" as first among his top five priorities. "We need a countywide growth plan, agreed on by all governmental entities and enforceable," argued the county chair. The president of the DuPage Mayors and Managers Conference, Mayor Betty Cheever of Downers Grove, justifiably complained: "We're not being consistent. If we really are concerned about all this growth, we shouldn't be out promoting a convention center, a high-tech corridor."[109] In true post-suburban fashion, DuPage Countians welcomed the jobs and tax revenues that high-tech development generated, but they also clung to the life style of suburbia, the quiet neighborhoods, and the small-town charm that contrasted so sharply with the big city. The problem facing Cheever, Knuepfer, and Zver, as well as their counterparts on Long Island or in Orange County, was to maintain a balance that would not endanger the best of the past.

Consequently, DuPage County communities pursued a schizoid existence similar to that of the "big-little-city" of Anaheim. In one community after another reaffirmations of village life were as commonplace as the opening of high-tech headquarters. Naperville was one of the nation's fastest growing high-tech cities, yet throughout the 1980s community leaders sought to emphasize its quaint past through the preservation of its small-town business district and the creation of a living history museum known as Naper Settlement, in the heart of the city. In her campaign literature, Mayor Margaret Price insisted: "One of Naperville's most valuable assets is our heritage. I believe it is important to shape the future, but never lose sight of the past." Moreover, one commentator perceptively noted that the sponsors of Naper Settlement had "attained their measure of public approbation because they ha[d] successfully created some semblance of small-town intimacy in a community otherwise known as a center of phenomenal growth."[110] Downtown preservation efforts yielded similar results, and a visitor to the center of Naperville at the close of the 1980s would find a pristine, small-town Main Street, a century removed from the Bell Labs campus on the edge of the city. Meanwhile, Downers Grove, a municipality of 43,000 residents, retained a village form of government under Illinois law, and locals consistently referred to it as "the village." Despite the controversial office-hotel complexes, Mayor Cheever insisted, "We see ourselves as primarily, and fundamentally, a residential community." Similarly, Glen Ellyn, a community of 24,000 inhabitants, refused to relinquish its past image, retaining a volunteer fire department. A song written for the town's 1984 sesquicentennial expressed a sentiment appealing to many residents: "No matter where I go, Glen Ellyn is my home town."[111] With their fingernails dug firmly into the past, residents of Glen Ellyn, Downers Grove, and Naperville tenaciously held on to the hometown qualities of their communities while simultaneously being lured by the tax dollars of developers.

The residents of Oakland and Saint Louis Counties shared these feelings, though the sentiments perhaps were less pervasive in political rhetoric. In the Oakland community of Birmingham, for example, candidates for public office vowed to maintain "the delicate balance between . . . residential and commercial areas" and to "monitor growth to maintain a healthy downtown business area which compliment[ed] rather than compete[d] with the residential area." In nearby Bloomfield Hills, the Woodward Corridor Protection Group battled against office developers who seemed to threaten the tranquillity of the community's millionaire homeowners. "We're going to keep the whole city as residential as possible," promised the group's president. Likewise, some residents of Novi in southwestern Oakland County organized Citizens for Responsible Development to halt construction of a shopping center that "would serve as a magnet, drawing people and development into [the] area."[112] Oakland's West Bloomfield and Commerce townships sought to purchase open spaces and thereby limit development. "There is a lot of community pressure to be more aggressive about acquiring land that could go to development," reported West Bloomfield's director of parks and recreation.[113] In 1988 residents of the Oakland city of Wixom voted on a similar land purchase scheme. "The last person who moved to Wixom wants to be the last person to move into Wixom," explained the city manager.[114]

Saint Louis Countians were likewise concerned about the paving over of their domain. "Increased urban development in St. Louis County has resulted in rapidly disappearing private open spaces," warned a planning report from 1985. Residents of fast-growing Chesterfield in the western half of the county were well aware of this onslaught of urbanization. Repeatedly they attended planning commission meetings to protest commercial projects that would generate traffic and threaten the suburban way of life. For example, in March 1988 about seventy Chesterfield residents attended a public hearing to complain about a giant Toys-R-Us store proposed for an intersection in their neighborhood. Increased traffic was the chief concern, but one new resident raised an aesthetic objection. "We're from Middletown, N.J., and Toys-R-Us [stores] are prevalent there," she said. "They are the worst buildings you've ever seen."[115] Six months later a proposed shopping center was the object of the residents' wrath. Two hundred protesters attended a public hearing and, according to a city councilman, "certainly made their wishes known."[116]

Even in the pioneering post-suburban city of Clayton, citizens would turn out to oppose development. In 1988 the board of aldermen received petitions signed by 102 residents who opposed the construction of a 334-room Hilton Hotel and parking garage, whereas petitions in favor of the project contained only 49 names. Opponents raised the standard objection that the hotel would create "extraordinary traffic jams," and condominium owners in the adjacent Old Town area did not want the parking garage in their neighborhood. "I'm very much opposed to the garage," complained one senior citizen "The Old Town of Clayton was very attractive to a couple of old goats who wanted to get into the condominium life. [The garage] wasn't what I bargained for."[117]

But Saint Louis Countians, like other post-suburbanites, not only sought to preserve greenery and residential property values, they also remained devoted to the village ideal of suburbia. Amid the growing number of office complexes, the rhetoric of neighborliness and small-town life survived. In a history written to commemorate the municipality of Glendale's seventy-fifth birthday, a devotee of the community extolled the residents' endeavors "to keep and maintain Glendale" in its existing state with "neighbor helping neighbor; . . . a City Administration concerned about the well-being of all the citizens; [and] civic and private organizations and clubs dedicated to keep up the city's garden aspects."[118] Despite the economic changes in the surrounding county, Glendale remained true to the village ideal, a bastion of suburban virtue in a post-suburban world.

In the minds of too many Americans, however, the ideals and advantages of communities like Glendale seemed endangered. In Orange County this threat ignited a bitter fight over Measure A, and on Long Island it produced a wave of upzoning ordinances and a clash over the pine barrens. Residents of DuPage were also waving "No Growth" placards at public hearings, and in Wixom foes of further development were dedicated to retiring the community's welcome wagon. By the late 1980s the post-suburban counties had gained much-deserved recognition as business hubs. But their economic victories bore a price tag in terms of quality of life which a growing number of residents were unwilling to pay.

REASSERTING THE GOVERNMENTAL BALANCE

Just as devotees of the suburban way of life were attempting to curb the power of developers, so they were also endeavoring to check the ambitions of post-suburban imperialists in county government. During the 1970s and early 1980s leaders like Lawrence Roos, Gene McNary, and Jack Knuepfer seemed bent on expanding the county's role as coordinator of local governmental services. Governmental fragmentation had fallen from favor, and these chieftains believed a new era of county hegemony was dawning. Their schemes for asserting this hegemony had stirred opposition in the 1970s, but during the following decade resistance mounted, and McNary, Knuepfer, and others were to discover the enduring strength of the village ideal. Though the outward appearance of DuPage, Saint Louis, and Orange Counties was post-suburban, the prevailing governmental ideology remained firmly suburban. Residents of such hometown communities as Glen Ellyn and Tustin were no fonder of big government than of big development and they were as suspicious of centralized rule as they were of high-rise office parks. During the 1980s this persistent devotion to small-scale government was to prove the undoing of the post-suburban imperialists.

Nowhere was the clash between the small-scale municipalities and the county authorities so pronounced as in Saint Louis County. During the 1960s and 1970s, the county government had gained the upper hand, expanding its role as a provider and coordinator of municipal services. County executives Roos and McNary had used the *Graeler* decision of 1963 to block major annexation attempts and had thereby eliminated defensive incorporation initiatives. Consequently, a growing portion of the population lived in unincorporated areas, depending on the county for services and looking to Gene McNary as their virtual mayor. In fact, by the 1980s forty percent of Saint Louis Countians resided in unincorporated territory and the other sixty percent were the target of the county's continuing efforts to compensate for fragmentation through county-wide coordination of services.

In 1983, however, the Missouri Supreme Court handed down a decision that upset the existing balance of power between the county and the municipalities. The litigation arose from a 1977 attempt by the city of Town and Country to double its size and triple its tax base through annexation of rich commercial territory. The zone to be annexed included a shopping center, two office parks, and the lucrative facilities of Western Electric and McGraw-Hill. According to county officials, the annexation would garner an additional $2 million in sales taxes alone for Town and Country, $1.2 million of which would otherwise go to the county. Understandably, McNary and his subordinates viewed this as a tax grab detrimental to the interests of the county as a whole and challenged its validity. The trial court upheld the annexation, but in 1982 the Missouri Court of Appeals applied the *Graeler* decision and ruled in favor of the county.[119]

The Missouri Supreme Court thought otherwise, and the following year it reversed the appeals court judgment, overruled *Graeler*, and upheld the annexation. The supreme court emphasized the right of the voters in the area to be annexed to decide their own fate. When *Graeler* was handed down, Missouri law did not give residents in unincorporated areas any voice in the annexation procedure, and consequently, the supreme court believed that it had fallen "to the judiciary to safeguard the interests of the 'community' of residents of unincorporated county areas through its scrutiny of proposed annexations." But following the *Graeler* decision, Missouri's legislature had granted residents of unincorporated areas a veto over boundary changes, so the 1983 court believed that there was no longer any need for such heightened judicial scrutiny. Moreover, in its *Town and Country* ruling the Missouri Supreme Court asserted that the annexation laws were intended to protect the interests of the residents in areas to be annexed and not the interests of governments, which might be adversely affected by boundary changes. Referring to the self-serving arguments of the Saint Louis County government, the court noted that the state legislature sought to provide for the needs of the citizenry and "not the needs of government in a continuing quest to serve itself."[120]

Observers immediately recognized the potential impact of this holding. "As

I see it, any municipality now will be able to look along its boundaries and annex any commercial establishment close by just for the sake of their tax money," Gene McNary complained, adding, "We are going to look for legislation to correct this." Likewise, the county counselor remarked, "With these facts it's going to be tough to oppose any annexation."[121] Moreover, the mayor of Bellefontaine Neighbors concluded that under the new rules of the game, "you've got to grab all the money you can while the pot's hot."[122] An attorney for the Missouri Municipal League, which intervened in the case on the side of Town and Country, viewed the decision more favorably. "We said people should determine which bureaucracy they want to serve them. It's called democracy," explained this counselor. "St. Louis [County] has no interest in perpetuating its bureaucracy if people don't want it." The attorney representing Town and Country summed up the impact of the ruling best: "This decision removes the club the county has been able to wield in barring annexation. It simply takes the county out of that role and puts the decision more meaningfully in the hands of residents."[123]

McNary had good reason to fear the loss of this club, for annexation deprived the county of both sales and utility tax revenues. The county levied a property tax on both incorporated and unincorporated areas, but it could impose sales and utility taxes, which provided 29 percent of county operating revenues, only on unincorporated territory. Moreover, Town and Country was not the only community with a pending annexation proposal. In 1979 voters had approved the annexation of the tax-rich Six Flags amusement park to Eureka, and with *Graeler* overruled, court approval of that boundary change also appeared inevitable.

The Eureka and Town and Country forays were only the beginning of the attack on the county's tax resources. Within two months after the *Town and Country* decision, more than ten cities presented proposals to annex extensive tracts. "A range war is on for the unincorporated areas of St. Louis County," reported one local journal. Among the warriors was Creve Coeur, which coveted twenty-one square miles, including both Chesterfield Mall and West Port Plaza shopping centers.[124] Likewise, Overland's board of aldermen voted unanimously to proceed with plans for the annexation of almost seven square miles with a valuation of $70 million. The *St. Louis Business Journal* attacked this "last land grab" as "an example of government at its worst." But the mayor of Jennings was more sympathetic, remarking: "If I were in Creve Coeur or Overland, I would do it (annex). You would be some kind of damn fool if you didn't."[125]

Gene McNary, however, was not willing to stand by and preside over the dissolution of his empire. Instead, he arranged a series of meetings with municipal officials, and in December 1983 several agreed to impose a moratorium on their annexation plans until a commission could study the issue. Some municipalities did proceed with annexation elections, but voters rejected most boundary changes. In the election of April 1984 only two of the seven annexation proposals in the county won voter approval, and one of the successful boundary changes involved only thirty acres. A relieved McNary commented: "We're pleased that voters in unincorporated areas are satisfied with county government services. It may settle the entire annexation situation down."[126]

But the possibility of further land grabs was also stirring renewed interest in defensive incorporation. Residents of unincorporated Maryland Heights especially felt threatened by neighboring municipalities eager to snatch their richest properties. Bridgeton sought to absorb the Riverport and Earth City commercial areas in Maryland Heights, and Overland and Creve Coeur wanted West Port Plaza shopping center. Consequently, Maryland Heights residents petitioned to incorporate, a move opposed not only by neighboring Overland but also by the county authorities who feared a further loss of revenue. Maryland Heights residents, however, opted for autonomy, and in November 1984 they voted to become a municipality. Encompassing over twenty square miles and 26,000 inhabitants, Maryland Heights was a major loss to McNary's empire and planners estimated the incorporation would cost the county $2 million annually in tax receipts.[127]

Meanwhile, residents in booming Chesterfield in the western county were making plans to incorporate as well. According to the *St. Louis Post-Dispatch,* "some county officials worry that as Chesterfield goes, so will go many of the other remaining areas of unincorporated county." By 1985 county leaders were clearly on the defensive. "We're massing troops here," joked one county official, pointing on the map to Chesterfield. "We're putting in bunkers here and we have some fortifications across the river." Yet it was no joking matter to McNary, who referred to the "governmental chaos," "jurisdictional jungle," and "fragmented conglomeration of local governments." Fearful that the county would be left with only the poorest fragments that no municipality wanted, the county executive sadly warned, "Our tax base is being devoured."[128]

McNary was not the only one to worry. The renewal of annexation and incorporation battles also spurred action by Confluence St. Louis, a metropolitan citizens group founded in 1983 to address the major issues confronting the region. For decades civic invigoration had been close to an obsession among Saint Louis area leaders, and Confluence was just the latest in a long line of organizations that sought to arouse local interest in metropolitan problems. In 1985 this organization established a task force "to study governmental multiplicity," and over the next year this investigatory body held twenty-four open meetings to consider whether the area had too many governmental units.[129] Not surprisingly, in 1986 the task force seconded the findings of every other good-government group that had studied the same issue and concluded that the Saint Louis area did indeed suffer from an excess of governments. Moreover, by 1987 the task force had prepared a series of recommendations to remedy the problem. Among these was a proposal to eliminate unincorporated territory in the county by ensuring that all land fell within the boundaries of some municipality. The county government would no longer have to provide municipal services for unincorporated areas but could concentrate on countywide responsibilities and serve as a regional government handling regional problems. The task force also recommended that each municipality ideally have a population between 25,000 and 75,000. Thus many of the smaller municipalities would have to merge to form larger, and supposedly more efficient, units.[130] The bottom line was that the majority of villages and cities within the county would disappear from the map and larger cities and a regional county government would provide public services.

The Confluence St. Louis proposal appealed to McNary, and in fall 1986 he initiated his own crusade for the radical reform of local government. To aid in the effort, he asked the county planning department to draw up a scheme for reorganization. The resulting plan closely resembled the Confluence proposal. The "cornerstone" of the planners' proposal was "the full incorporation of St. Louis County into a limited number of larger municipalities." As compared to the ninety existing municipalities, there would be only twenty-one cities, each with an ultimate population of at least 25,000 (see figure 4). Freed of responsibility for providing municipal services to unincorporated areas, the county government would perform traditional county functions as well as those "services best provided on a regional basis" that required "a high level of countywide coordination or technical expertise."[131]

Actually neither the plan of the Confluence task force nor that of the county planners was very new or original. Both schemes were strikingly similar to the "county-municipal partnership" envisioned in the 1960s by the father of post-suburban imperialism, Lawrence Roos. In 1964 Roos told a planning workshop that his partnership scheme would entail "the eventual incorporation of all of the heavily populated areas of the County into municipalities large enough to be capable of providing municipal services efficiently" and would "involve consolidation of many . . . smaller towns and villages into entities sufficiently large to function efficiently." According to Roos, "the County, in turn, would be responsible for providing those services which can best be performed on an

FIGURE 4.   New municipalities proposed by the Saint Louis County, Missouri, Department of Planning, 1987. *Source:* Based on Saint Louis County Department of Planning, "A Comprehensive Proposal for Local Government Reorganization in St. Louis County," in *City/County Board of Freeholders Community Involvement and Public Information Resource Document* (Clayton, MO: Board of Freeholders, 1988), p. 13a.

area-wide basis regardless of municipal boundaries."[132] The proposals of the 1980s were, then, simply a restatement of the long-standing aims of county leaders. In the 1960s Roos had dreamed of municipal consolidation and county coordination. Now Confluence St. Louis and Gene McNary were mounting a campaign to realize that dream.

In accord with the provisions of the Missouri constitution, proponents of reorganization called for the creation of a board of freeholders to consider a plan for restructuring the local government, and in fall 1987 such a board convened. At the board's hearings municipal officials predictably denounced the proposals for consolidation. The St. Louis County Municipal League, which represented seventy-seven cities and villages, contended that "an existing municipality should not be eliminated without an affirmative vote of . . . the residents of the municipality" and claimed that "the desirable goal of universal incorporation of St. Louis County [could] be achieved without the dismantling of existing municipal government." It proposed a "phased process" of universal incorporation under the supervision of a commission similar to California's LAFCOs. This commission would draft a general plan for incorporation and render judgments on the merit of incorporation and annexation proposals.[133] The mayors of the county's larger cities also jointly objected to the McNary-backed proposal of the county planning department, arguing that "a majority of the residents in St. Louis County ha[d] strong emotional ties to their communities" and that "smaller governments appeal[ed] to citizens because they consider them more responsive and accessible." The mayors could only conclude that "any attempt to change municipal boundaries through forced consolidation or merger of existing cities would be divisive and would jeopardize acceptance of any plan by the voters."[134]

Individual city officials reiterated these points in the documents they submitted to the board of freeholders. The mayor of Crestwood objected to her city of 12,800 residents "being swallowed up into a new community of 60,000 persons" and thereby losing its identity. The city of Creve Coeur transmitted a similar complaint, remarking that "citizens of municipalities in St. Louis County like[d] being part of a smaller city with its own identity" and which provided "responsive local government . . . concerned with the needs of its citizens." Lottie Mae Williams, mayor of Velda Village, complained that the county's reorganization plan would deprive African Americans of political power by destroying the many small, increasingly black municipalities, such as her own, in the northeastern part of the county. "One look at the Reorganization map as presented by St. Louis County shows that all black elected officials in St. Louis County would be eliminated," Mayor Williams protested. She concluded, "I raise my voice in harmony with the other mayors and elected officials who loudly say 'LEAVE US ALONE.'"[135]

Repeatedly, Saint Louis Countians expressed the typical suburban desire for self-determination and small-scale government that could respond to the needs of the fragment and that reflected each fragment's ethnic or class interests. Perhaps no one expressed the persistent village ideal so well as a resident of Calverton Park. "We are small (1800 residents, no businesses, by choice) and feel that large is not necessarily better," she informed the board of freeholders. "Our police officers know the area and residents well, respond to calls quickly, and on patrol, recognize anything out of the ordinary. Our Board of Trustees are readily available if there are concerns or problems." Government in Calverton Park was, then, on a human scale, devoid of the bureaucracy associated with the big city or the county—and this resident and many of her fellow citizens wanted to keep it that way.[136]

The board of freeholders, however, thought differently, and in September 1988 it completed drafting a reorganization proposal that would reduce the number of municipalities from ninety to thirty-seven. Under the freeholders' plan, the county would continue to have charge of health clinics, arterial road maintenance, major parks, specialized police services, and the county jail and courts. But the county would exercise new powers as well. It would have the authority to draft a land-use master plan and veto any municipal zoning changes that did not conform to that plan. Moreover, the county would be able to impose a minimum housing code on all areas within its boundaries and would be responsible for building inspection countywide. Thus county authorities, and not municipalities, would have ultimate authority over development and construction. Each municipality would no longer be able to use zoning powers to serve its parochial purposes, regardless of the welfare of the county as a whole. A county commission would also oversee fire and emergency services, thereby ensuring uniform standards. In its report the board of freeholders estimated that these proposed reforms would increase the cost of government and recommended a new 1-percent earnings tax.[137]

If anything, the freeholders' plan aroused even greater furor than the Mc-Nary-backed planning department scheme. A group called Countians Against High Taxes and Loss of Local Control, chaired by a former Florissant city council member, was organized to lead the opposition to the forced merger of existing municipalities. According to the group's treasurer, "the freeholders have totally disregarded the basic American right of self-determination. St. Louis County communities and their residents have the right to join with one another or to remain as they are. It is their choice."[138] Mayor Shirley Sweet of Des Peres attacked the proposed merger of her city with neighboring Kirkwood, calling it a "shotgun wedding," and another Des Peres official described the freeholders' proposal as "a cynical attempt to erode democracy."[139] Kirkwood's city council was no happier with the plan, denouncing it as a "misguided, expensive and potentially destructive overreaction to the problems of St. Louis County."[140] Other municipal officials labeled the scheme "vindictive" and "out of touch with the real world." A Maplewood city councilman compared the board of freeholders to "Big Brother" in George Orwell's *1984.* "George Orwell was only four years off in St. Louis County," the councilman bitterly remarked.[141]

Especially controversial were the proposals for a new tax levy and for county control of zoning and building. Repeatedly, municipal officials complained that "city zoning would be subservient to the county government land use plans," and one report issued by opponents claimed, "[The] proposed uniform building code in St. Louis County . . . seeks to impose sameness on all county municipalities, prohibiting innovation or standards of excellence."[142] Moreover, consolidation had been sold as a means of reducing taxes, not raising them, and now an angry public rebelled. "Why . . . does the Freeholder plan call for the elimination of Cool Valley, whose mayor makes $1.00 per year and is in touch with her community, yet makes no provision for reducing the $75,000 salary of the County Executive, who probably doesn't even know where Cool Valley is," asked one irate taxpayer.[143] But even the county executive was troubled by the proposal for a new tax and blamed it on the refusal of the board to eliminate many wasteful municipalities. "I went in with a plan of 21 cities, and I believed 21 was even too many," McNary commented. In fact, he claimed that he was "unsure" about whether he would support the freeholders' proposal. "Just like everyone else, I'll study it and then make up my mind."[144] The St. Louis County Municipal League, however, had no problem making up its mind. Its members voted unanimously to reject the board of freeholders' scheme. "We were promised efficiency and reduced costs," complained the league's president. "Instead we have a plan, which when the final bill is tallied, may result in at least a 15 percent tax increase."[145]

Bolstering the Municipal League's position was a report issued in September 1988 by the Washington-based Advisory Commission on Intergovernmental Relations. This scholarly survey rejected the traditional academic bias in favor of consolidation and found much to admire in the fragmented pattern prevailing in Saint Louis County. "Today, propositions linking the fragmentation of jurisdictions with disorganization and ineffectiveness can no longer be accepted as self-evident," the report asserted. Moreover, it claimed that "the experience of the St. Louis area in metropolitan organization ha[d] much to teach the rest of metropolitan America."[146] The researchers discovered that Saint Louis County's many small municipalities had coped imaginatively with fragmentation through cooperative arrangements, sharing the burden of services while maintaining local autonomy. Thus, just when consolidationists seemed most threatening, the report added scholarly imprimatur to the arguments of devotees of localism.

In a special election scheduled for June 20, 1989, Saint Louis County voters were to cast their ballots for or against the adoption of the freeholders' plan. Just five days before that date, however, the United States Supreme Court scuttled the controversial proposal when it decided a case brought by opponents of the scheme. Missouri's constitution restricted membership on the board of freeholders to real property owners, and the federal Supreme Court held this to be a denial of equal protection of the laws in violation of the Fourteenth Amendment.[147] Thus the process whereby the plan was developed was invalid; the freeholders had had no legal authority to draw up any proposal.

Meanwhile, the fortunes of the imperial county had continued to decline during the long debate over governmental reorganization. In spring 1988 Chesterfield became a municipality, withdrawing twenty-six square miles and 33,000 people from McNary's unincorporated domain and adding one more unit of government to the scores already existing. The county planning department warned that Chesterfield's incorporation would have a "substantial negative fiscal impact" on the county government, but residents of the area sought incorporation to ensure greater control over local zoning. Rejecting county rule for further fragmentation, the cochair of the pro-incorporation campaign declared that "the citizens in Chesterfield wanted to govern themselves." A concerned McNary, however, announced plans to call a "Budget Summit" to deal with the revenue loss resulting from Chesterfield's new independence.[148]

The following year McNary's budget woes mounted when voters overwhelmingly rejected a ½ percent county sales tax hike to fund a long list of capital improvements. Again fears of big government seem to have doomed a McNary-backed proposal. Opponents of McNary's reorganization scheme viewed the proposed tax increase as part of a pattern of government from the top down. A lack of public participation in determining which projects should be included in the improvement plan only added to suspicions of a county government out of kilter with the suburban ideal of grass-roots rule. The mayor of Saint John accused McNary of "a power and money grab," and the bulk of the electorate appeared to agree.[149]

With the reorganization plan stymied and his tax scheme defeated, McNary had little hope of realizing his long-term goals. Fortunately for the embattled executive, the Bush administration intervened and offered him the federal post of Commissioner of Immigration and Naturalization. In fall 1989 McNary accepted the Washington position and resigned as executive, leaving behind a legacy of confrontation and ill will between the county and the municipalities.

One major reform, however, did result from the reorganization debate of the late 1980s. The Missouri legislature approved the municipal league's proposal for a county boundary commission to review and vote on incorporation, annexation, and consolidation proposals. If the commission approved a proposal, it would then submit it to the voters of the area affected, who thereby retained their voice in the process of boundary change. Beginning in January 1990, this boundary commission set to work to end the chaotic border wars of the previous decade and within the next two years received thirty-two proposals for adjustments of municipal limits.[150] Rather than accepting a wholesale remapping of the region as proposed by McNary, Saint Louis Countians thus followed a course of gradual change coordinated by a county commission.

Such a pragmatic compromise was typical of post-suburban governmental development. True to their devotion to small-scale, grass-roots government, Saint Louis Countians had rebelled against a gargantuan plan of consolidation and opted instead for countywide coordination that promised more efficient and effective rule without destroying the multiple municipalities so dear to the suburban ideal. The imperialist county executive had retired in defeat whereas the county municipal league's compromise proposal had prevailed. Once again post-suburbanites had demonstrated a devotion to their suburban ideological roots and an aversion for the centralization associated with the big city.

Meanwhile, in DuPage County Jack Knuepfer was facing obstacles in his long-standing struggle to create a county supergovernment. Though Knuepfer dominated DuPage County politics during the 1980s, he eventually overreached himself and suffered the voters' rebuke. Moreover, as Knuepfer attempted to expand the county's realm, he aroused an increasingly powerful countervailing force in the form of the DuPage Mayors and Managers Conference. This association of municipal officials was to wield new clout in county politics and offer an alternative to centralization of authority in the hands of county officials.

The battle over Lake Michigan water played a key role in the new militancy of municipal officials. Since the 1950s DuPage mayors had investigated the possibility of constructing a water pipeline system that would link the inland municipalities with the Chicago system and thus draw on the lake's vast water supply. In the early 1980s concerned municipalities organized a water commission, which drafted plans for financing the pipeline and negotiated contracts with Chicago to purchase this water. But in 1984 the Illinois legislature shifted control of the pipeline project to the county-dominated DuPage Water Commission, a body consisting of six members appointed by county board chair Jack Knuepfer and five members chosen by the mayors of municipalities purchasing the water. Characteristically, Knuepfer believed that water supply was a countywide problem requiring a countywide solution. And Knuepfer and his allies won this round of the battle with the municipalities.

Yet the cities and villages did not accept defeat quietly. The *Chicago Tribune* correctly observed that "mayors feared that the 1984 law . . . was the first step in a power play by Jack T. Knuepfer . . . to take over local mains, pumping stations, water towers and wells, giving the county a monopoly on an important source of local revenue."[151] Consequently, the municipalities brought suit to overturn the legislation, and withdrew their court challenge only when the county agreed that the commission would act solely as a wholesaler of water, purchasing it from Chicago and selling it to the individual municipalities. Each city or village would retain control of local mains and of the retail sale of water to households and businesses. But this agreement did not lull municipal officials into a state of complacency. Instead, the water dispute activated the Mayors and Managers Conference, and conference president Mayor Betty Cheever of Downers Grove later viewed this conflict as "the real turning point" for her organization.[152] Henceforth, the mayors and managers were on the alert and prepared to repel Knuepfer-led forays against municipal power.

This was evident in later struggles over storm water drainage. DuPage County suffered severe flooding in August 1987, and both the county and municipalities recognized the need for joint action to prevent a reoccurrence of this natural disaster. The Stormwater Management Committee, consisting of equal numbers of municipal and county appointees, prepared a budget for flood control improvements, but in November 1988 the county board's finance committee approved a marked revision in the budget, reallocating the lion's share of the funds to communities along the flood-prone Salt Creek. The Mayors and Managers Conference erupted in protest at this high-handed county maneuver. "I think we, as municipalities, have been short changed. We have been shot down," complained Roselle village board member Joseph Devlin. Mayor A. Eugene Rennels of West Chicago saw the county board's action as an attempt to drive a wedge between the Salt Creek municipalities and the other villages and cities in DuPage. He claimed the county's policy was "to divide and conquer." Moreover, Rennels warned ominously, "if they divide us, we are lost."[153]

Despite such setbacks the Mayors and Managers Conference continued to grow in significance in DuPage policymaking. According to Betty Cheever, the conference made a "concerted effort to join forces" with the county to seek solutions to regional problems. And Cheever's successor as conference president, Sonya Crawshaw of Hanover Park, reiterated this stance when she emphasized the need to keep "lines of communication open" between the municipalities and the county to ensure an equal voice in the discussion and resolution of area concerns.[154] In the minds of both Cheever and Crawshaw, the municipalities were to be partners with the county in regional governance, not subordinates goose-stepping to the orders of Jack Knuepfer.

Yet Knuepfer's grandiose visions of county rule continued to unnerve municipal officials and other devotees of traditional grass-roots suburban rule. By the late 1980s the ambitious county chair was not only seeking to build stadiums for the Chicago Bears and White Sox, he was also campaigning for the construction of a convention center, the founding of a state university in DuPage, and the $100 million expansion of the county's airport. Major-league sports teams, convention complexes, giant universities, and busy airports all were signs that an urban area had come of age. Knuepfer realized this and wished to advertise to the world that DuPage was, in fact, a major metropolis, a post-suburban hub that had emerged from the shadow of Chicago. But to the many DuPage residents who clung to a suburban vision, Knuepfer's plans seemed to connote only higher taxes, more traffic, and greater congestion.

Moreover, Knuepfer continued to push for the centralization of authority in the hands of the county, thus threatening one more tenet of the traditional suburban creed. Speaking before a business group in 1988, the imperial county chair observed, "DuPage is really one large municipality, but it doesn't have the municipal government, and that is part of the problem." Repeatedly the chair seemed to advocate one supergovernment for divided DuPage, and he continued to target governmental fragmentation as the source of many evils. In 1988 he told a journalist, "Municipalities will not deal responsibly with something like solid-waste disposal, because they keep trying to dump it off on someone else."[155] Centralized coordination was Knuepfer's answer to such problems, but this was an answer that made the mayors and managers squirm.

The discomfort of municipal officials, however, did not deter Knuepfer and his supporters from formulating plans for the restructuring of DuPage government. In 1987 the county board chair appointed a task force to submit a scheme for reforming county rule, and this committee's report was exactly what Knuepfer desired. It proposed the creation of an elected county executive with broad administrative authority and recommended that the county board be reduced from twenty-five to sixteen members. DuPage would be ruled, in effect, by a mayor-council form of government appropriate to a large urban area. Supporting the recommendations, Knuepfer commented, "You need some unit of government that is larger than a municipality. If you grant the need for certain county services, then, to have any efficiency at all, you need some sort of chief executive officer."[156] In other words, Knuepfer envisioned an enhanced county government that required a strong executive at the helm.

Predictably, the task force's report raised fears of a total takeover by Jack Knuepfer. A member of a conservative Republican organization said of the proposed county executive, "You would be giving far too much power and veto to that person." Moreover, she complained that the reformed county board would become "a paper tiger."[157] "A smaller board and county manager is part of a move to the centralized government Knuepfer favors," warned another DuPage resident. When a local newspaper asked voters for their opinions, a Naperville resident replied, "I am in favor of anything that would end the dictatorship of Knuepfer," and a respondent from Glen Ellyn answered, "No single individual should have the control and power that Knuepfer has enjoyed."[158] Meanwhile, a majority of the county board opposed any change that would deny nine of them positions.[159] Faced with such opposition, the reform plan was soon tabled. Later Knuepfer concluded that the scheme failed because "there was no constituency to make the change. By and large, the average citizen does not know what county government is and does not have much interest unless he/she gets a ticket or tax bill."[160]

By 1989 and early 1990, however, more DuPage residents were showing an interest in county government, an interest that Knuepfer would regret. Antagonism to the ambitious county chair was mounting, as county board members organized to challenge his authority and ordinary citizens blamed his grand dreams for their burdensome tax bills. In April 1989 Knuepfer's opponents on the board sought a change in the body's procedure, so that a simple majority, rather than two-thirds, would be able to overturn a ruling of the county chair. One newspaper reported on the "bitter debate, . . . filled with name-calling and insinuation." For the moment Knuepfer's forces triumphed, but one board member said of the conflict: "It was a total fiasco. It brought county government to a new low."[161]

The following year Knuepfer confronted a Republican primary challenge. He had won his position in 1978, 1982, and 1986 without facing a Republican opponent, but now lawyer Aldo Botti and county board member Judith Crane Ross both entered the race against the post-suburban imperialist. Botti especially sought to exploit antitax sentiment, promising lower levies for burdened DuPage citizens. And both Botti and Ross attacked Knuepfer's potentially expensive schemes for providing DuPage with the accoutrements of a metropolis. Speaking of possible county expenditures for a convention center, Botti complained, "If [the county leaders] have the money, . . . use it to educate little kids about alcohol and drug problems." Referring to Chicago's successful convention center, Knuepfer replied, "Can you imagine how many people in Chicago would be out of business if they closed down McCormick Place?"[162]

In the midst of the campaign, Knuepfer further fueled the opposition by asserting that DuPage was indeed a home rule county and thus could impose a broad range of taxes without the approval of the state legislature. Despite the defeat of home rule in 1972, Knuepfer claimed that the county chair was a county executive, and under Illinois law any county electing an executive automatically enjoyed home rule status. "The thing that scares people about a home rule county is the taxes," Knuepfer correctly observed, and his bold assertion of home rule status did nothing to allay the fears of rising taxes and dictatorial, centralized rule by a power-grabbing executive.[163] During debates over the home rule question, Botti supporters picketed the DuPage County Government Center with signs saying, "East Germany had the Berlin Wall— We have Jack Knuepfer" and "Give Jack the Boot."[164]

The courts were not to uphold Knuepfer's home rule argument and DuPage voters were not to award him a fourth term. In the March 1990 primary, DuPage Republicans chose the antitax Aldo Botti as their candidate for county chair. Botti won 44,000 votes, Ross 29,500, and Knuepfer ran a humiliating third, with only 23,000 votes, or less than a quarter of the total ballots cast. Knuepfer's campaign had outspent both Botti and Ross by a large margin, but all the handbills, advertisements, and yard signs had not overcome DuPage Countians' aversion to big government as represented by the incumbent county chair.[165] The *Naperville Sun* correctly concluded that "the voters rejected Jack Knuepfer in favor of Aldo Botti's siren song of lower taxes and a lower profile county government." Botti himself recognized that the vote was less an endorsement of himself and more a stinging rebuke of Knuepfer. "Flattery would say the voters wanted me in there," Botti remarked. "But I don't think that's the full case." Some lamented the loss of the visionary architect of post-suburban DuPage. "I think the county is going to lose a man of great vision," announced one Knuepfer backer. "Say what you want about Jack Knuepfer, but he has done marvelous things for the county. He brought DuPage forward."[166]

In the minds of most DuPage Countains, however, Knuepfer had been pushing the county too far forward. Whereas the county chair viewed DuPage as the emerging metropolis of the future, the majority of his constituents clung to the suburban past. Their vision of DuPage remained focused on well-maintained homes, top-notch schools, and homogeneous neighborhoods, characteristics increasingly alien to the big city. A big-time convention center and multi-million-dollar airport expansion program were not part of their dreams for the county.

Thus in DuPage, as in Saint Louis County, the 1980s ended with defeat for the forces of post-suburban imperialism. Advocates of centralized county rule such as Gene McNary and Jack Knuepfer lost ground, whereas the municipal leagues assumed greater responsibility for coordinating local government services. The balance between the fragment and the whole was maintained and the Knuepfers and McNarys who had threatened that balance fell from power. The traditional suburban ideal of small-scale, grass-roots government survived, even though the municipal leagues in both counties were increasingly aware that the many miniature polities could no longer act as isolated islands of authority.

The late 1980s also witnessed the dissolution of much of the empire of the Orange County Board of Supervisors. Centralization of authority and county coordination were not the hallmarks of these years, but instead a new wave of municipal incorporation engulfed the county, resulting in border wars reminiscent of the 1950s. The forces of fragmentation again prevailed, and the number of municipalities mounted. The future of Orange seemed to rest increasingly with its municipal officials, who would curb the authority of the county.

This resurgence in municipal incorporation was in part a result of changing California law. No new municipalities were created in Orange between 1971 and 1987, but in 1978 the passage of Proposition 13 was to increase the appeal of incorporation. Proposition 13 was a state constitutional amendment that capped property tax rates. One of the chief arguments against incorporation proposals had been that they would result in higher property taxes. After 1978, however, property levies could not rise above a fixed limit; hence previous fears of a mounting tax burden were disspelled. Moreover, the property tax limit forced local governments to rely more heavily on sales, hotel, and other miscellaneous taxes. Thus communities could benefit from incorporation if they included within their boundaries lucrative shopping malls. And incorporation would ensure that sales or hotel tax revenues funded services in the immediate community rather than contributing toward countywide functions. Throughout California, then, municipal independence appeared increasingly attractive. Before the passage of Proposition 13, approximately two new municipalities incorporated in California per year; during the eight years following its adoption, the rate increased to five per year.[167]

The traditional suburban desire for enhanced local control, however, also spurred incorporation advocates. A 1985 public opinion poll found that 63 percent of Orange County respondents opposed any merger of city and county governments, and when asked whether the municipalities or county should have more responsibility, 58 percent chose the cities and only 28 percent opted for the county.[168] Repeatedly in the incorporation campaigns of the late 1980s, Orange Countians expressed their exasperation with distant county authority and their opposition to the creation of mammoth municipalities unresponsive to the individual voter. "The people are very frustrated with dealing with [the county] bureaucracy and the size of it," commented one advocate of incorporation. Another, who opposed the abortive incorporation of sprawling Saddleback Valley and preferred a smaller municipality including only Laguna Hills, expressed his contempt for bigness when he told a reporter: "I do not buy the idea that bigger is better. We want the smallest city that is fiscally viable. We need local government that is truly local."[169]

These sentiments produced five new incorporations between 1987 and 1991, beginning with the creation of the city of Mission Viejo. In November 1987, 57 percent of those casting ballots in the planned community opted for municipal status. Cries of home rule were frequently heard in the Mission Viejo campaign for cityhood. Following the election, a satisfied advocate of incorporation announced: "Now the residents have access to local leadership for local problems, such as transportation safety, public safety, and waste. They will have a greater voice."[170]

More turbulent was the struggle to incorporate nearby Dana Point. An overwhelming majority of the coastal community's residents favored incorporation, but conflict arose over whether the new city should include the coastal section of adjoining Laguna Niguel, a community also seeking municipal status. In an advisory referendum, 61 percent of the residents of the disputed coastal subdivisions favored union with swank Dana Point. "We believe we'll get local control along the coast with a coastal city, as opposed to in a sprawling inland city of Laguna Niguel where they're more concerned about an eight-screen movie house or a bus station," commented one proponent of union with Dana Point.[171] But homeowners in the remainder of Laguna Niguel protested vigorously the loss of the coastline. Laguna Niguel's developers had used the slogan "sea country" to market the area's homes, but if the coastal strip joined Dana Point, the remainder of Laguna Niguel would be landlocked and unable to sell itself as an oceanfront community. Moreover, the coastal strip boasted of the posh Ritz-Carlton Hotel, and additional expensive hostelries were planned. Together they were expected to produce $4.4 million annually in hotel taxes.[172] The prospective municipality of Laguna Niguel did not want to lose that revenue source to neighboring Dana Point.

Orange County's LAFCO was caught in the crossfire between Laguna Niguel and Dana Point. At one hectic LAFCO meeting, nearly four hundred Laguna Niguel residents packed the hearing room, many dressed in red, white, and blue and carrying signs and balloons. Before the hearing, an ardent foe of the coastal land grab led his neighbors in cheers. "Give me an L!" he shouted as the protesters spelled out "Laguna Niguel," and they ended their cheers with chants of "sea country, sea country." Sheriff's deputies had to be called to control the crowd, and a county supervisor serving on LAFCO threatened to have the sheriff remove the rowdiest Laguna Niguel residents.[173]

The cheers and chants, however, were to no avail. In June 1988 Dana Point became Orange County's twenty-eighth municipality, including within its boundaries the coastal section of Laguna Niguel. Planners on the LAFCO staff originally recommended that the remainder of Laguna Niguel join with Laguna Hills to form a large municipality. But protests from the two communities forced a change in the recommendation. LAFCO acceded to traditional suburban localism and allowed Laguna Niguel and Laguna Hills to incorporate as two separate municipalities. "Although LAFCO staff continues to harbor grave concerns over the formation of several relatively small cities," wrote the LAFCO executive officer, "it is also recognized the south county residents may prefer smaller cities."[174] A leader of the Laguna Hills incorporation drive welcomed the opportunity to pursue a separate existence. Rejecting "the mega-city concept," she claimed voters wanted "the smallest city possible that's feasible."[175] Local control was the campaign slogan in both Laguna Hills and Laguna Niguel, and following the incorporation of the latter community, one resident happily concluded: "It's going to be easier to have a voice. Hopefully, we will have control over our own community now." In words that summed up the suburban creed of the past half century, another Laguna Niguel enthusiast proclaimed, "We want a place to call home and to a lot of people, 'city[hood]' means community and local control."[176]

In 1991 El Toro became the fifth new municipality created in Orange County since 1987. Again the desire for local control prompted the adoption of city status. "Without cityhood, we have to wait to see what happens," said the vice chair of the Community Coalition for Incorporation. "With cityhood, we can make it happen."[177]

Big county government had not, then, superseded the suburban tradition of localism. In Orange County, as in DuPage and Saint Louis Counties, municipal rule was alive and well and the units of local government were actually proliferating. County planners had to yield to demands for smaller units, and Dana Point and Laguna Niguel engaged in border conflicts similar to those of the more chaotic 1950s. Angry residents still demanded self-determination and fought neighbors for revenue-rich territory. Despite the changing outward appearance of the post-suburban region, with its high-rises, mammoth malls, and performing arts centers, the rhetoric of local leaders remained remarkably unchanged. Local control was still an unquestioned virtue and dictation by distant county authorities a danger to be avoided. The Orange County edition of the *Los Angeles Times* may have observed that "the splintering off of cities" seemed "to encourage a parochial view of government at a time when common problems increasingly transcend[ed] boundaries."[178] But for most Orange Countians, centralization of authority outweighed parochialism as an evil.

By the early 1990s the wave of incorporations had so weakened county authority that Orange residents apparently had little to fear from county imperialists. Rather than appearing to be the government of the future, the county seemed a relic of the past and some questioned its continued utility. The county administrative officer estimated that the five recent incorporations had cost the county $21 million in property and sales taxes. Such tax losses contributed to the county's mounting financial woes, and, according to the *Los Angeles Times,* those figures made "it clear why county administrators shudder[ed] at the word 'cityhood.'"[179] One editorial announced, "Thoughtful citizens, not only in Orange County but throughout the state, are wondering aloud whether county government has outlived its usefulness."[180] And Orange County supervisor Roger Stanton likewise felt compelled to respond to the question of whether "county government [had] outlived its usefulness." The supervisor dismissed as "specious" arguments positing a future diminished role for county government, but even he would have admitted that the county no longer wielded as much authority over the charting of the post-suburban future.[181] Stanton and others mentioned the future coordinating function of the county, as more governmental fragments cluttered the map of Southern California. Yet in Orange, as in Saint Louis and DuPage Counties, the post-suburban imperialists had lost ground to the persistent localism basic to the suburban ideal.

On post-suburban Long Island the multitude of local governments also survived with powers intact. At the close of 1989 Congressman Thomas Downey proposed a special commission to "streamline" Long Island's local government and thereby relieve the heavy tax burden. "We have more units of government than any of us can name, let alone describe," complained Downey.[182] Three years later Downey had lost his seat in Congress, but scores of supposedly unknown governmental units had not lost their powers. Moreover, in the early 1990s the unifying grasp of the Nassau County Republican organization slackened notably, producing an unwonted fragmentation of political power. Shattering GOP hegemony, two of the county's three townships elected Democratic supervisors, an occurrence unknown in the glory days of Russel Sprague. The office of county executive remained in Republican hands, but with the townships of North Hempstead and Oyster Bay in the enemy camp, the executive and Republican party leader wielded less clout than in past years. At the same

time, Suffolk's townships remained fiercely jealous of their authority, perpetuating that county's chaotic political tradition. Despite budgetary problems in
both Nassau and Suffolk, the counties continued to exercise broad powers, but
the townships and villages appeared no nearer to extinction than they had
three decades earlier.

Meanwhile, in Oakland County Daniel Murphy stayed at the county's helm
until the beginning of 1993. Though the newspapers labeled Murphy, the
mayor of Detroit, and the leaders of Wayne and Macomb Counties as the "Big
Four" of southeastern Michigan, the Oakland executive did not use his powerful position to upset the balance of power between the county and the municipalities.[183] Never a crusader for consolidation in the mold of Gene McNary or
Jack Knuepfer, Daniel Murphy survived eighteen years as county executive
and, unlike his DuPage counterpart, retired voluntarily. He accommodated
himself to the persistent localism of his domain rather than combating it. Like
Russel Sprague before him, he recognized that suburbanites would accept
pragmatic initiatives aimed at coordinating services, but most did not wish to
move beyond that. Thus in the early 1990s exclusive Franklin, "the town time
forgot," and elegantly aloof Bloomfield Hills maintained their independence,
free from the forces of social and political homogenization.

The legacy of the 1980s was, then, a perpetuation of the governmental balance in post-suburban America. Just as most post-suburban residents did not
choose to abandon their villages and towns to the mercies of profit-hungry
commercial developers, so they refused to sell out to post-suburban imperialists who equated consolidation with efficiency and good government. By 1990
few cows grazed the pastures of Saint Louis and DuPage Counties and the citrus groves of Orange had largely disappeared, but residents of these areas still
sought to ensure that their hometowns as closely resembled the suburban
dream as possible. Big development and big government were for big cities and
both were at best necessary evils in the post-suburban counties. For the sake of
efficiency, employment, convenience, or lower taxes, they might be tolerated.
But unless centralized rule and high rises in some way enhanced the suburban
way of life, they were unwelcome.

7

The Pragmatic Compromise

Referring to county chair Jack Knuepfer, one DuPage County resident commented in the late 1980s: "He thinks we want DuPage County to become Cook County with big convention centers, huge highways, etc. We live in DuPage County because it isn't like Cook County and will leave if Knuepfer's so-called improvements continue."[1] This summed up the persistent suburban mindset of post-suburban America. The bigness of Chicago's Cook County was bad, and DuPage County had to be spared the by-products of the big city. DuPage had almost 800,000 inhabitants, a population density of more than 2,000 people per square mile, and a full complement of corporate offices, research centers, hotels, and shopping malls, but DuPage residents remained devoted to the traditional suburban ideal. The growing body of literature on edge cities and technoburbs correctly identified the changes occurring along the metropolitan fringe. Its physical appearance had altered as six-lane highways supplanted country roads and big-league stadiums arose in former cornfields and orange groves. Moreover, economic data indicated that a new world had developed in DuPage County and its counterparts from Long Island to Southern California. The casual observer and statistician alike could testify to the new post-suburban reality. Yet in their hearts DuPage Countians remained suburban. Outward appearance indicated a new post-suburban world, but as Jack Knuepfer was to discover, voting returns demonstrated the persistence of the suburban dream.[2]

Post-suburbia was, in fact, a marriage of convenience, an uneasy union based on practical necessity. Though remaining true in their hearts to the suburban ideal, residents of outlying areas warmed to the promise of tax revenues, jobs, shopping opportunities, regionally coordinated water and sewer projects, and county parks. Thus they joined in a pragmatic alliance with commercial developers and government centralizers. To the outside world the post-suburban areas generally appeared a happy combination of homes and commerce, of villages and regional authorities, but the marriage was a rocky one, built on perceived practical advantages rather than genuine devotion. The slow-growth campaigns of the 1980s were outward signs of the tension underlying this shaky alliance as were the revolts against the centralizing schemes of McNary and Knuepfer. The post-suburban union survived these spats, but it was clearly not a love match. If governmental centralization and commercial development had not paid off, residents of Nassau, Naperville, and Newport Beach would have gladly walked out on the post-suburban marriage of convenience.

Thus despite some appearances to the contrary, post-suburbia in many ways remained suburban. By the 1980s Long Island, Oakland, DuPage, Saint Louis, and Orange Counties were not suburban in the sense of primarily serving as bedrooms for central cities. They were not a conglomeration of residential satellites rotating around a dominant central-city downtown. But they remained suburban in the sense that residents continued to reject much that smacked of the big city. During the 1980s DuPage Countians had no more desire to imitate life in Chicago than they had in the 1930s. Oakland Countians were no more enamored of Detroit than they had been fifty years earlier, and Long Islanders remained just as suspicious of New York City. In the 1980s as in the 1930s, "urban" had a negative connotation among residents of the metropolitan edge.

This persistent suburban vision was in marked contrast to the notions that had molded urban America. In the nineteenth century a spirit of urban boosterism had prevailed; bigger was automatically better. Growth was good, and noise, smoke, and traffic were signs of success. Suburbanites and their post-suburban heirs questioned this. In their hierarchy of values, homogeneity, intimacy, and placidity ranked higher than growth, hustle and bustle, and bigness. They recognized that some benefits resulted from commercial growth and development, and they embraced those benefits. But they were wary, for development in their minds was not an unquestioned good.

Moreover, residents on Long Island and in Oakland and DuPage remained staunchly suburban in their governmental ideals. Despite the persistent ridicule and diatribes of generations of so-called experts on local government, hundreds of small-scale polities survived from Suffolk County in the east to Orange County in the west. During the 1970s and 1980s metropolitan councils of government had limped along, propped up by the supposed experts and the federal government. But scores of purportedly anachronistic and incompetent village governments had weathered the storms of proposed reform and were still organizing community Fourth of July celebrations on the village green in 1990 just as they had in 1940.

In fact, given the persistent suburban ideal of government, the village regimes were not anachronisms. Instead, the metropolitan schemes were out of line with prevailing beliefs and ill-suited to win acceptance among political leaders or voters. Metropolitanism was based on an anachronistic view of metropolitan areas, a view that emphasized the social and economic ties linking city and suburb. Yet by the 1960s and 1970s there was actually a decreasing community of interest between the urban core and outlying municipalities. No longer was one workplace and the other bedroom; they did not complement each other but rather competed for offices, factories, and retailing. Race, class, and politics further divided them, as the central city was increasingly black, poor, and Democratic, whereas the outlying municipalities generally remained white, middle or upper-middle class, and Republican. And the persistent suburban vision of government was yet another factor distinguishing the fringe from the center. The grounds for agreement were, then, diminishing, and the political fragmentation of the metropolis reflected existing social, economic, and ideological divisions. Fragmentation was not out of step with the realities of the age. It very much reflected those realities.

After 1960 residents of outlying areas rejected the excessive fragmentation of the 1940s and 1950s, and the new municipalities of the 1980s were not of the same miniature scale as many units created in earlier decades. Moreover, voters were willing to accept a degree of coordination by county agencies or special-purpose metropolitan authorities if such coordination promised practical returns in terms of superior services. But from Long Island to Orange residents still deemed bigness as a bane that should be tolerated only for the sake of efficiency or fiscal viability. The notion of government by friends and neighbors retained a lasting appeal, and threats to grass-roots rule faced heated resistance as Lawrence Roos, Gene McNary, and Jack Knuepfer learned during the 1970s and 1980s.

Moreover, by the 1990s nothing indicated an imminent change in attitude among residents of the six post-suburban counties. Some authors continued to deplore metropolitan fragmentation and espoused central-city annexation of suburban areas.[3] Others still dreamed of metropolitan governments of the ilk proposed in the Saint Louis area in the late 1950s and early 1960s. But given the long-standing devotion to grass-roots rule and the repeated defeats suffered by government centralizers, there was little chance of a radical redistribution of authority along the metropolitan fringe. The city of Saint Louis was about as likely to annex Saint Louis County as the United States was to make Mexico the fifty-first state. And the likelihood of Detroit absorbing Oakland County within its boundaries was even more remote.

As post-suburban politicians assumed increasing prominence in national and state government, the chances for a successful assault on grass-roots government further diminished. In 1995 third-term Senator Alfonse D'Amato, a former supervisor of Hempstead township and a product of the Nassau County Republican organization, assumed the chair of the Senate Banking, Housing, and Urban Affairs Committee. Federal legislation dealing with urban affairs had to pass the muster of this Nassau politician, a man dedicated to the pragmatic compromise of Russel Sprague. By the mid 1990s both the speaker of the Illinois House of Representatives and the state senate majority leader were DuPage County Republicans, staunchly committed to the interests of their post-suburban county and suspicious of any legislative initiative from the big city of Chicago. The Republicans controlled the Illinois legislature, and DuPage County controlled the Republicans.

Reflecting the growing impact of the suburban mindset, opposition to big government became a national crusade during the 1990s, and this powerful anti-bigness sentiment also did not augur well for the creation of metropolitan gargantuans on Long Island or in Oakland or DuPage. The ranks of government centralizers seemed to be thinning, and the news columns offered little encouragement for latter-day Jack Knuepfers. For example, in 1994 when Orange County went bankrupt owing to the reckless investment policies of the county treasurer, faith in countrywide rule and coordination suffered yet another blow. None of the miniature polities of post-suburbia had proven such poor guardians of public funds as the Orange County treasurer. With the Orange County debacle, grass-roots advocates could point to one more example that the bigger unit of government was not necessarily better.

Whether they liked it or not, then, policymakers had to face the fact that the suburban ideology had survived largely intact in post-suburban areas. No countervailing post-suburban ideology had arisen to effectively dislodge rosy visions of the grass-roots village from the minds of millions of Americans. Thus in any conflict over regional reform, the burden of proof rested on the proponents of change. Reformers could not benefit from any preexisting predilection for centralized rule. They had to win their case on the basis of hard dollars-and-cents evidence.

Given this disadvantage, it is not surprising that the electoral verdict on regional reform was often negative. With unusual consistency, residents along the metropolitan fringe opposed the destruction of local units of government, which they associated with grass-roots democracy. Regional restructuring was possible if voters believed it would improve the standard of public service and not prove too threatening to the ideal of government by friends and neighbors. But lawmakers had to tread lightly, because in post-suburbia, as in suburbia, big government and centralization of authority were suspect. The government of the post-suburban future was in large measure a product of the ideology inherited from the suburban past. In post-suburbia a dose of pragmatism leavened the localism so dominant in the suburban mindset. But in the post-suburban world, localism remained strong, posing a major obstacle to metropolitan reform and the development of regional government.

Notes

Chapter 1—New Government for a New Metropolis

1. Christopher B. Leinberger and Charles Lockwood, "How Business Is Reshaping America," *Atlantic* 258 (October 1986): 43.
2. Robert Fishman, *Bourgeois Utopias: The Rise and Fall of Suburbia* (New York: Basic Books, 1987), p. 184.
3. Joel Garreau, *Edge City: Life on the New Frontier* (New York: Doubleday, 1991), p. 3.
4. See, for example, Joel Garreau, "Edge Cities," *Landscape Architecture* 78 (December 1988): 48–55; Joel Garreau, "Cities on the Edge," *Architecture* 80 (December 1991): 45–47, 114–15.
5. Richard Ingersoll, "The Disappearing Suburb," *Design Book Review* 26 (Fall 1992): 5.

Chapter 2—The Age of the Suburban Haven

1. *Birmingham Eccentric,* 17 May 1928, p. 24; *St. Louis Post-Dispatch,* 7 May 1939, p. 4C; Lois L. Leipper, *Clarendon Hills: The Village of Volunteers* (Clarendon Hills, Ill.: Fiftieth Anniversary Committee, 1974), not paged; *New York Times,* 29 April 1928, sec. 12, p. 4.
2. *Birmingham Eccentric,* 17 May 1928, pp. 35, 24; *New York Times,* 1 May 1927, sec. 11, p. 6.
3. *Birmingham Eccentric,* 17 May 1928, p. 24; *New York Times,* 1 May 1927, sec. 11, p. 7.
4. Dennis P. Sobin, *Dynamics of Community Change. The Case of Long Island's Declining "Gold Coast"* (Port Washington, N.Y.: Ira J. Friedman, Inc., 1968), p. 49; Edward J. Smits, *Nassau: Suburbia, U.S.A.* (Syosset, N.Y.: Friends of the Nassau County Museum, 1974), pp. 121, 126; Monica Randall, *The Mansions of Long Island's Gold Coast* (New York: Rizzoli, 1987), p. 15.
5. Roger L. Rosentreter, "Michigan's 83 Counties: Oakland," *Michigan History* 72 (September-October 1988): 10; Marion Knoblauch, ed., *DuPage County: A Descriptive and Historical Guide, 1831–1939* (Elmhurst, Ill.: Irwin A. Ruby, 1948), pp. 55–56, 83; Richard A. Thompson, ed., *DuPage Roots* (Wheaton, Ill.: DuPage County Historical Society, 1985), pp. 71–72, 253; Robert E. Hannon, ed., *St. Louis: Its Neighborhoods and Neighbors, Landmarks and Milestones* (Saint Louis: St. Louis Regional Commerce and Growth Association, 1986), p. 176.
6. *New York Times,* 10 May 1925, sec. 11, p. 1; *New York Times,* 14 February 1926, sec. 11, p. 2; *Birmingham Eccentric,* 17 May 1928, p. 30; Shirley McLellan, *Briefly Berkley* (Berkley, Mich.: Berkley Public Library, 1982), p. 51; Arthur A. Hagman, ed., *Oakland County Book of History* (Pontiac, Mich.: Sesqui-Centennial Committee, 1970), pp. 175, 195; Thompson, *DuPage Roots,* pp. 67–68.

7. *New York Times,* 29 April 1928, sec. 12, p. 17; see also *New York Times,* 1 May 1927, sec. 11, p. 2; Manhasset Community Liaison Committee, comp., *Manhasset: The First Three Hundred Years* (Manhasset, N.Y.: Manhasset Chamber of Commerce, 1980), p. 41.

8. Thompson, *DuPage Roots,* pp. 204, 220–21.

9. Sobin, *Dynamics of Community Change,* p. 100.

10. Kate Van Bloem, *History of the Village of Lake Success* (Lake Success, N.Y.: Village of Lake Success, 1968), pp. 30–31; Meade C. Dobson, ed., *This Is Long Island: The Sunrise Homeland* (New York: Long Island Association, 1942).

11. Manhasset Community Liaison Committee, *Manhasset,* p. 67; Sobin, *Dynamics of Community Change,* p. 60.

12. Manhasset Community Liaison Committee, *Manhasset* pp. 42, 35, 41.

13. C. Ray Ballard, *The History of Huntington Woods: The City of Homes* (Huntington Woods, Mich.: Huntington Woods Study Club, 1976), pp. 38–39; Leipper, *Clarendon Hills.*

14. Hannon, *St. Louis,* p. 176; Harland Bartholomew and Associates, *A Preliminary Report upon a City Plan: City of Ladue, Missouri* (Saint Louis: Harland Bartholomew and Associates, 1939), p. 10.

15. *Hempstead Sentinel,* 1 October 1936, p. 1.

16. *Royal Oak Daily Tribune,* 4 March 1932, p. 1; 2 April 1932, p. 1; 4 April 1932, p. 1; 7 April 1932, p. 1; 18 April 1932, p. 1; 17 May 1932, p. 1; McLellan, *Briefly Berkley,* pp. 56–57.

17. Smits, *Nassau,* p. 57.

18. *Hempstead Sentinel,* 4 March 1926, p. 1.

19. *Hempstead Sentinel,* 1 March 1934, pp. 1, 4; 15 March 1934, p. 1; 5 December 1935, p. 9; 23 January 1936, p. 6; 6 February 1936, p. 6. In some Suffolk County villages that had not yet succumbed to suburbanization, Republican-Democrat contests were the norm before World War II. In many of that county's villages, however, the tradition of local parties and unopposed elections prevailed.

20. *Royal Oak Daily Tribune,* 23 April 1932, p. 1 (see also McLellan, *Briefly Berkley,* p. 50); *St. Louis Post-Dispatch,* 3 April 1933, p. 6A; 5 April 1933, p. 6A; 3 April 1935, p. 8C; *New York Times,* 17 March 1926, p. 3.

21. *New York Times,* 13 March 1927, p. 9; 15 March 1927, p. 16; 16 March 1927, p. 52; 21 March 1928, p. 4.

22. *St. Louis Post-Dispatch,* 2 April 1941, p. 4C; 4 April 1943, p. 2B.

23. Mildred H. Smith, *History of Garden City* (Manhasset, N.Y.: Channel Press, 1963), pp. 107–11; *Annual Report of the Incorporated Village of Garden City, New York, 1946* (Garden City, N.Y.: Village of Garden City, 1946), pp. 11–12. For additional information on the history of Garden City, see M. H. Smith, *Garden City, Long Island in Early Photographs, 1869–1919* (Mineola, N.Y.: Dover Publications, 1987).

24. Milton S. Meyer, *Village of Lawrence, N.Y.: A Brief History of a Long Island Community* (Lawrence, N.Y.: Village of Lawrence, 1977), pp. 23–24.

25. *Glen Ellyn News,* 8 January 1937, pp. 1–2; 26 February 1937, p. 1; 23 April 1937, p. 1; 13 January 1939, p. 1; 3 March 1939, p. 1; 21 April 1939, p. 1.

26. Knoblauch, *DuPage County,* p. 98; Timothy H. Bakken, *Hinsdale* (Hinsdale, Ill.:

Hinsdale Doings, 1976), p. 294; Hugh G. Dugan, *Village on the County Line: A History of Hinsdale* (Chicago: Lakeside Press, 1949), p. 164.

27. Leipper, *Clarendon Hills.*

28. *Hempstead Sentinel,* 20 February 1936, p. 6; *Report of Garden City, 1946,* p. 13.

29. Leipper, *Clarendon Hills.*

30. Smits, *Nassau,* p. 59; Ballard, *Huntington Woods,* p. 39; Manhasset Community Liaison Committee, *Manhasset,* p. 46; Smits, *Nassau,* p. 59.

31. Thomas H. Reed, *The Government of Nassau County* (Mineola, N.Y.: Nassau County, 1934), pp. 4, 58; Victor Jones, *Metropolitan Government* (Chicago: University of Chicago Press, 1942), p. 76; *A Home Rule Charter for St. Louis County* (Saint Louis: Governmental Research Institute, 1946), p. 5; Richard Bigger, James D. Kitchen, Lyndon R. Musolf, and Carolyn Quinn, *Metropolitan Coast: San Diego and Orange Counties, California* (Los Angeles: Bureau of Governmental Research, UCLA, 1958), p. 80; Thomas H. Reed, *Oakland County: A Survey of County and Township Administration and Finance* (Birmingham, Mich.: n.p., 1932), p. 7.

32. Reed, *Nassau County,* p. 61; Reed, *Oakland County,* p. 7.

33. Reed, *Oakland County,* p. 8; Reed, *Nassau County,* p. 6.

34. John Gardner, "Dewey's Nassau County Boss," *New Republic* 119 (4 October 1948): 13; Alden Hatch, "The Men Around Dewey," *Harper's Magazine* 197 (October 1948): 39–40.

35. See Sprague's obituary, *New York Times,* 18 April 1969, p. 43.

36. Smits, *Nassau,* p. 59.

37. Hatch, "Men Around Dewey," p. 40.

38. *Hempstead Sentinel,* 20 February 1936, p. 1; 5 March 1936, p. 1.

39. *Staff Papers on Government Organization for Metropolitan Southeast Michigan* (Detroit: Citizens Research Council of Michigan, 1965), sec. III, chap. 5, p. 11; William P. Lovett, "Incorporation of Metropolitan Districts Authorized by Constitutional Amendment in Michigan," *American City* 36 (May 1927): 653; *Royal Oak Daily Tribune,* 15 April 1930, p. 1. See also *Royal Oak Daily Tribune,* 2 April 1930, p. 1.

40. *Royal Oak Daily Tribune,* 15 April 1930, p. 1; Ralph T. Jans, *The Urban Fringe Problem: Solutions under Michigan Law* (Ann Arbor: Bureau of Government, University of Michigan, 1957), p. 42.

41. Reed, *Oakland County,* foreword, pp. 7, 42–50.

42. *Royal Oak Daily Tribune,* 15 March 1932, p. 1.

43. Thompson, *DuPage Roots,* pp. 91–92; Knoblauch, *DuPage County,* p. 4.

44. Griffenhagen and Associates, *Report on the Organization, Procedures, Expenditures, and Finances of the DuPage County Government* (n.p.: DuPage County Taxpayers Council, 1936), pp. I-9, I-13.

45. Paul W. Wager, ed., *County Government across the Nation* (Chapel Hill: University of North Carolina Press, 1950), pp. 805–7; Bigger et. al, *Metropolitan Coast,* p. 82.

46. Commission on the Government of Nassau County, *Report to the Board of Supervisors of Nassau County* (n.p.: Nassau County Association, 1918), pp. 3, 5, 10.

47. Ibid., p. 11.

48. *New York Times,* 17 March 1918, sec. 3, p. 11; Smits, *Nassau,* p. 66.

49. Smits, *Nassau,* p. 67.

214 Notes to Pages 35–41

50. For an outline of the proposed charter, see *Hempstead Sentinel,* 29 October 1925, p. 13.

51. *Hempstead Sentinel,* 12 April 1923, p. 1; *New York Times,* 11 April 1923, p. 36.

52. *Hempstead Sentinel,* 22 March 1923, p. 1; 29 March 1923, p. 1.

53. *Hempstead Sentinel,* 29 October 1925, p. 1. See also *Hempstead Sentinel,* 22 October 1925, p. 1; *New York Times,* 29 October 1925, p. 14; 3 November 1925, p. 4.

54. *Hempstead Sentinel,* 29 October 1925, p. 1.

55. *Hempstead Sentinel,* 5 November 1925, p. 2. See also *Hempstead Sentinel,* 5 November 1925, p. 1; *New York Times,* 4 November 1925, p. 4; 5 November 1925, p. 22.

56. Reed, *Nassau County,* p. 22.

57. James C. Shelland, "The County Executive: A Case Study of the Office in Nassau County, New York," Ph.D. diss., New School for Social Research, 1975, p. 139. See also *New York Times,* 17 March 1927, p. 2.

58. *New York Times,* 4 March 1928, p. 1; 28 December 1930, sec. 11 and 12, p. 3.

59. Smits, *Nassau,* p. 69; *Hempstead Sentinel,* 24 October 1935, p. 2.

60. *Hempstead Sentinel,* 31 October 1935, p. 6; 10 October 1935, p. 1. For reaction to the Cuff charter, see also *New York Times,* 27 February 1933, p. 14; 1 October 1933, sec. 2, p. 3; Shelland, "County Executive," pp. 141–42.

61. *Hempstead Sentinel,* 7 November 1935, p. 1; *New York Times,* 6 November 1935, p. 19; Shelland, "County Executive," p. 142; *Nassau Daily Review,* 17 July 1934, as quoted in Shelland, "County Executive," p. 142.

62. Reed, *Nassau County,* pp. 4–5.

63. Smits, *Nassau,* p. 70.

64. For the discussion of the proposed charter by the board of supervisors, see *Proceedings of the Board of Supervisors for the Fiscal Year 1936* (Hempstead, N.Y.: Countywide Press, 1936), pp. 109–11; for a detailed description and explanation of the charter, see the series of articles in the *Hempstead Sentinel,* 20 August 1936, p. 7; 27 August 1936, p. 4; 3 September 1936, p. 4; 10 September 1936, p. 4; 17 September 1936, p. 8; 24 September 1936, p. 8; 1 October 1936, p. 8; 8 October 1936, p. 8; 22 October 1936, p. 8. See also J. Russel Sprague, "The Nassau County Charter," in *Long Island: A History of Two Great Counties, Nassau and Suffolk,* ed. Paul Bailey, 2 vols. (New York: Lewis Historical Publishing, 1949): 2: 231–38; J. Russel Sprague, *Nassau County Government* (Mineola, N.Y.: Nassau County, 1940).

65. *Hempstead Sentinel,* 9 January 1936, p. 6.

66. Sprague, "Nassau County Charter," pp. 224–25. Almost identical wording is found in Sprague, *Nassau County Government,* pp. 17–18.

67. Sprague, "Nassau County Charter," p. 225. The same sentiment is worded slightly differently in Sprague, *Nassau County Government,* p. 18.

68. *Hempstead Sentinel,* 29 October 1936, p. 12.

69. *New York Times,* 1 November 1936, sec. 2, p. 1. See also *Hempstead Sentinel,* 22 October 1936, p. 1.

70. *New York Times,* 1 November 1936, sec. 2, p. 1. For two accounts of the charter campaign, see Shelland, "County Executive," pp. 152–57, and Smits, *Nassau,* pp. 71–72.

71. *Hempstead Sentinel,* 5 November 1936, p. 1; *New York Times,* 4 November 1936, p. 6; Shelland, "County Executive," pp. 157–58; Smits, *Nassau,* p. 72; Sobin, *Dynamics of Community Change,* pp. 106–7.

72. Gardner, "Dewey's Nassau County Boss," p. 15; Shelland, "County Executive," p. 190.

73. Gardner, "Dewey's Nassau County Boss," p. 15; James Munves, "Portrait of a Boss," *The Nation* 173 (18 August 1951): 128, 129; Shelland, "County Executive," p. 193.

74. Gardner, "Dewey's Nassau County Boss," p. 14.

Chapter 3—The Emerging Post-Suburban Pattern

1. *New York Herald Tribune,* 18 May 1958, sec. 11, pp. 2, 7, 15, 18.

2. Harold L. Wattel and Rita D. Kaunitz, "Roosevelt Field: A Privately Planned and Operated Regional Center," in *Developing Long Island,* ed. Harold L. Wattel, (Hempstead, N.Y.: Bureau of Business and Community Research, 1959), p. 83.

3. Edward J. Smits, *Nassau: Suburbia, U.S.A.* (Syosset, N.Y.: Friends of the Nassau County Museum, 1974), p. 197; *Detroit Free Press,* 29 March 1953, p. 9B; *Detroit News,* 15 March 1957, p. 68; Anaheim City Planning Department, *Community Surveys of Anaheim, Social and Economic* (Anaheim: City Planning Commission, 1957), p. 10; John M. Findlay, *Magic Lands: Western Cityscapes and American Culture after 1940* (Berkeley: University of California Press, 1992), p. 98; Victor Gruen Associates, *The Comprehensive General Plan: Buena Park, California* (Buena Park: City of Buena Park, 1962), p. 1; *Fullerton News Tribune,* 27 October 1955, p. 24.

4. Orange County Planning Commission, *Orange County Planning, 1960* (Santa Ana: Orange County Planning Commission, 1960), not paged; Ernest A. Engelbert, ed., *Metropolitan California: Papers Prepared for the Governor's Commission on Metropolitan Area Problems* (Sacramento: Governor's Commission on Metropolitan Area Problems, 1961), p. 58; *New York Herald Tribune,* 18 May 1958, sec. 11, p. 9; *Naperville Clarion,* 13 September 1956, p. 2.

5. "Land Development in Oakland County," *Planning Quarterly* 1 (October 1958): 3 (see also "Population Growth in Oakland County," *Planning Quarterly* 2 [July 1959]: 1–7); Northeastern Illinois Planning Commission, *A Report on Forest Preserves, DuPage County* (Chicago: Northeastern Illinois Planning Commission, 1965), pp. 3, 19; Wattel, *Developing Long Island,* statistical app. A; *New York Herald Tribune,* 18 May 1958, sec. 11, p. 14.

6. Jean Moore, *Build Your Own Town: The Carol Stream Story* (West Chicago: West Chicago Printing Co., 1984), p. 25.

7. George Robert Willenborg, "Woodridge: Origin and Growth of a Suburb," master's thesis, University of Illinois, 1971, p. 16; *Chicago Tribune,* 16 July 1989, sec. 18, p. 1. See also *Reporter/Progress Newspapers,* 15–16 June 1989, Woodridge anniversary supplement.

8. *Newsday* (Garden City, N.Y.), 30 September 1957, 4 October 1957; *New York Herald Tribune,* 22 September 1957, sec. 7, p. 4.

9. "Housing, Up from the Potato Fields," *Time* 56 (3 July 1950): 69.

10. *Newsday,* 30 September 1957; *New York Herald Tribune,* 22 September 1957, sec. 7, p. 6.

11. *Newsday,* 30 September 1957; 3 October 1957; *New York World-Telegram and Sun,* 8 August 1957; *New York Times,* 29 September 1957, p. 33.

12. *New York Times,* 29 September 1957, p. 33; 23 December 1957, p. 14; William N. Leonard, "Schools in Crisis," *Nassau-Suffolk Business Conditions* 2 (February 1955): 10.

13. *New York World-Telegram and Sun,* 8 August 1957; *Newsday,* 3 October 1957. See also Joseph F. Maloney, "'The Lonesome Train' in Levittown," in *State and Local Government Case Book,* ed. Edwin A. Bock (Tuscaloosa: University of Alabama Press, 1963), pp. 49–65.

14. Robert Moses, "The Future of Nassau and Western Suffolk," *Long Island Business* 2 (September 1955): 6; M. Eugene Baughman, *Metropolitan Metamorphosis: The Story of the Change of St. Louis County, Missouri, from a Rural to an Urban Area* (Clayton, Mo.: Saint Louis County Planning Commission, 1955), pp. 37, 39; Saint Louis County Planning Commission, *Guide for Growth: Research and Analysis of the Land Use Components* (Clayton, Mo.: Saint Louis County Planning Commission, 1962), p. 47.

15. Saint Louis County Planning Commission, *Look to Tomorrow Today* (Clayton, Mo.: Saint Louis County Planning Commission, 1951), p. 4; E. W. Moeller, ed., *A Plan of Progress for Greater Anaheim, California* (Anaheim: Anaheim Chamber of Commerce, 1954), p. 2; Clawson Plan Commission, *General Development Plan, City of Clawson, Michigan* (Clawson: Clawson Plan Commission, 1956), p. 25; *Port Jefferson Record,* 10 January 1957, p. 14; John C. Dowling, "The Town of Oyster Bay's Comprehensive Zoning Plan," in Wattel, *Developing Long Island,* p. 27; Carl L. Gardner and Associates, *Comprehensive Village Plan, Itasca, Illinois* (Chicago: Carl L. Gardner and Associates, 1959), p. 19.

16. Evert Kincaid and Associates, *A Review of the Comprehensive City Plan, University City, Missouri* (Chicago: Evert Kincaid Associates, 1958), p. 24; Evert Kincaid and Associates, *Plans for University City, Missouri* (Chicago: Evert Kincaid and Associates, 1958), p. 4.

17. Hinsdale Plan Commission, *Tollways and their Effects on Hinsdale* (Hinsdale, Ill.: Hinsdale Plan Commission, 1958), p. 21.

18. *Suffolk County News* (Sayville, N.Y.), 31 October 1957, p. 9; Edgar Gray and William N. Leonard, "Park That Industry," *Long Island Business* 4 (October 1957): 4.

19. *New York Herald Tribune,* 18 May 1958, sec. 11, p. 3; see also Harold L. Wattel, "The Westbury Industrial Park," in Wattel, *Developing Long Island,* pp. 35–37; Saint Louis County Planning Commission, *Guide for Growth,* p. 53.

20. James W. Jones, "Employment Prospects for Oakland County," *Planning Quarterly* 5 (1964): 5.

21. Trout Pomeroy, *Oakland County: Making It Work in Michigan* (Chatsworth, Calif.: Windsor Publications, 1990), p. 26; "Manufacturing Profile of Oakland County," *Planning Quarterly* 3 (July 1960): 6.

22. Pomeroy, *Oakland County,* p. 26; Arthur A. Hagman, ed., *Oakland County Book of History* (Pontiac, Mich.: Sesqui-Centennial Committee, 1970), p. 82.

23. Smits, *Nassau,* pp. 94–119; William F. Clarke, "Aircraft: Long Island's Industrial Lift," *Long Island Business* 3 (September 1956): 9–12; Robert B. MacKay, Geoffrey L. Rossano, and Carol A. Traynor, eds., *Between Ocean and Empire: An Illustrated History of Long Island* (Northridge, Calif.: Windsor Publications, 1985), pp. 194–97.

24. Spencer C. Olin, "Globalization and the Politics of Locality: Orange County, California, in the Cold War," *Western Historical Quarterly* 22 (May 1991): 151; Anaheim City Planning Department, *Community Surveys,* p. 22; Olin, "Globalization," p. 151.

25. Jacqueline Overton and Bernice Marshall, *Long Island's Story, With a Sequel—The Rest of the Story, 1929–1961* (Port Washington, N.Y.: Ira J. Friedman, 1963), p. 21 of "The Rest of the Story"; Baughman, *Metropolitan Metamorphosis,* p. 37.

26. Bureau of the Census, *County and City Data Book, 1952* (Washington, D.C.: U.S. Government Printing Office, 1953), pp. 262, 294; Bureau of the Census, *County and City Data Book, 1967* (Washington, D.C.: U.S. Government Printing Office, 1967), pp. 218, 258.

27. Robert E. Chisholm, ed., *Profile 68: A Statistical Profile of Oakland County, Michigan, and Seven County Detroit Region* (Pontiac, Mich.: Oakland County Planning Commission, 1968), pp. 5, 42–43.

28. *Shopping Centers, Principles and Policies—Urban Land Institute Technical Bulletin No. 20* (Washington, D.C.: Urban Land Institute, 1953), pp. 57–59; Hagman, *Oakland County*, pp. 83, 273, 279; Pomeroy, *Oakland County*, p. 26; Katharine Mattingly Meyer and Martin C. P. McElroy, eds., *Detroit Architecture A.I.A. Guide* (rev. ed.) (Detroit: Wayne State University Press, 1980), p. 148.

29. *Shopping Centers*, p. 57; *Detroit Free Press*, 21 September 1959, p. 9.

30. *Spotlight on Southfield* (Southfield, Mich.: Southfield High School, 1959), pp. 28–29; Hagman, *Oakland County*, p. 83.

31. Daniel R. Fusfeld, "Shopping Centers: The New Main Streets," *Nassau-Suffolk Business Conditions* 2 (April 1955): 3–5; *Time* 68 (16 July 1956): 80–81; Smits, *Nassau*, pp. 252–53; Wattel and Kaunitz, "Roosevelt Field," pp. 80–84.

32. Smits, *Nassau*, p. 252.

33. Dickson Terry, *Clayton: A History* (Clayton, Mo.: City of Clayton, 1976), p. 243, Earl W. Kerston, Jr. and D. Reid Ross, "Clayton: A New Metropolitan Focus in the St. Louis Area," *Annals of the Association of American Geographers* 58 (December 1968): 642.

34. Robert E. Hannon, ed., *St. Louis: Its Neighborhood and Neighbors, Landmarks, and Milestones* (Saint Louis: St. Louis Region Commerce and Growth Association, 1986), pp. 174, 189; Saint Louis County Planning Commission, *Guide for Growth*, p. 30.

35. "Disneyland," *Life* 39 (15 August 1955): 39; Findlay, *Magic Lands*, pp. 62, 100.

36. *Port Jefferson Record*, 9 May 1957, p. 16; Charles E. Stonier, *Long Island's Transportation: Resources and Needs* (Hempstead, N.Y.: Hofstra College Bureau of Business and Community Research, 1957), pp. 1, 6; Harland Bartholomew and Associates, *Growth of the Community, Report Number One: Population Distribution and Density, Prepared for the Town of Huntington Planning Board* (Saint Louis: Harland Bartholomew and Associates, 1962), p. 4; Saint Louis County Planning Commission, *Guide for Growth*, p. 21; see *Planning Report No. 2, Village of Villa Park, Illinois* (n.p., 1961), chap. 3, p. 3.

37. *New York Times*, 23 December 1957, p. 14; Charles E. Stonier, "Long Island's Transportation," in Wattel, *Developing Long Island*, pp. 38–39.

38. Bureau of the Census, *U. S. Census of Population, 1960: Subject Reports—Journey to Work* (Washington, D.C.: U.S. Government Printing Office, 1963), pp. 20, 34, 61, 77, 80, 102.

39. Mildred H. Smith, *History of Garden City* (Manhasset, N.Y.: Channel Press, 1963), p. 131; *Royal Oak Tribune*, 8 April 1958, p. 1.

40. *Detroit Free Press*, 21 September 1959, p. 9.

41. J. Raymond McGovern, "Creation, Control and Supervision of Cities and Villages by the State," *Brooklyn Law Review* 20 (April 1954): 162–63; Donald A. Walsh, "Twentieth Century Laws for Twentieth Century Villages," *Brooklyn Law Review* 20 (April 1954): 195; Samuel F. Thomas, *Nassau County: Its Governments and Their Expenditure and Revenue Patterns* (New York: City College Press, 1960), p. 5.

42. Thomas, *Nassau County,* p. 4; Suffolk County Planning Department, *Report on Local Government Analysis* (Riverhead, N.Y.: Suffolk County, 1962), pp. 64–65.

43. Thomas, *Nassau County,* pp. 36–38; Suffolk County Planning Department, *Report on Local Government Analysis,* pp. 64–68.

44. Thomas, *Nassau County,* p. 77.

45. *City of Lathrup Village: An Administrative Survey* (Detroit: Citizens Research Council of Michigan, 1965), pp. 1–2; Hagman, *Oakland County,* pp. 205, 207.

46. *Royal Oak Tribune,* 22 May 1953, p. 13.

47. *Spotlight on Southfield,* p. 15; Hagman, *Oakland County,* pp. 208, 279; Vicki Goldbaum, *Southfield, Yesterday and Today* (n.p., 1983), p. 6.

48. *Royal Oak Tribune,* 13 May 1953, p. 19; *Spotlight on Southfield,* p. 16.

49. *Royal Oak Tribune,* 13 May 1953, p. 19; 14 May 1953, p. 17; 16 May 1953, p. 1; 19 May 1953, pp. 11, 14; 26 May 1953, p. 1.

50. *Royal Oak Tribune,* 9 May 1953, pp. 1–2; 13 May 1953, p. 19; 14 May 1953, p. 17; 16 May 1953, p. 1; 19 May 1953, pp. 11, 14; 26 May 1953, p. 1.

51. *Royal Oak Tribune,* 9 May 1953, p. 2; 26 May 1953, p. 1.

52. *Royal Oak Tribune,* 14 May 1953, p. 17; 16 May 1953, p. 1; 19 May 1953, p. 11.

53. *Spotlight on Southfield,* p. 16.

54. *Detroit News,* 9 June 1972, p. 3B.

55. Bettie Waddell Cannon, *All about Franklin from Pioneers to Preservation* (Franklin, Mich.: Franklin Historical Society, 1979), pp. 117–18; *Spotlight on Southfield,* p. 16.

56. Cannon, *All about Franklin,* p. 118.

57. Hagman, *Oakland County,* pp. 395–96; *Spotlight on Southfield,* p. 17.

58. *Spotlight on Southfield,* p. 18; Hagman, *Oakland County,* p. 392; League of Women Voters of Birmingham-Bloomfield, *Know Your Town, Beverly Hills, Michigan* (Birmingham, Mich.: League of Women Voters of Birmingham-Bloomfield, 1970), p. 4.

59. *Pontiac Press,* 26 March 1958, p. 5, 22 April 1958, p. 17; *Royal Oak Tribune,* 22 April 1958, pp. 1–2; Goldbaum, *Southfield,* p. 6; Hagman, *Oakland County,* p. 281.

60. *Royal Oak Tribune,* 22 April 1958, p. 1.

61. Robert J. Mowitz and Deil S. Wright, *Profile of a Metropolis: A Case Book* (Detroit: Wayne State University Press, 1962), p. 590.

62. Hagman, *Oakland County,* p. 424; Mowitz and Wright, *Profile of a Metropolis,* pp. 586–87, 597.

63. Mowitz and Wright, *Profile of a Metropolis,* pp. 603–4. See also *Detroit Free Press,* 27 October 1958, p. 6.

64. Mowitz and Wright, *Profile of a Metropolis,* pp. 610, 597, 622.

65. *Northville Record* (centennial ed.), 17 July 1969, as copied in "Novi History," a typewritten compilation in the files of the Novi Public Library, Novi, Michigan; Rowena Salow, "The Story of Novi's Development," Master's thesis, Wayne State University, 1961, p. 25; *Detroit Free Press,* 11 August 1957; *Pontiac Press,* 6 August 1957, p. 17; 18 March 1958, p. 15; Hagman, *Oakland County,* p. 222.

66. *Detroit News,* 17 April 1955, p. A19. See also Hagman, *Oakland County,* p. 214.

67. Hagman, *Oakland County,* p. 293.

68. *Naperville Clarion,* 7 June 1956, p. 1; *Naperville Clarion,* 28 June 1956, p. 1. See also *Naperville Clarion,* 12 July 1956, p. 6; *Naperville Sun,* 14 June 1956, p. 5; 28 June 1956, p. 3.

69. Winston W. Crouch, Jack Goldsmith, and Robert Giordano, *Agricultural Cities: Paradoxes in Politics of a Metropolis* (Los Angeles: Department of Political Science, University of California, Los Angeles, 1964), pp. 19, 26; *Fullerton News Tribune,* 12 October 1955, p. 1.

70. *Fullerton News Tribune,* 11 October 1955, p. 1; 25 October 1955, p. 9; 26 October 1955, p. 1.

71. *Fullerton News Tribune,* 26 October 1955, p. 8; *Santa Ana Register,* 27 June 1956, p. B11. See also *Santa Ana Register,* 25 June 1956, p. B2, and *Fullerton News Tribune,* 27 June 1956, p. 1.

72. Crouch, Goldsmith, and Giordano, *Agricultural Cities,* pp. 32–46.

73. Saint Louis County Planning Commission, *Let's Get Together: A Report on the Advantages of an Integrated Community* (Clayton, Mo.: Saint Louis Planning Commission, 1952), p. 17.

74. *Wellston Journal,* 1 March 1950, p. 1A.

75. Saint Louis County Planning Commission, *Let's Get Together,* pp. 6, 32; Baughman, *Metropolitan Metamorphosis,* p. 99.

76. Governmental Research Institute, *A Report on the Proposed Consolidation of the Municipalities of Ladue, Frontenac, and Huntleigh Village, Missouri* (Saint Louis: Governmental Research Institute, 1958), p. 36.

77. Alan K. Campbell, "Planning Suburbia: America's New Frontier," in Wattel, *Developing Long Island,* pp. 6–7. See also Thomas, *Nassau County,* pp. 6, 100.

78. Suffolk County Planning Department, *Report on Local Government Analysis,* p. 63.

79. *Pontiac Press,* 12 August 1957, p. 17; Richard Bigger, James D. Kitchen, Lyndon R. Musolf, and Carolyn Quinn, *Metropolitan Coast: San Diego and Orange Counties, California* (Los Angeles: Bureau of Governmental Research, University of California, 1958), p. 92.

80. William Glennon, "New Control over Municipal Formation and Annexation," *Santa Clara Lawyer* 4 (Fall 1963): 125–26.

81. Robert A. Cohn, *The History and Growth of St. Louis County, Missouri* (Clayton, Mo.: Saint Louis County, 1974), p. 41.

82. Ibid., p. 42.

83. Governmental Research Institute, *A Home Rule Charter for St. Louis County* (Saint Louis: Governmental Research Institute, 1946), pp. 2–5.

84. *Watchman Advocate* (Clayton, Mo.), 28 January 1949, p. 1; Cohn, *St. Louis County,* p. 12.

85. Cohn, *St. Louis County,* p. 42.

86. *St. Louis Globe-Democrat,* 23 March 1949, p. 2C.

87. Ibid.; "Counties Seek New Charters," *National Municipal Review* 38 (October 1949): 457; *Watchman Advocate,* 23 September 1949, p. 1; "Women Voters Propose Manager for St. Louis Co.," *National Municipal Review* 38 (November 1949): 509.

88. *Watchman Advocate,* 9 September 1949, p. 3.

89. "Women Voters Propose Manager," p. 509.

90. *Home Rule Charter for St. Louis County, Mo.* (n.p., 1950), pp. 13–14.

91. *St. Louis Globe-Democrat,* 19 March 1950, p. 6F; 30 March 1950, p. 2C; *St. Louis Post-Dispatch,* 24 March 1950, p. 2D.

92. *Webster News-Times* (Webster Groves, Mo.), 9 March 1950, p. 2; *Wellston Journal,* 22 March 1950, p. 11; *Webster News-Times,* 9 March 1950, p. 4.

93. *Watchman Advocate,* 24 March 1950, p. 1; *St. Louis Globe-Democrat,* 19 March 1950, p. 6F; *St. Louis Post-Dispatch,* 24 March 1950, p. 2D.
94. *Webster News-Times,* 23 March 1950, p. 4.
95. *Watchman Advocate,* 31 March 1950, p. 1; *St. Louis Globe-Democrat,* 26 March 1950, p. 3A; *St. Louis Post-Dispatch,* 29 March 1950, p. 1A.
96. *Watchman Advocate,* 24 March 1950, p. 1.
97. *Watchman Advocate,* 17 March 1950, p. 1; "St. Louis County Adopts Home Rule Charter," *National Municipal Review* 39 (May 1950): 249; *St. Louis Globe-Democrat,* 26 March 1950, p. 3A.
98. *St. Louis Globe-Democrat,* 26 March 1950, p. 3A; *Wellston Journal,* 1 February 1950, p. 1A; *Webster News-Times,* 23 March 1950, p. 4.
99. *St. Louis Globe-Democrat,* 29 March 1950, p. 1A; *St. Louis Post-Dispatch,* 29 March 1950, pp. 1A, 6A; *Wellston Journal,* 29 March 1950, pp. 1A, 12A; *Watchman Advocate,* 31 March 1950, p. 1; "St. Louis County Adopts Home Rule Charter," p. 249.
100. Saint Louis County Planning Commission, *Look to Tomorrow Today,* p. 1; Metropolitan St. Louis Survey, *Background for Action* (University City, Mo.: Metropolitan St. Louis Survey, 1957), p. 45.
101. Metropolitan St. Louis Survey, *Background for Action,* pp. 45–46; John C. Bollens, ed., *Exploring the Metropolitan Community* (Berkeley: University of California Press, 1961), p. 76.
102. *Parks on Parade: The Story of St. Louis County Parks System* ([Saint Louis]: St. Louis County Water Company, 1978), p. 1; Saint Louis County Planning Commission, *Look to Tomorrow Today,* pp. 1, 31.
103. Saint Louis County Planning Commission, *The Challenge of Growth: A Study of Major County and Regional Park Needs* (Clayton, Mo: Saint Louis County Planning Commission, 1965), pp. 2–1, 2–2.
104. *St. Louis Post-Dispatch,* 26 June 1953, p. 3A.
105. Cohn, *History of St. Louis County,* p. 46.
106. *St. Louis Post-Dispatch,* 27 June 1953, p. 3A; 28 June 1953, p. 3A.
107. Cohn, *History of St. Louis County,* p. 47; Bollens, *Exploring the Metropolitan Community,* pp. 75–76; *St. Louis Post-Dispatch,* 24 October 1954, pp. 16A, 3H; 3 November 1954, p. 1A.
108. *New York Times,* 13 February 1956, p. 21; 17 February 1956, pp. 1, 8.
109. "Charter Proposed for Suffolk County, N.Y.," *National Municipal Review* 45 (January 1956): 30; *New York Times,* 4 December 1955, p. 50.
110. Nancy Ann Edwards, "New Government for Suffolk County," *Long Island Business* 3 (May 1956): 4–5. See also *New York Times,* 6 March 1956, p. 33; 13 March 1956, p. 34.
111. Edwards, "New Government," pp. 3, 5. See also "Suffolk County, N.Y., Charter Proposed," *National Municipal Review* 45 (April 1956): 183–85.
112. *New York Times,* 15 March 1956, p. 27; 24 April 1956, p. 33; "Governor Vetoes Charter for Suffolk County, N.Y.," *National Municipal Review* 45 (May 1956): 240. See also *Port Jefferson Record,* 24 January 1957, p. 20; 7 February 1957, p. 1.
113. "Charter Commission Appointed for Suffolk County, N.Y.," *National Municipal Review* 45 (September 1956): 398, 404; *Port Jefferson Record,* 24 January 1957, p. 20.

114. *Port Jefferson Record,* 21 March 1957, p. 16. See also *Port Jefferson Record,* 3 January 1957, p. 16; 10 January 1957, p. 20; 14 February 1957, pp. 4, 16; 21 February 1957, p. 8; 21 March 1957, p. 2; 28 March 1957, p. 1; 4 April 1957, p. 4.

115. *Port Jefferson Record,* 2 May 1957, pp. 1, 4. See also "N.Y. Governor Again Vetoes Charter for Suffolk County," *National Municipal Review* 46 (June 1957): 309.

116. *Suffolk County News* (Sayville, N.Y.), 27 February 1958, pp. 1, 8.

117. *Port Jefferson Record,* 13 February 1958, p. 1. See also: *Port Jefferson Record,* 2 January 1958, p. 1; 13 March 1958, pp. 1–2; *Suffolk County News,* 13 February 1958, pp. 1, 3; 6 March 1958, pp. 1, 3; *New York Times,* 8 February 1958, p. 21; 25 February 1958, p. 17; 23 March 1958, p. 54; "Suffolk County to Vote on New Charter," *National Municipal Review* 47 (May 1958): 238.

118. Marilyn Gittell, "The Role of the Urban County in Solving Metropolitan Problems in New York State," Ph.D. diss., New York University, 1960, p. 130; "Suffolk Co. to Vote on New Charter," *National Municipal Review* 47 (June 1958): 287–88; *Suffolk County News,* 23 October 1958, sec. 3, p. 4.

119. *Suffolk County News,* 23 October 1958, p. 9; *Port Jefferson Record,* 9 October 1958, p. 4.

120. *Suffolk County News,* 23 October 1958, p. 9; *Port Jefferson Record,* 9 October 1958, p. 4. See also *Suffolk County News,* 17 July 1958, p. 9; 30 October 1958, pp. 1, 3; *New York Times,* 2 November 1958, p. 58.

121. *Suffolk County News,* 6 November 1958, pp. 1, 8; *Port Jefferson Record,* 6 November 1958, p. 1; *New York Times,* 5 November 1958, p. 26; 6 November 1958, p. 73; "Suburban County Charters: One Approved, One Rejected," *National Municipal Review* 47 (December 1958): 575.

122. Delos Hamlin, "Highlights," *1962 Planning Conference Papers—Oakland County Planning Commission* (1962), p. 82; *Planning Quarterly* 8 (February 1969): not paged. See also *Detroit News,* 30 October 1958, p. 14; Hagman, *Oakland County,* pp. 130–31.

123. Hamlin, "Highlights," pp. 82–83; *Detroit News,* 17 December 1959, p. 6F.

124. Hamlin, "Highlights," p. 83.

125. "Plans and Work Progress of the Oakland County Department of Public Works," *Planning Quarterly* 3 (April 1960): not paged. For the difficulties of operating under the drain commissioner, see Mowitz and Wright, *Profile of a Metropolis,* pp. 517–78.

126. "Plans and Work Progress"; Hagman, *Oakland County,* pp. 135–36.

127. "Plans and Work Progress."

128. *Detroit News,* 30 October 1958, p. 14; *Royal Oak Tribune,* 2 November 1959, p. 11.

129. *Orange County Planning, 1960.* See also *Orange County Planning Commission, 1957–58* (Santa Ana: Orange County Planning Commission, 1958), p. 13.

130. *Orange County Planning, 1959.*

131. *Orange County Planning, 1960.* Regional Parks Advisory Committee, *The Proposed Master Plan of Regional Parks for Orange County* (Santa Ana: Regional Parks Advisory Committee, 1963), p. 7; *Orange County Planning 1961* (Santa Ana: Orange County Planning Commission, 1961), not paged. See also *Orange County Planning Commission, 1957–58,* p. 25.

Chapter 4—Maintaining the Balance of Power

1. Robert A. Willier and Associates, *Mid-America's New Executive City: Clayton, Missouri* (Clayton, Mo.: Clayton Chamber of Commerce, 1968), p. 12.
2. Ibid., p. 6; Dickson Terry, *Clayton: A History* (Clayton, Mo.: City of Clayton, 1976), pp. 6, 249–50; Earl W. Kersten, Jr. and D. Reid Ross, "Clayton: A New Metropolitan Focus in the St. Louis Area," *Annals of the Association of American Geographers* 58 (December 1968): 643–44.
3. Willier, *Executive City*, p, 5; Terry, *Clayton*, pp. 7, 260–62; Kersten and Ross, "Clayton," p. 644; Clayton Chamber of Commerce, *This is Clayton, Missouri: Historical and Statistical* (Clayton, Mo.: Clayton Chamber of Commerce, 1967), not paged.
4. Terry, *Clayton*, pp. 262–63; Willier, *Executive City*, p. 6.
5. Terry, *Clayton*, p. 275.
6. Clayton Chamber of Commerce, *This is Clayton*, not paged; Willier, *Executive City*, p. 22.
7. Willier, *Executive City*, p. 7; Kersten and Reid, "Clayton," pp. 639, 637, 649.
8. *A Report of Civic Progress, 1959–60* (Clayton, Mo.: City of Clayton, 1960), not paged; *Clayton Annual, 1966* (Clayton, Mo.: City of Clayton, 1966), p. 11; *Clayton Annual, 1969* (Clayton, Mo: City of Clayton, 1969), p. 3; *Clayton Annual, 1970* (Clayton, Mo.: City of Clayton, 1970), p. 7.
9. *Report of Civic Progress, 1959–60; Clayton Annual, 1969*, p. 3.
10. *Clayton Annual, 1966*, pp. 11–12; *Clayton Annual, 1970*, p. 1; Bureau of the Census, *Census of Population and Housing: 1970* (Washington, D.C.: U.S. Government Printing Office, 1972).
11. Regional Plan Association, *The Future of Nassau County* (New York: Regional Plan Association, 1969), p. 3. See also William Hamovitch, Albert M. Levenson, and Alfred J. Van Tassel, *A Look Ahead at Long Island Employment* (Hempstead, N.Y.: Hofstra University Center for Business and Urban Research, 1982), pp. 6–7.
12. "A Center for the Suburbs," *Regional Plan News* no. 78 (May 1965): 1–2.
13. Ibid., p. 6; *Newsday* (Garden City, N.Y.), 8 April 1965.
14. Vicki Goldbaum, *Southfield, Yesterday and Today*, 2d rev. ed. (Southfield, Mich.: Vicki Goldbaum, 1983), p. 38; Vicki Goldbaum, *Southfield, Yesterday and Today*, 1st ed. (Southfield, Mich.: Vicki Goldbaum, 1974), p. 15.
15. *Southfield: Focus on Progress* (Southfield, Mich.: Community Relations Seminar, Southfield High School, 1964), p. 4.
16. Goldbaum, *Southfield*, 2d rev. ed., pp. 39–40; Goldbaum, *Southfield*, 1st ed., p. 21; Trout Pomeroy, *Oakland County: Making It Work in Michigan* (Chatsworth, Calif.: Windsor Publications, 1990), p. 31; Arthur A. Hagman, ed., *Oakland County Book of History* (Pontiac, Mich.: Sesqui-Centennial Executive Committee, 1970), p. 275.
17. *Southfield: Focus on Progress*, p. 5.
18. *Detroit Free Press*, 31 October 1971, p. 10B; *Detroit News*, 15 February 1981, p. 11A; *Southfield Eccentric*, 24 February 1986, p. 7A.
19. Bureau of the Census, *Census of Population, 1970: Subject Reports—Journey to Work* (Washington, D.C.: U.S. Government Printing Office, 1973), pp. 74–75.
20. *Detroit News*, 26 March 1969, p. 3A.
21. Robert Cassidy, "Planning for Polo, Not People," *Planning* 40 (April/May 1974): 34–35; Robert Bruegmann, "Schaumburg, Oak Brook, Rosemont, and the Recentering

of the Chicago Metropolitan Area," in *Chicago Architecture and Design 1923–1993: Reconfiguration of an American Metropolis,* ed. John Zukowsky (Chicago: Art Institute of Chicago, 1993), p. 170; *Chicago Tribune,* 16 October 1983, sec. 2, pp. 1–2; Richard A. Thompson, ed., *DuPage Roots* (Wheaton, Ill.: DuPage County Historical Society, 1985), pp. 212–13.

22. *Suburban Life,* 17 March 1993, sec. 4, p. 3.
23. J. Ross McKeever, *Business Parks, Office Parks, Plazas, and Centers: A Study of Development Practices and Procedures* (Washington, D.C.: Urban Land Institute, 1970), p. 53.
24. Cassidy, "Planning for Polo," pp. 34–35.
25. Ibid., p. 34; Bruegmann, "Schaumburg, Oak Brook," pp. 168, 170; *Chicago Tribune,* 16 October 1983, sec. 2, pp. 1–2; Thompson, *DuPage Roots,* p. 212.
26. Cassidy, "Planning for Polo," p. 35.
27. Allen L. Kracouver and Associates and DuPage County Regional Planning Commission, *Housing in DuPage County* (Wheaton, Ill.: DuPage County Regional Planning Commission, 1972), pp. 24, 28–29.
28. Cassidy, "Planning for Polo," p. 37; Thompson, *DuPage Roots,* p. 212.
29. Cassidy, "Planning for Polo," p. 37.
30. Thompson, *DuPage Roots,* p. 213.
31. Cassidy, "Planning for Polo," pp. 34, 37.
32. Nathaniel M. Griffin, *Irvine: The Genesis of a New Community* (Washington, D.C.: Urban Land Institute, 1974), pp. 16–17; Wilsey and Ham, *General Plan for the City of Irvine* (Irvine, Calif.: City of Irvine, 1974), p. i–4; Michael M. Hertel, *Irvine Community Associations* (Claremont, Calif.: Claremont Urban Research Center, 1969), pp. 13–16.
33. *Newport Center: Growth Center of Exploding Southern California* (n.p.: [c. 1968]), not paged; Economic Research Department, Security Pacific National Bank, *Irvine Industrial Complex, A Special Report* (Los Angeles: Security Pacific National Bank, 1969), not paged.
34. *Newport Center.*
35. Press release from Irvine Company, in vertical files of City Planning and Landscape Architecture Library, University of Illinois, Urbana, Illinois; David Gebhard and Robert Winter, *A Guide to Architecture in Los Angeles and Southern California* (Santa Barbara: Peregrine Smith, 1977), p. 428.
36. Press release from Irvine Company; Economic Research Department, *Irvine Industrial Complex,* not paged.
37. Griffin, *Irvine,* pp. 20, 22.
38. Ibid., pp. 62–67; Hertel, *Irvine Community Associations,* pp. 18–23.
39. Mission Viejo Company Planning Department, *Mission Viejo, California: A New Town* (Mission Viejo, Calif.: Mission Viejo Company, 1969), pp. 2, 11; J. A. Prestridge, *Case Studies of Six Planned New Towns in the United States* (Lexington: Institute for Environmental Studies, University of Kentucky Research Foundation, 1973), pp. 8, 10–12.
40. *Mission Viejo Reporter,* January 1970, p. 3.
41. Mission Viejo Planning Department, *Mission Viejo,* p. 14.
42. *Mission Viejo Reporter,* June 1969, p. 1.

43. Metropolitan St. Louis Survey, *Background for Action* (University City, Mo.: Metropolitan St. Louis Survey, 1957), pp. 33–34; Robert A. Cohn, *The History and Growth of St. Louis County, Missouri* (Clayton, Mo.: Saint Louis County, 1974), p. 59.

44. Metropolitan Survey, *Background for Action*, p. 34; Cohn, *St. Louis County*, p. 59.

45. "Annexation by Municipality of Adjacent Area in Missouri: Judicial Attitude toward the Sawyer Act," *Washington University Law Quarterly* 1961 (April 1961): 162–63. See also Cohn, *St. Louis County*, pp. 60–61; Metropolitan Survey, *Background for Action*, p. 36; Steven H. Goldberg, "Annexations in Urban Counties: Missouri's Scheme and a Plan for Reform," *Washington University Journal of Urban and Contemporary Law* 29 (Winter 1985): 189–91; Advisory Commission on Intergovernmental Relations, *Metropolitan Organization: The St. Louis Case* (Washington, D.C.: Advisory Commission on Intergovernmental Relations, 1988), p. 39. The annexation legislation is known both as the "Sawyer" and "Sawyers" Act.

46. Cohn, *St. Louis County*, p. 59.

47. *St. Louis Post-Dispatch*, 7 April 1960, p. 2B; 29 December 1963, p. 3A; 7 January 1965, pp. 5N, 7N. See also *St. Louis County Observer* (Maplewood, Mo.), 17 October 1962, pp. 1A-2A.

48. *City of Olivette v. Graeler I*, 338 S.W.2d 830 (1960); *City of Olivette v. Graeler II*, 369 S.W.2d 87–89, 93 (1963); Cohn, *St. Louis County*, p. 61; *St. Louis Post-Dispatch*, 4 June 1963, p. 10A.

49. *City of Olivette v. Graeler I*, 338 S.W.2d 830; Cohn, *St. Louis County*, p. 61; *St. Louis Post-Dispatch*, 7 April 1960, p. 2B; "Annexation by Municipality of Adjacent Area," pp. 163–64.

50. *City of Olivette v. Graeler I*, 338 S.W.2d 838; Cohn, *St. Louis County*, p. 61; "Annexation by Municipality of Adjacent Area," pp. 164–65; Goldberg, "Annexations in Urban Counties," pp. 197–99; T. E. Lauer, "Municipal Law in Missouri," *Missouri Law Review* 28 (1963): 581.

51. *City of Olivette v. Graeler II*, 369 S.W.2d 86; Goldberg, "Annexations in Urban Counties," p. 199.

52. *City of Olivette v. Graeler II*, 369 S.W.2d 94–95.

53. Ibid., p. 95; Cohn, *St. Louis County*, p. 61; Lauer, "Municipal Law in Missouri," p. 581; Goldberg, "Annexations in Urban Counties," pp. 200–201; *St. Louis Post-Dispatch*, 4 June 1963, pp. 1A, 10A.

54. Lauer, "Municipal Law in Missouri," p. 582.

55. *St. Louis Post-Dispatch*, 6 January 1966, p. 1N; Cohn, *St. Louis County*, p. 62.

56. *St. Louis County v. Village of Champ*, 438 S.W.2d 214; Cohn, *St. Louis County*, pp. 61–62; Goldberg, "Annexations in Urban Counties," pp. 203–5.

57. *St. Louis Post-Dispatch*, 27 March 1964, p. 1A; 30 March 1964, p. 2C; 10 January 1968, p. 3S; Cohn, *St. Louis County*, p. 62.

58. *St. Louis Post-Dispatch*, 9 January 1967, p. 2C; 28 January 1967, p. 4A.

59. *St. Louis Post-Dispatch*, 27 January 1967, p. 3A; 10 January 1968, p. 3S; Cohn, *St. Louis County*, p. 62.

60. *St. Louis Post-Dispatch*, 20 January 1967, p. 1N; Cohn, *St. Louis County*, p. 62.

61. *St. Louis Post-Dispatch*, 27 March 1964, p. 1A.

62. *St. Louis Post-Dispatch*, 27 March 1964, p. 1A; 30 March 1964, p. 2C.

63. *St. Louis Post-Dispatch*, 9 January 1967, p. 2C.

64. *St. Louis Post-Dispatch,* 10 January 1968, p. 3S.

65. *St. Louis Post-Dispatch,* 4 April 1962, p. 1A; Cohn, *St. Louis County,* p. 62.

66. *Final Report of the Assembly Interim Committee on Municipal and County Government* (Sacramento: California State Printing Office, 1961), p. 44; Richard T. LeGates, *California Local Agency Formation Commissions* (Berkeley: Institute of Governmental Studies, University of California, Berkeley, 1970), p. 17; William E. Glennon, "New Control over Municipal Formation and Annexation," *Santa Clara Lawyer* 4 (Fall 1963): 126.

67. *Final Report of Interim Committee,* pp. 15–18; LeGates, *California Local Agency Formation Commissions,* p. 15.

68. *Final Report of Interim Committee,* p. 33; LeGates, *California Local Agency Formation Commissions,* p. 16.

69. John Goldbach, "Local Formation Commissions: California's Struggle over Municipal Incorporations," *Public Administration Review* 25 (September 1965): 214.

70. Ibid.; LeGates, *California Local Agency Formation Commissions,* pp. 19–20; Glennon, "New Control," pp. 129–31.

71. David Curry, "Irvine: The Case for a New Kind of Planning," *Cry California* 6 (Winter 1970/71): 35.

72. Ibid., pp. 30–31.

73. Ibid., p. 31; Griffin, *Irvine,* p. 62; Barton-Aschman Associates, *Orange County, Santa Ana, and Irvine: Recommendations for Making the Development of Irvine a Countywide Success* (Chicago: Barton-Aschman Associates, 1971), p. 49.

74. *Santa Ana Register,* 16 September 1970, p. C1.

75. Barton-Aschman Associates, *Orange County, Santa Ana, and Irvine,* p. 46.

76. Ibid., pp. 46–47.

77. *Santa Ana Register,* 14 January 1971, p. C1; *Fullerton News Tribune,* 14 January 1971, p. B6; Curry, "Irvine," pp. 27–28. See also Earl Finkler, *Nongrowth as a Planning Alternative: A Preliminary Examination of an Emerging Issue* (Chicago: American Society of Planning Officials, 1972), p. 43.

78. *Santa Ana Register,* 11 February 1971, pp. A1-A2; *Fullerton News Tribune,* 11 February 1971, p. C1.

79. *Fullerton News Tribune,* 11 February 1971, p. C1. For more on the Irvine incorporation, see *Fullerton News Tribune,* 7 January 1971, p. A14; *Santa Ana Register,* 7 January 1971, p. C1. For another account of the Irvine incorporation battle, see Martin J. Schiesl, "Designing the Model Community: The Irvine Company and Suburban Development, 1950–88," in *Post-Suburban California: The Transformation of Orange County since World War II,* ed. Rob Kling, Spencer Olin, and Mark Poster (Berkeley: University of California Press, 1991), pp. 69–72.

80. California Council on Intergovernmental Relations, *Local Agency Formation Commissions* (Sacramento: California Council on Intergovernmental Relations, 1971), pp. 3, 9, 13; Griffin, *Irvine,* pp. 59, 61. See also *Santa Ana Register,* 1 February 1971, p. A6. For information on a later border war between Anaheim and Yorba Linda, which occurred despite the LAFCO reforms, see *Los Angeles Times* (Orange County edition), 3 June 1982, pt. 2, pp. 1, 14; 27 October 1982, pt. 2, pp. 1, 6; 28 October 1982, pt. 2, pp. 1, 17.

81. Maureen J. Par, *Annexation Practices in Michigan: The City Perspective* (Ann Arbor: Michigan Municipal League, 1988), pp. 5–6.

82. *Report on Local Government Analysis* (Riverhead, N.Y.: Suffolk County, 1962), preface; *Annual Report to the Suffolk County Board of Supervisors, 1963* (Riverhead, N.Y.: Suffolk County, 1963), cover letter. See also *Annual Report to the Suffolk County Board of Supervisors, 1966* (Riverhead, N.Y.: Suffolk County, 1966), cover letter.

83. *Smithtown Messenger,* 17 May 1962, pt. 2, p. 3.

84. Jon C. Teaford, *City and Suburb: The Political Fragmentation of Metropolitan America, 1850–1970* (Baltimore: Johns Hopkins University Press, 1979), pp. 103–4, 119–20, 133–34, 138–41, 143–44, 148–56.

85. Cohn, *St. Louis County,* p. 10.

86. Advisory Commission on Intergovernmental Relations, *Factors Affecting Voter Reactions to Governmental Reorganization in Metropolitan Areas* (Washington, D.C.: Advisory Commission on Intergovernmental Relations, 1962), p. 65; Cohn, *St. Louis County,* p. 54.

87. Henry J. Schmandt, Paul G. Steinbicker, and George D. Wendel, *Metropolitan Reform in St. Louis: A Case Study* (New York: Holt, Rinehart and Winston, 1961), pp. 36–40; Scott Greer, *Metropolitics: A Study of Political Culture* (New York: John Wiley and Sons, 1963), pp. 62–71.

88. *News-Times* (Webster Groves, Mo.), 24 September 1959, p. 1. See also *Watchman-Advocate* (Clayton, Mo.), 2 October 1959, p. 1.

89. *News-Times,* 24 September 1959, p. 1.

90. *News-Times,* 29 October 1959, p. 1. See also *News-Times,* 1 October 1959, p. 1.

91. *News-Times,* 8 October 1959, p. 1.

92. *News-Times,* 29 October 1959, p. 8; *News-Times,* 8 October 1959, p. 1. See also *News-Times,* 22 October 1959, p. 1.

93. *Watchman-Advocate,* 25 September 1959, p. 8; *News-Times,* 29 October 1959, p. 8.

94. *Watchman-Advocate,* 16 October 1959, p. 1; 2 October 1959, p. 2.

95. *Watchman-Advocate,* 16 October 1959, p. 1; Schmandt, Steinbicker, and Wendel, *Metropolitan Reform in St. Louis,* p. 36.

96. *St. Louis Post-Dispatch,* 23 October 1959, p. 3A.

97. *St. Louis Post-Dispatch,* 4 November 1959, pp. 1A, 13A.

98. Frank S. Sengstock, Phillip A. Fellin, Lawrence E. Nicholson, and Charles I. Mundale, *Consolidation: Building a Bridge between City and Suburb* (Saint Louis: Heffernan Press, 1964), pp. 54–56; Cohn, *St. Louis County,* p. 55.

99. *St. Louis Post-Dispatch,* 27 October 1962, p. 4A; Sengstock et al., *Consolidation,* pp. 87–88; Cohn, *St. Louis County,* p. 55.

100. Sengstock et al., *Consolidation,* p. 87; *Watchman-Advocate,* 30 October 1962, p. 1; *St. Louis County Observer* (Maplewood, Mo.), 31 October 1962, p. 2A.

101. *Watchman-Advocate,* 30 October 1962, pp. 3, 1; *St. Louis County Observer,* 17 October 1962, p. 2A.

102. Helen G. McMahon, *Shrewsbury of All Places: A History of Our Town* (Shrewsbury, Mo.: City of Shrewsbury, 1978), p. 98.

103. *Watchman-Advocate,* 30 October 1962, p. 1; *St. Louis Post-Dispatch,* 18 October, p. 8N; 1 November 1962, p. 7S.

104. *St. Louis County Observer,* 31 October 1962, pp. 1A-2A; *Watchman-Advocate,* 30 October 1962, p. 4.

105. *Watchman-Advocate,* 1 November 1962, p. 4.

106. *St. Louis Post-Dispatch,* 7 November 1962, p. 5A; Cohn, *St. Louis County,* p. 56.

107. *Watchman-Advocate,* 7 November 1962, p. 1. *St. Louis County Observer,* 14 November 1962, p. 1A.

108. *Watchman-Advocate,* 7 November 1962, pp. 1, 6; *St. Louis Post-Dispatch,* 8 November 1962, p. 3A; *St. Louis County Observer,* 14 November 1962, p. 1A.

109. Nicholas P. Thomas, "The Roundtables of Metroplex: A Comparison of the Supervisors Inter-County Committee (Detroit), the Metropolitan Regional Council (New York), and the Metropolitan Washington (D.C.) Council of Governments," Ph.D. diss., Syracuse University, 1967, p. 71.

110. Ibid., p. 72.

111. Ibid., pp. 209–10; Michael N. Danielson and Jameson W. Doig, *New York: The Politics of Urban Regional Development* (Berkeley: University of California Press, 1982), p. 152.

112. *Newsday,* 2 October 1959, as quoted in Thomas, "Roundtables of Metroplex," p. 220; Joan B. Aron, *The Quest for Regional Cooperation: A Study of the New York Metropolitan Regional Council* (Berkeley: University of California Press, 1969), p. 49.

113. *New York Times,* 7 October 1962, sec. 6, p. 47; Danielson and Doig, *New York,* p. 152.

114. *Long Island Press,* 24 October 1960, as quoted in Aron, *Quest for Regional Cooperation,* p. 50.

115. *Port Jefferson Times,* 18 May 1962, pp. 1, 13; Thomas, "Roundtables of Metroplex," pp. 238–39; Aron, *Quest for Regional Cooperation,* p. 52; Danielson and Doig, *New York,* p. 153.

116. *Port Jefferson Times,* 18 May 1962, pp. 1, 13; Aron, *Quest for Regional Cooperation,* p. 52; Thomas, "Roundtables of Metroplex," p. 238; *Northport Journal,* 17 May 1962, p. 1.

117. *Northport Journal,* 17 May 1962, p 1; *Port Jefferson Times,* 18 May 1962, p. 1; *Smithtown Messenger,* 24 May 1962, sec. 2, p. 3; Aron, *Quest for Regional Cooperation,* p. 52; Thomas, "Roundtables of Metroplex," p. 236; Danielson and Doig, *New York,* p. 153.

118. Thomas, "Roundtables of Metroplex," p. 239; *Northport Journal,* 17 May 1962, p. 1.

119. Aron, *Quest for Regional Cooperation,* p. 53; Thomas, "Roundtables of Metroplex," p. 239.

120. Aron, *Quest for Regional Cooperation,* pp. 53–54.

121. *Port Jefferson Times,* 25 May 1962, p. 4; *Smithtown Messenger,* 24 May 1962, sec. 2, p. 2.

122. *Staff Papers on Governmental Organization for Metropolitan Southeast Michigan* (Detroit: Citizens Research Council of Michigan, 1965), sec. IV, pp. 7–19; C. J. Hein, Joyce M. Keys, and G. M. Robbins, *Regional Governmental Arrangements in Metropolitan Areas: Nine Case Studies* (Washington, D.C.: Office of Research and Development, U.S. Environmental Protection Agency, 1974), pp. 14–15; Thomas, "Roundtables of Metroplex," pp. 65–68.

123. Hein, Keys, and Robbins, *Regional Governmental Arrangements,* p. 15.

124. Committee of One Hundred, *A Proposal for a Voluntary Council of Governments in Southeast Michigan* (Detroit: Committee of One Hundred, 1966), pp. 1, 2, 11.

125. Hein, Keys, and Robbins, *Regional Governmental Arrangements,* p. 17.
126. *Royal Oak Tribune,* 4 November 1967, p. 10.
127. Ibid. See also *Royal Oak Tribune,* 4 November 1967, p. 2.
128. *Royal Oak Tribune,* 4 November 1967, p. 10; *Detroit News,* 20 May 1967, p. 4A.
129. *Detroit News,* 10 July 1969, n.p.; *Detroit Free Press,* 22 August 1970, p. 3A; *Detroit News,* 29 August 1971, p. 16A.
130. *Detroit Free Press,* 24 February 1969, p. 12C.
131. *Detroit News,* 12 March 1970, n.p.
132. *Detroit Free Press,* 22 August 1970, p. 3A; *Detroit News,* 29 August 1971, p. 16A; *Detroit Free Press,* 22 August 1970, p. 3A.
133. *Detroit Free Press,* 24 February 1969, p. 12C; 24 May 1970, p. 7B.
134. *Detroit News,* 29 August 1971, p. 16A.
135. William Fulton and Morris Newman, "When COGs Collide," *Planning* 58 (June 1992): 12–13. For a positive view of SCAG, see *Fullerton News Tribune,* 24 May 1967, p. A2. See also Peter Douglas, *The Southern California Association of Governments: A Response to Federal Concern for Metropolitan Areas* (Los Angeles: Institute of Government and Public Affairs, UCLA, 1968).
136. *Orange County Register* (Santa Ana, Calif.), 25 September 1980, p. B4; 1 November 1988, p. B9.
137. *Orange County Register,* 1 November 1988, p. B9.

Chapter 5—Post-Suburban Imperialists

1. *Detroit Free Press,* 22 August 1970, p. 3A.
2. *St. Louis Post-Dispatch,* 3 January 1975, p. 2B. For more on Roos's life and views, see David R. Brown, Justin L. Faherty, and Mary Kimbrough, *Movers and Shakers: Men Who Have Shaped Saint Louis* (Tucson: Patrice Press, 1992), pp. 115–20.
3. *St. Louis Post-Dispatch,* 7 January 1963, p. 3A.
4. *St. Louis Post-Dispatch,* 3 January 1964, p. 3A. See also Robert A. Cohn, *The History and Growth of St. Louis County, Missouri* (Clayton, Mo.: Saint Louis County, 1974), pp. 63–64.
5. *St. Louis Post-Dispatch,* 8 January 1965, p. 3A; 5 January 1968, p. 10A.
6. Cohn, *St. Louis County,* pp. 49–51. See also *St. Louis Post-Dispatch,* 27 January 1967, p. 7A; 25 March 1968, p. 2B.
7. *Watchman-Advocate* (Clayton, Mo.), 15 February 1968, pp. 1, 8. See also *Watchman-Advocate,* 12 February 1968, p. 1.
8. *Community News* (Overland, Mo.), 14 March 1968, p. 1; *Watchman-Advocate,* 7 March 1968, p. 8. See also *Florissant Valley Reporter* (Florissant, Mo.), 21 March 1968, p. 1; *Watchman-Advocate,* 28 March 1968, p. 3.
9. *Florissant Valley Reporter,* 21 March 1968, p. 4.
10. Cohn, *St. Louis County,* p. 52; *Watchman-Advocate,* 3 April 1968, p. 1; 4 April 1968, p. 8; *St. Louis Post-Dispatch,* 3 April 1968, pp. 1A, 2D.
11. *St. Louis Post-Dispatch,* 3 April 1968, p. 9A.
12. *St. Louis County, 1970* (Clayton, Mo.: Saint Louis County, 1971), p. 6.
13. Cohn, *St. Louis County,* p. 69; *St. Louis Post-Dispatch,* 22 October 1970, p. 7W.
14. *St. Louis Post-Dispatch,* 22 October 1970, p. 8B.
15. *St. Louis Post-Dispatch,* 9 January 1970, p. 11A.

16. *St. Louis Post-Dispatch,* 22 October 1970, p. 8B.
17. *St. Louis Post-Dispatch,* 4 November 1970, p. 1A; Cohn, *St. Louis County,* p. 69.
18. *St. Louis County, 1970,* p. 6; Cohn, *St. Louis County,* p. 69.
19. *St. Louis County, 1970,* p. 1.
20. Cohn, *St. Louis County,* p. 69; *St. Louis County Observer* (Maplewood, Mo.), 23 June 1971, p. 1A.
21. *St. Louis County Observer,* 18 August 1971, p. 1A; 25 August 1971, p. 8A.
22. *St. Louis County Observer,* 21 July 1971, p. 1A; *Florissant Valley Reporter,* 28 October 1971, pp. 1, 6.
23. *St. Louis Post-Dispatch,* 8 January 1971, p. 4A.
24. *Watchman-Advocate,* 29 October 1971, p. 1.
25. *St. Louis County Observer,* 27 October 1971, pp. 1A-2A.
26. *Watchman-Advocate,* 21 October 1971, p. 1; *St. Louis Post-Dispatch,* 31 October 1971, p. 19A.
27. *St. Louis County Observer,* 15 September 1971, pp. 1A-2A; *Watchman-Advocate,* 1 November 1971, p. 1.
28. *St. Louis Post-Dispatch,* 3 November 1971, pp. 1A, 5A; Cohn, *St. Louis County,* p. 69.
29. *St. Louis Post-Dispatch,* 7 January 1973, p. 1A.
30. *St. Louis County Observer,* 10 November 1971, p. 10A; *Florissant Valley Reporter,* 11 November 1971, p. 1.
31. *St. Louis Post-Dispatch,* 4 November 1971, p. 3A; Cohn, *St. Louis County,* p. 70.
32. *St. Louis Post-Dispatch,* 7 January 1972, p. 3A; 7 January 1973, p. 8A.
33. *St. Louis Post-Dispatch,* 3 November 1974, p. 1K.
34. *St. Louis Post-Dispatch,* 29 October 1978, p. 3B; 19 January 1979, p. 1B; 4 February 1979, p. 2B; 14 February 1979, p. 1D.
35. *St. Louis Post-Dispatch,* 16 February 1979, p. 2B.
36. *St. Louis Post-Dispatch,* 16 February 1979, p. 2B; 22 February 1979, p. 2B.
37. *St. Louis Post-Dispatch,* 23 February 1979, p. 1B.
38. *St. Louis Post-Dispatch,* 23 February 1979, p. 1B; 26 February 1979, p. 2B.
39. *Proposed St. Louis County Charter* (Clayton, Mo.: Saint Louis County, 1979), p. v.
40. *St. Louis Post-Dispatch,* 1 November 1979, p. 1W.
41. *St. Louis Post-Dispatch,* 7 November 1979, p. 1C.
42. Cohn, *St. Louis County,* p. 13; Confluence St. Louis Task Force, *Too Many Governments? An Analysis of the Present Governmental Structure in St. Louis City and County* (Saint Louis: Confluence St. Louis, 1986), p. 39; Saint Louis County Department of Planning, *The Challenges of Transition: General Plan Update, 1985—St. Louis County* (Clayton, Mo.: Saint Louis County Department of Planning, 1986), pp. 12–13; Advisory Commission on Intergovernmental Relations, *Metropolitan Organization: The St. Louis Case* (Washington, D.C.: Advisory Commission on Intergovernmental Relations, 1988), p. 20.
43. Saint Louis County Department of Planning, *St. Louis County, Missouri, Fact Book, 1977* (Clayton, Mo.: Saint Louis County Department of Planning, 1977), p. 82.
44. *St. Louis Post-Dispatch,* 7 November 1979, p. 1C; "St. Louis County Voters Approve Charter Changes," *National Civic Review* 69 (January 1980): 45.
45. St. Louis County Department of Planning, *Fact Book, 1977,* pp. 82, 85.
46. *St. Louis Post-Dispatch,* 18 January 1980, p. 1B; Saint Louis County Department of

Planning, *Fact Book, 1982, St. Louis County, Missouri* (Clayton, Mo.: Saint Louis County Department of Planning, 1982), p. 69.

47. *St. Louis Post-Dispatch,* 18 January 1980, p. 1B; *St. Louis County, 1971* (Clayton, Mo.: Saint Louis County, 1972), p. 9.

48. *St. Louis Currents: The Community and Its Resources* (Saint Louis: Leadership St. Louis, 1986), p. 39.

49. Laurel Lunt Prussing, "County Government in Downstate Illinois," in *Illinois Local Government: A Handbook,* ed. James F. Keane and Gary Koch (Carbondale: Southern Illinois University Press, 1990), p. 81; Jean Moore and Hiawatha Bray, *DuPage at 150 and Those Who Shaped Our World* (Wheaton, Ill.: DuPage County Sesquicentennial Steering Committee, 1989), p. 241.

50. Thomas Dwight Wilson, "Patterns of Change in Illinois County Government, 1960 to 1974," Ph.D. diss., University of Illinois at Urbana-Champaign, 1975, p. 78.

51. *Wheaton Daily Journal,* 15 November 1978, p. 4; *Downers Grove Reporter,* 2 February 1972, p. 17.

52. Ted Gregory, "Jack Knuepfer of DuPage: 'Mayor Daley' of the Suburbs," *Illinois Issues* 13 (November 1987): 16.

53. *Commission on Local Government Report to Governor Richard B. Ogilvie and Members of the 76th Illinois General Assembly* (Springfield: State of Illinois, 1969), pp. 5, 44, 56.

54. *Downers Grove Reporter,* 12–13 January 1972, sec. 2, p. 1; *Wheaton Daily Journal,* 2 March 1972, p. 2.

55. *Naperville Sun,* 16 March 1972, p. 9.

56. *Wheaton Daily Journal,* 2 March 1972, p. 2; *Downers Grove Reporter,* 15–16 March 1972, sec. 2, p. 7; *Wheaton Daily Journal,* 21 March 1972, p. 4.

57. *Wheaton Daily Journal,* 2 March 1972, p. 2.

58. *Downers Grove Reporter,* 2–3 February 1972, sec. 2, p. 3.

59. *Downers Grove Reporter,* 29–30 March 1972, sec. 2, p. 6.

60. David R. Beam, Alex Pattakos, and David Tobias, eds., *County Home Rule in Illinois* (DeKalb: Center for Governmental Studies, Northern Illinois University, 1977), p. 33.

61. *Chicago Tribune,* 19 March 1972, sec. W10, p. 11; *Naperville Sun,* 16 March 1972, p. 4; *Downers Grove Reporter,* 15 March 1972, p. 6; *Wheaton Daily Journal,* 21 March 1972, p. 4.

62. *Downers Grove Reporter,* 26–27 January 1972, sec. 2, p. 1; Beam, Pattakos, and Tobias, *County Home Rule in Illinois,* p. 27.

63. *Wheaton Daily Journal,* 23 February 1972, p. 8; Beam, Pattakos, and Tobias, *County Home Rule in Illinois,* p. 27; *Naperville Sun,* 16 March 1972, p. 4; *Downers Grove Reporter,* 15 March 1972, p. 6.

64. *Downers Grove Reporter,* 15 March 1972, p. 1; Beam, Pattakos, and Tobias, *County Home Rule in Illinois,* p. 28.

65. *Naperville Sun,* 16 March 1972, p. 9.

66. *Downers Grove Reporter,* 2 February 1972, p. 17.

67. *Chicago Tribune,* 19 March 1972, sec. W10, p. 11. See also *Wheaton Daily Journal,* 18 February 1972, p. 1; 23 February 1972, p. 8.

68. *Wheaton Daily Journal,* 2 March 1972, p. 2; 14 March 1972, p. 8.

69. *Wheaton Daily Journal,* 8 March 1972, p. 17.

70. *Chicago Tribune,* 23 March 1972, sec. 1A, p. 2; *Wheaton Daily Journal,* 22 March 1972, p. 1.
71. "Home Rule Report—Round One," *Illinois County and Township Official* 32 (May 1972): 22; *Chicago Tribune,* 23 March 1972, sec. 1A, p. 2.
72. "Home Rule Report," p. 22; Jay Smith, "County Home Rule: Doesn't Anybody Want It?," in *County Alternatives: The Structure, Functions, and Management of Illinois Counties,* ed. Thomas D. Wilson (n.p.: 1976), p. 67.
73. *Chicago Tribune,* North DuPage County Supplement, 19 October 1982, p. 4; Gregory, "Knuepfer of DuPage," p. 14.
74. *Chicago Tribune,* North DuPage County Supplement, 11 March 1983, p., 2.
75. Gregory, "Knuepfer of DuPage," p. 14.
76. Richard A. Thompson, *DuPage Roots* (Wheaton, Ill.: DuPage County Historical Society, 1985), pp. 91–92.
77. *This is DuPage* (Wheaton, Ill.: League of Women Voters of DuPage County, 1974), p. 19; League of Women Voters, *The Key to Our Local Government,* 3d ed. (Chicago: Citizens Information Service of Illinois, 1972), p. 209.
78. *Progress Report, DuPage County Regional Planning Commission, 1976* (Wheaton, Ill.: DuPage County Regional Planning Commission, 1976), p. 12.
79. Ibid., unpaged introductory letter, p. 9.
80. Ibid., p. 13. See also *Intergovernmental Cooperation in Illinois* (Springfield: State of Illinois, 1976), pp. 116–17.
81. *Royal Oak Tribune,* 7 November 1963, p. 2.
82. Ibid., p. 1.
83. *Oakland Press* (Pontiac, Mich.), 2 November 1980, p. A2; *Detroit Free Press,* 30 October 1984, p. 11A.
84. *St. Louis Post-Dispatch,* 25 March 1968, p. 5A.
85. *Birmingham Observer and Eccentric,* 1 August 1974, p. 12A; *Royal Oak Tribune,* 2 August 1974, p. 17; Barbara Kukes Goldman, ed., *Oakland County Government* (Birmingham, Mich.: Leagues of Women Voters, 1982), pp. 11–12.
86. *Birmingham Observer and Eccentric,* 1 August 1974, p. 12A; *Royal Oak Tribune,* 2 August 1974, p. 17.
87. *Southfield Observer and Eccentric,* 1 August 1974, p. 18A; *Birmingham Observer and Eccentric,* 1 August 1974, p. 16 A.
88. *Royal Oak Tribune,* 1 August 1974, p. 29.
89. Ibid., p. 34. See also *Birmingham Observer and Eccentric,* 1 August 1974, p. 4A.
90. *Royal Oak Tribune,* 7 August 1974, pp. 1–2, 25; 22 August 1974, p. 19; *Oakland Press,* 7 August 1974, pp. A2, A10; *Southfield Observer and Eccentric,* 8 August 1974, p. 1A.
91. *Royal Oak Tribune,* 1 August 1974, p. 34; *Oakland Press,* 1 November 1974, p. E1.
92. Ibid. See also *Royal Oak Tribune,* 1 November 1974, pp. 3, 17; *Southfield Observer and Eccentric,* 4 November 1974, p. 7A.
93. *Royal Oak Tribune,* 6 November 1974, p. 2. See also *Oakland Press,* 6 November 1974, pp. A1, A9; 8 November 1974, pp. A1, A3; *Southfield Observer and Eccentric,* 7 November 1974, pp. 3A, 17A; *Detroit Free Press,* 7 November 1974, p. 12A.
94. *Detroit Free Press,* 7 November 1984, p. 14A; *Oakland Press,* 3 November 1976, p. A1.
95. *Oakland Press,* 2 November 1980, p. A2; 5 November 1980, p. D1.

96. *Oakland Press,* 4 November 1984, p. E7; 7 November 1984, A6.

97. *Detroit Free Press,* 30 October 1984, p. 11A.

98. *Detroit Free Press,* 4 November 1976, p. 16A; *Oakland Press,* 1 November 1974, E1.

99. *Oakland Press,* 4 November 1984, unpaged advertising supplement.

100. *Royal Oak Tribune,* 2 November 1977, Tribune Plus, p. 9.

101. Ibid.

102. Goldman, *Oakland County Government,* pp. 99–104, for airport, see pp. 104–5.

103. *Oakland Press,* 4 November 1984, unpaged advertising supplement; Goldman, *Oakland County Government,* p. 104.

104. Goldman, *Oakland County Government,* pp. 27, 114–16.

105. Ibid., pp. 109–10, 28–29, 113.

106. Cortus T. Koehler, *Managing California Counties* (Sacramento: County Supervisors Association of California, 1983), p. 27; *Orange County Register* (Santa Ana, Calif.), 9 January 1980, p. B1.

107. *Orange County Register,* 25 September 1980, p. B6.

108. *Fullerton News Tribune,* 23 May 1967, p. A3.

109. Ibid., p. A1; *Santa Ana Register,* 27 May 1967, p. A8. See also *Anaheim Bulletin,* 24 May 1967, p. A1.

110. *Santa Ana Register,* 27 May 1967, p. A8.

111. *Fullerton News Tribune,* 23 May 1967, p. A3.

112. *Los Angeles Times* (Orange County edition), 10 September 1984, pt. 2, p. 1.

113. *Fullerton News Tribune,* 3 February 1971, p. A8; *Santa Ana Register,* 1 February 1971, p. A1; 2 February 1971, p. A1.

114. *Fullerton News Tribune,* 11 January 1971, p. B1.

115. *Santa Ana Register,* 4 February 1971, p. D10; 7 February 1971, p. J10.

116. *Santa Ana Register,* 9 February 1971, p. A1; 11 February 1971, p. E10; *Fullerton News Tribune,* 9 February 1971, p. A4.

117. *Fullerton News Tribune,* 4 February 1971, p. B14; 8 February 1971, p. B12.

118. *Fullerton News Tribune,* 8 February 1971, p. A1; *Santa Ana Register,* 10 February 1971, p. A3.

119. *Santa Ana Register,* 9 February 1971, p. A1; 10 February 1971, p. A3; *Fullerton News Tribune,* 9 February 1971, pp. A1-A4.

120. *Los Angeles Times* (Orange County edition), 10 September 1984, pt. 2, p. 3.

121. *Los Angeles Times* (Orange County edition), 9 September 1984, pt. 2, p. 1.

122. *Los Angeles Times* (Orange County edition), 12 September 1984, pt. 2, p. 1; 10 September 1984, pt. 2, p. 3.

123. *Los Angeles Times* (Orange County edition), 9 September 1984, pt. 2, p. 4.

124. *Los Angeles Times* (Orange County edition), 7 January 1985, pt. 2, p. 7.

125. Ibid.

126. *Los Angeles Times* (Orange County edition), 13 September 1984, pt. 2, p. 1.

127. *Los Angeles Times* (Orange County edition), 12 September 1984, pt. 2, p. 6.

128. *Los Angeles Times* (Orange County edition), 10 September 1984, pt. 2, p. 3.

129. See, for example, *Orange County Register,* 10 January 1979, pp. A3, C1; 7 January 1981, p. B1; 8 November 1989, p. B1; *Los Angeles Times* (Orange County edition), 6 January 1982, pt. 2, pp. 1, 6; 9 June 1982, pt. 2, pp. 1, 11; 6 January 1983, pt. 2, p. 11; 9 September 1984, pt. 2, p. 4.

130. Office of State Controller, *Annual Report of Financial Transactions Concerning Transit Operators and Non-Transit Claimants under the Transportation Development Act, Fiscal Year 1981–82* (Sacramento: State of California, 1982), p. 127.

131. *Orange County Register,* 7 January 1975, p. B3. See also *Orange County Register,* 7 January 1975, p. B1; 9 January 1979, p. B2. For the creation of the Orange County Transportation Commission, a countywide transportation planning body, see *Orange County Register,* 1 October 1976, p. A3, and *Los Angeles Times,* 1 October 1976, pt. 1, pp. 3, 30; 27 December 1976, pt. 2, pp. 1–2.

132. *Los Angeles Times* (Orange County edition), 9 September 1984, pt. 2, p. 3; 14 September 1984, pt. 2, p. 7.

133. *Los Angeles Times* (Orange County edition), 14 September 1984, pt. 2, p. 7.

134. For the referendum defeat of a sales tax to finance countywide transportation projects, see *Los Angeles Times* (Orange County edition), 27 May 1984, pt. 2, p. 16; 3 June 1984, pt. 2, pp. 1, 9, 14; 6 June 1984, pt. 1, pp. 1, 3.

135. *Los Angeles Times* (Orange County edition), 1 April 1984, pt. 2, p. 4.

136. Ibid., pt. 2, p. 6.

137. Ibid., pt. 2, pp. 1, 9.

Chapter 6—Recognition and Rebellion

1. Bureau of the Census, *State and Metropolitan Area Data Book, 1991* (Washington, D.C.: U.S. Government Printing Office, 1991), pp. 102, 114, 132, 144, 162.

2. "How Long Island Beats the Slump," *Business Week,* 2755 (6 September 1982): 60.

3. Douglas R. Gabel, "Long Island's Human Resources," in *An Exploration of the Multidimensional Nature of Long Island's Identity,* ed. Elaine Sherman (Hempstead, N.Y.: Hofstra University, 1988), p. 420; *Newsday* (Garden City, N.Y.), 28 January 1985, pt. III, p. 2.

4. *County of Nassau, 1990 Comprehensive Annual Financial Report* (Mineola, N.Y.: Nassau County, 1991), p. 119.

5. "How Long Island Beats the Slump," p. 60.

6. *Newsday,* 4 April 1985, p. 7.

7. *County of Nassau, New York, Comprehensive Annual Financial Report for the Year Ended December 31, 1987* (Mineola, N.Y.: Nassau County, 1988), p. 9; *County of Nassau, New York, Comprehensive Annual Financial Report for the Year Ended December 31, 1988* (Mineola, N.Y.: Nassau County, 1989), p. 4.

8. *New York Times,* 3 January 1987, p. 25.

9. Gioia Parente, "Hotels and Tourism: Establishing a Unique Long Island Identity," in Sherman, *Long Island's Identity,* p. 242.

10. Michael Villaplana, "High Technology vs. Traditional Aerospace Industry on Long Island," in Sherman, *Long Island's Identity,* p. 370.

11. *Newsday,* 28 January 1985, pt. III, p. 3.

12. "How Long Island Beats the Slump," p. 60.

13. *Barron's* 62 (18 October 1982): 34; Donald D. Rienzo, Sr., "Long Island Responds, 'America, I Hear Your Calling,'" *Barron's* 62 (18 October 1982): 36.

14. Robert B. McKay, Geoffrey L. Rossano, and Carol A. Traynor, eds., *Between Ocean and Empire: An Illustrated History of Long Island* (Northridge, Calif.: Windsor Publications, 1985), p. 220.

15. Gabel, "Long Island's Human Resources," pp. 423, 418.
16. Steven Goldberg, "The Image of Long Island and Its Relationship to and Implication for the Region's Advertising and Media Industries" in Sherman, *Long Island's Identity,* p. 201.
17. "How Long Island Beats the Slump," p. 61.
18. *1989 Annual Report, Oakland County Department of Community and Economic Development* (Pontiac, Mich.: Oakland County, 1990), p. ii.
19. Ibid. See also *Detroit News,* 17 January 1986, p. 3A.
20. Trout Pomeroy, *Oakland County: Making It Work in Michigan* (Chatsworth, Calif.: Windsor Publications, 1990), p. 46.
21. *Southfield Eccentric,* 14 January 1985, p. 3A; *Detroit Free Press,* 22 October 1984, p. 4D; 11 March 1985, p. 2B.
22. *Southfield Eccentric,* 21 February 1986, p. 1; *Detroit News,* 15 May 1988, p. 1G.
23. *Detroit Free Press,* 11 March 1985, p. 2B; *Detroit News,* 1 June 1986, p. 18A. See also *Southfield Eccentric,* 24 February 1986, p. 7A; *Detroit News,* 24 May 1984, p. 1A.
24. Pomeroy, *Oakland County,* p. 142.
25. Ibid., pp. 143, 34.
26. *Southfield Eccentric,* 29 August 1985, p. 1.
27. Pomeroy, *Oakland County,* p. 38.
28. *Detroit Free Press,* 22 December 1985, p. 23A.
29. Pomeroy, *Oakland County,* p. 28. See also *Detroit Free Press,* 28 September 1987, pp. 3A, 15A.
30. Division of County Planning, *Summary of Development Oakland County, Michigan—1988* (Pontiac, Mich.: Oakland County, 1989), pp. 11, 39, 41.
31. Oakland Economic Development Group, *Oakland County, Michigan* (Pontiac, Mich.: Oakland County, 1985), not paged; Pomeroy, *Oakland County,* pp. 59–60.
32. Alan DiGaetano and John S. Klemanski, "Restructuring the Suburbs: Political Economy of Economic Development in Auburn Hills, Michigan," *Journal of Urban Affairs* 13 (no. 2, 1991): 143–45; Pomeroy, *Oakland County,* pp. 40–45.
33. Pomeroy, *Oakland County,* pp. 43, 45.
34. *Detroit News,* 24 May 1984, p. 1A; 15 May 1987, pp. 1A, 10A; *Michigan Manual, 1989–1990* (Lansing: Legislative Service Bureau, 1989), pp. 929, 934.
35. *Chicago Sun-Times,* 5 November 1982, p. 91.
36. *Chicago Tribune,* 25 October 1987, sec. 10, pp. 10–11.
37. *Chicago Tribune,* 17 February 1985, sec. 4, p. 1.
38. *Crain's Chicago Business,* 14–20 January 1991, p. 13.
39. *Downers Grove Reporter,* 15 December 1982, p. 3A; *Chicago Tribune,* 25 October 1987, sec. 10, p. 20.
40. *Chicago Tribune,* 26 June 1988, sec. 18, p. 3.
41. Robert T. Dunphy, "Suburban Mobility: Reducing Reliance on the Auto in DuPage County, Illinois," *Urban Land* 46 (December 1987): 7.
42. Blair Kamin, "Shall We Dance? The Suburban Context of Oakbrook Terrace Tower," *Inland Architect* 32 (November/December 1988): 52–57.
43. Ibid., p. 53.
44. *Naperville Sun,* 26 August 1987, DuPage Profile Section, p. 8.

45. *St. Louis County Development Profile, 1991–1992* (Clayton, Mo: Saint Louis County Department of Planning and Saint Louis County Economic Council, 1992), p. 2.
46. *St. Louis Post-Dispatch,* 24 January 1986, p. 1B.
47. *The Challenges of Transition: General Plan Update, 1985—St. Louis County* (Clayton, Mo.: Saint Louis County, 1985), p. 19; *St. Louis County Development Profile,* p. 3.
48. "RCGA's Profile of the St. Louis Economy, 1994–1995," *St. Louis Commerce* 7 (May 1994): 13A.
49. Alan J. Beaudette, "Orange County," *Urban Land* 46 (September 1987): 8.
50. *Los Angeles Times,* 6 March 1988, pt. VIII, p. 7. See also Beaudette, "Orange County," p. 8; *Los Angeles Times,* 28 September 1986, pt. IV, pp. 1, 4, 9.
51. *Los Angeles Times,* 6 July 1982, pt. II, p. 4; Allan Carpenter, comp., *Facts about the Cities* (New York: H.W. Wilson Co., 1991), p. 26.
52. *Los Angeles Times,* 6 July 1982, pt. II, p. 4.
53. Gladwin Hill, "Big But Not Bold: Irvine Today," *Planning* 51 (February 1986): 19.
54. *Los Angeles Times,* 10 June 1984, pt. IV, p. 6.
55. Ibid.; Dan Walters, *The New California: Facing the Twenty-First Century,* 2d ed. (Sacramento: California Journal Press, 1992), p. 41.
56. Robert Cervero, *Suburban Gridlock* (New Brunswick, N.J.: Center for Urban Policy Research, 1986), pp. 156–57.
57. *Los Angeles Times* (Orange County edition), 30 September 1986, pt. I, p. 20; Trevor Bailey, "Orange County," *Horizon* 30 (January/February 1987): 49.
58. *Los Angeles Times* (Orange County edition), 29 September 1986, pt. VI, p. 1; 30 September 1986, pt. I, p. 1.
59. *Los Angeles Times,* 28 September 1986, pt. V, p. 4.
60. *Los Angeles Times* (Orange County edition), 30 September 1986, pt. II, p. 1.
61. Judith and Neil Morgan, "Orange, A Most California County," *National Geographic* 160 (December 1981): 778.
62. *Los Angeles Times* (Orange County edition), 3 April 1982, pt. 1A, p. 1.
63. *Los Angeles Times* (Orange County edition), 5 April 1982, pt. II, p. 6; 27 October 1982, pt. II, pp. 1, 7; 4 November 1982, pt. II, pp. 2, 5.
64. *Los Angeles Times* (Orange County edition), 6 January 1983, pt. II, p. 1; 9 January 1983, pt. X, p. 2.
65. *Los Angeles Times* (Orange County edition), 6 November 1986, pt. II, p. 2; 25 November 1986, pt. II, p. 1; 26 November 1986, pt. I, pp. 1, 21.
66. *Los Angeles Times* (Orange County edition), 25 November 1986, pt. II, p. 1; 26 November 1986, pt. I, pp. 1, 21; 27 November 1986, pt. II, pp. 1, 3; *Orange County Register,* 3 April 1987, pp. B1, B12.
67. *Los Angeles Times* (Orange County edition), 5 June 1988, pt. II, p. 3.
68. John Landis and Cynthia Kroll, "The Southern California Growth War," in John J. Kirlin and Donald R. Winkler, eds., *California Policy Choices, Volume Five* (Los Angeles: University of Southern California School of Public Administration, 1989), pp. 125–26; *Los Angeles Times* (Orange County edition), 7 December 1987, pt. II, p. 4; 5 June 1988, pt. II, p. 3.
69. *Orange County Register,* 8 June 1988, p. A1; *Los Angeles Times* (Orange County edition), 7 December 1987, pt. II, p. 4.

70. *Orange County Register,* 1 June 1988, p. B4.
71. *Orange County Register,* 5 June 1988, p. H5.
72. *Orange County Register,* 8 June 1988, p. A10.
73. *Anaheim Bulletin,* 3 June 1988, p. A11; *Los Angeles Times* (Orange County edition), 7 December 1987, pt. II, p. 4.
74. *Anaheim Bulletin,* 4 June 1988, p. A1; 8 June 1988, p. A1; *Los Angeles Times* (Orange County edition), 26 May 1988, pt. II, p. 1.
75. *Anaheim Bulletin,* 3 June 1988, p. A12; *Orange County Register,* 1 June 1988, p. B8.
76. *Anaheim Bulletin,* 4 June 1988, p. A7. See also *Orange County Register,* 2 June 1988, pp. B1, B5.
77. *Orange County Register,* 2 June 1988, p. B10; 3 June 1988, p. B9.
78. *Anaheim Bulletin,* 4 June 1988, p. A1.
79. *Fullerton News Tribune,* 19 May 1988, pp. 1A-2A; *Anaheim Bulletin,* 4 June 1988, p. A7. See also *Los Angeles Times* (Orange County edition), 26 May 1988, pt. II, pp. 1, 6–7.
80. *Anaheim Bulletin,* 8 June 1988, p. A7. See also *Anaheim Bulletin,* 4 June 1988, p. A15.
81. *Anaheim Bulletin,* 8 June 1988, pp. A1, A6; *Los Angeles Times* (Orange County edition), 8 June 1988, pt. I, pp. 1, 21; *Orange County Register,* 8 June 1988, p. A1; Landis and Kroll, "Southern California Growth War," pp. 154–55.
82. *Orange County Register,* 8 June 1988, p. A10. See also Jane Glenn Haas, "Anti- Versus Pro-Growth Forces in Southern California: A Ballot Box Battle," *Urban Land* 47 (October 1988): 2–5.
83. *Orange County Register,* 8 June 1988, p. A10.
84. *Orange County Register,* 9 November 1988, p. A14; *Los Angeles Times* (Orange County edition), 29 October 1988, pt. II, pp. 3, 10–11; 6 November 1988, pt. II, p. 10.
85. *Orange County Register,* 7 November 1988, p. A6; 8 November 1988, p. B1.
86. *Los Angeles Times* (Orange County edition), 6 November 1988, pt. II, p. 6.
87. Landis and Kroll, "Southern California Growth War," pp. 156–57.
88. *Los Angeles Times* (Orange County edition), 9 November 1989, p. B18.
89. Elaine Sherman, "Summary and Conclusions," in Sherman, *Long Island's Identity,* pp. 529–30.
90. *Newsday,* 12 March 1985, p. 37. See also 17 October 1977, p. 16.
91. *Newsday,* 15 March 1989, p. 34. See also 22 March 1989, p. 33.
92. *Newsday,* 20 March 1989, p. 29; *New York Times,* 25 February 1990, sec. 12, p. 1; Paul Goldberger, "The Strangling of a Resort," *New York Times Magazine* (4 September 1983), p. 16.
93. *Newsday,* 22 March 1989, p. 33.
94. *Newsday,* 4 November 1985, pt. III, p. 12.
95. *Newsday,* 15 March 1985, p. 21; 17 March 1985, p. 21.
96. *Newsday,* 12 September 1985, p. 7.
97. *Newsday,* 1 November 1987, Voter's Guide, p. 4; Roberta Mincieli Lituchy, "Quality of Life on Long Island and Its Effect on Long Island's Image and Identity," in Sherman, *Long Island's Identity,* pp. 476–77.
98. *Newsday,* 4 November 1987, p. 26; 4 November 1989, pp. 7, 10.
99. *Newsday,* 5 December 1989, p. 72; *New York Times,* 25 February 1990, sec. 12, pp. 1,4.

100. *Newsday,* 3 November 1989, p. 81; 19 December 1989, p. 63; 4 November 1989, p. 7.

101. *Chicago Tribune,* 25 October 1987, sec. 10, p. 23.

102. Kamin, "Shall We Dance?," p. 53.

103. *Naperville Sun,* 22 March 1987, pp. 3A, 16A.

104. Kamin, "Shall We Dance?," p. 57; *Naperville Sun,* 26–27 August 1987, DuPage Profile Section, p. 9.

105. *Chicago Tribune,* 28 November 1986, sec. 1, p. 11.

106. *Wheaton Daily Journal,* 31 December 1986, p. 1; *Chicago Tribune,* 5 November 1986, sec. 1, p. 4.

107. *Chicago Tribune,* 27 August 1986, sec. 2, p. 2; 5 November 1986, sec. 1, p. 4; 6 November 1986, sec. 2, p. 7.

108. *Wheaton Daily Journal,* 31 December 1986, p. 1; *Chicago Tribune,* 5 November 1986, sec. 1, p. 4.

109. *Naperville Sun,* 16 March 1990, p. 2A; 26–27 August 1987, DuPage Profile Section, p. 10.

110. "Price for Mayor," pamphlet file, Nichols Library, Naperville, Illinois; Michael H. Ebner, "Technoburb," *Inland Architect* 37 (January/February 1993): 59.

111. *Naperville Sun,* 26–27 August 1987, DuPage Profile Section, p. 10; *150 Years: Glen Ellyn Sesquicentennial, 1834–1984* (n.p.), p. 32.

112. League of Women Voters of Birmingham-Bloomfield, *Voters' Guide, 1990* (Birmingham, Mich.: League of Women Voters of Birmingham-Bloomfield, 1990), not paged; *Birmingham Eccentric,* 6 April 1981, p. 3A; *Novi-Wixom Spinal Column,* 8 March 1989, as transcribed in "Novi History: Volume Two" in vertical file of Novi Public Library, Novi, Michigan.

113. *Detroit Free Press,* 16 July 1988, p. 3A.

114. Ibid. See also DiGaetano and Klemanski, "Restructuring the Suburbs," p. 142.

115. *Challenges of Transition,* p. 63; *St. Louis Post-Dispatch,* 21 March 1988, p. 2W.

116. *St. Louis Post-Dispatch,* 29 September 1988, pp. 7W–9W; 12 December 1988, pp. 1W, 8W; 15 December 1988, pp. 1W–2W.

117. *St. Louis Post-Dispatch,* 29 September 1988, pp. 1W, 4W.

118. Alexander C. Niven, *City of Glendale 75* (n.p.: [c. 1987]), not paged.

119. *St. Louis Post-Dispatch,* 25 September 1983, pp. 1B, 3B; *City of Town and Country v. St. Louis County,* 657 S.W.2d 598 (1983). See also *St. Louis Post-Dispatch,* 22 September 1983, p. 6W.

120. *City of Town and Country v. St. Louis County,* 657 S.W.2d 605, 606; *St. Louis Post-Dispatch,* 25 September 1983, p. 3B.

121. *St. Louis Post-Dispatch,* 25 September 1983, pp. 3B, 1B.

122. *St. Louis Business Journal,* 17–23 October 1983, p. 42.

123. *St. Louis Post-Dispatch,* 25 September 1983, p. 3B.

124. *St. Louis Business Journal,* 17–23 October 1983, pp. 1, 4, 42.

125. *St. Louis Post-Dispatch,* 29 September 1983, p. 1N; *St. Louis Business Journal,* 17–23 October 1983, pp. 4, 43.

126. Saint Louis County Department of Planning, *Report of the St. Louis County Annexation Study Commission* (Clayton, Mo.: Saint Louis County, 1985), p. 1; *St. Louis Post-Dispatch,* 4 April 1984, p. 1A; 5 April 1984, p. 3A. See also Confluence St. Louis Task Force, *Too Many Governments? An Analysis of the Present Government*

Structure in St. Louis City and County (Saint Louis: Confluence St. Louis, 1986), p. 9; *St. Louis Post-Dispatch,* 1 April 1984, pp. 1D-2D; 8 September 1985, p. 13C; 25 October 1985, pp. 1S-2S.

127. *St. Louis Post-Dispatch,* 17 October 1984, p. 3A; 8 September 1985, p. 13C.

128. *St. Louis Post-Dispatch,* 8 September 1985, p. 1C. See also *St. Louis Post-Dispatch,* 12 May 1986, pp. 1S-2S.

129. Confluence St. Louis Task Force, *Too Many Governments?,* pp. 34–35.

130. Confluence St. Louis, "Too Many Governments? Task Force Presentation to Board of Freeholders," in *St. Louis City/County Board of Freeholders Community Involvement and Public Information Resource Document* (Clayton, Mo.: Board of Freeholders, 1988).

131. Saint Louis County Department of Planning, "A Comprehensive Proposal for Local Government Reorganization in St. Louis County," in *Board of Freeholders Community Involvement,* p. 5.

132. Robert A. Cohn, *The History and Growth of St. Louis County, Missouri* (Clayton, Mo.: Saint Louis County, 1974), pp. 63–64.

133. "St. Louis County 2000 Commission," in *Board of Freeholders Community Involvement,* pp. 2–3; *St. Louis Post-Dispatch,* 4 June 1987, p. 3A.

134. "Statement for the Board of Freeholders by the Mayors of Large Cities," in *Board of Freeholders Community Involvement,* pp. 1–2.

135. "Reorganization of St. Louis County—A Position Paper for the City of Crestwood," in *Board of Freeholders Community Involvement,* p. 1; "Statement to the Board of Freeholders by the City of Creve Coeur," in *Board of Freeholders Community Involvement,* p. 1; Lottie Mae Williams, "Presentation to Board of Freeholders," in *Board of Freeholders Community Involvement,* pp. 4, 7.

136. Statement of Joanne Parrott, in *Board of Freeholders Community Involvement,* p. 2.

137. *St. Louis Post-Dispatch,* 8 September 1988, p. 1B.

138. *Naborhood Link News* (Lemay, Mo.), 21 September 1988, p. 1; *Florissant Valley Reporter* (Florissant, Mo.), 20 September 1988, p. 1; 4 October 1988, p. 1; *St. Louis Post-Dispatch,* 12 September 1988, p. 3A.

139. *Webster-Kirkwood Times* (Webster Groves, Mo.), 2–8 September 1988, p. 5; 22–29 December, p. 4.

140. *Webster-Kirkwood Times,* 22–29 December 1988, p. 4. See also *Webster-Kirkwood Times,* 2–8 September 1988, pp. 5, 11, 16–22 September 1988, p. 4.

141. *St. Louis Post-Dispatch,* 9 September 1988, p. 3A.

142. *Florissant Valley Reporter,* 20 September 1988, p. 7; *St. Louis Post-Dispatch,* 20 September 1988, p. 3A. See also *Florissant Valley Reporter,* 27 September 1988, p. 2; *Naborhood Link News,* 28 September 1988, p. 1; *St. Louis Post-Dispatch,* 14 September 1988, p. 16A; *Webster-Kirkwood Times,* 2–8 September 1988, pp. 10–11; 22–29 December 1988, p. 4.

143. *Florissant Valley Reporter,* 20 September 1988, p. 2.

144. *St. Louis Post-Dispatch,* 8 September 1988, p. 10A; *Naborhood Link News,* 21 September 1988, p. 1.

145. *Naborhood Link News,* 28 September 1988, p. 1; *Florissant Valley Reporter,* 27 September 1988, p. 1. See also *St. Louis Post-Dispatch,* 20 September 1988, p. 3A; 23 September 1988, p. 3A.

146. Roger B. Parks and Ronald J. Oakerson, *Metropolitan Organization: The St. Louis Case* (Washington, D.C.: Advisory Commission on Intergovernmental Relations, 1988), pp. 12, 168. See also Roger B. Parks and Ronald J. Oakerson, "Comparative Metropolitan Organization: Service Production and Governance Structures in St. Louis (MO) and Allegheny County (PA)," *Publius: The Journal of Federalism* 23 (Winter 1993): 19–39; Donald Phares, "Bigger Is Better, or Is It Smaller? Restructuring Local Government in the St. Louis Area," *Urban Affairs Quarterly* 25 (September 1989): 11.

147. *Quinn v. Millsap,* 491 U.S. 95 (1989); Phares, "Bigger Is Better," p. 15.

148. *St. Louis Post-Dispatch,* 31 March 1988, p. 3W; 6 April 1988, p. 9A.

149. *St. Louis Post-Dispatch,* 29 January 1989, pp. 1A, 6A, 7A; 31 January 1989, p. 1B; 8 February 1989, pp. 1A, 6A; 9 February 1989, pp. 1B, 2B.

150. *St. Louis County Boundary Commission Annual Legislative Report, 1991* (Clayton, Mo.: Saint Louis County, 1992), pp. 3–4. See also *St. Louis County Boundary Commission Annual Legislative Report, 1990* (Clayton, Mo.: Saint Louis County, 1990).

151. *Chicago Tribune,* 27 February 1985, sec. 8, p. 4.

152. Pat Raab, "Municipalities Work Together for a Better DuPage County," *DuPage Profile: DuPage County's Weekly Newsmagazine* (15–16 June 1988), p. 4. For more on the water issue, see Nancy Pohlman, "Lake Michigan Water: An Investment in DuPage's Future," *DuPage Profile: DuPage County's Weekly Newsmagazine* (31 August–1 September 1988), pp. 1, 4–5; *Chicago Tribune,* 1 June 1984, sec. 7, p. 8; 11 June 1984, sec. 2, p. 1; 12 June 1984, sec. 1, p. 14; sec. 2, p. 4; 24 June 1984, sec. 3, p. 8; 27 June 1984, sec. 2, p. 3; 30 June 1984, sec. 1, p. 5; 26 July 1984, sec. 1, p. 18; 27 July 1984, sec. 2, p. 3; 16 December 1984, sec. 4, pp. 1, 21.

153. *Chicago Tribune* (DuPage edition), sec. 2, 18 November 1988, pp. 1, 6.

154. Raab, "Municipalities Work Together," p. 4.

155. *Naperville Sun,* 27 May 1988, p. 1D; Tom Andreoli, "Can a 'County Executive' Help Suburbs Manage Growth?" *Chicago Enterprise* 3 (September 1988): 13.

156. *Naperville Sun,* 2 September 1987, DuPage Profile Section, p. 8.

157. *Naperville Sun,* 30 October 1987, p. 18A. See also *Naperville Sun,* 6 November 1987, p. 4A.

158. *Naperville Sun,* 19 August 1987, DuPage Profile Section, p. 6.

159. *Naperville Sun,* 30 October 1987, p. 18A.

160. Lowell W. Culver, ed., *Adapting County Government to the Challenges of Growth: Proceedings of the Conference on County Government Modernization in Northeastern Illinois, April 20, 1990* (University Park, Ill.: Institute for Public Policy and Administration Governors State University, 1991), p. 33.

161. *Chicago Tribune* (DuPage edition), 26 April 1989, sec. 2, pp. 1, 8. See also 25 April 1989, sec. 2, pp. 1, 4.

162. *Chicago Sun-Times,* 14 March 1990, p. 16.

163. *Chicago Tribune* (DuPage edition), 4 March 1990, sec. 2, p. 4.

164. *Chicago Tribune* (DuPage edition), 14 March 1990, sec. 1, p. 1. See also 19 March 1990, sec. 1, p. 8.

165. *Naperville Sun,* 23 March 1990, pp. 2A, 7A; *Chicago Sun-Times,* 22 March 1990, p. 6.

166. *Naperville Sun,* 23 March 1990, p. 4A; *Chicago Sun-Times,* 22 March 1990, p. 6; *Chicago Tribune* (DuPage edition), 22 March 1990, sec. 2, p. 1.

167. *Orange County Register,* 4 January 1987, p. B3. See also *Los Angeles Times* (Orange County edition), 5 November 1987, pt. II, p. 10.
168. *Los Angeles Times* (Orange County edition), 25 September 1985, pt. II, p. 1.
169. *Orange County Register,* 6 November 1988, p. B7.
170. *Los Angeles Times* (Orange County edition), 5 November 1987, pt. II, p. 1. See also 4 November 1987, pt. II, pp. 3–4; *Orange County Register,* 4 November 1987, pp. A1, A19.
171. *Los Angeles Times* (Orange County edition), 29 October 1987, pt. II, p. 1; *Orange County Register,* 4 November 1987, p. A1.
172. *Los Angeles Times* (Orange County edition), 29 October 1987, pt. II, p. 7.
173. *Los Angeles Times* (Orange County edition), 19 November 1987, pt. II, pp. 1, 5.
174. *Los Angeles Times* (Orange County edition), 8 June 1988, pt. II, pp. 1, 4; 9 June 1988, pt. II, pp. 2, 14; 9 February 1989, pt. II, p. 4; *Orange County Register,* 8 June 1988, p. A17.
175. *Orange County Register,* 8 November 1989, p. A19.
176. Ibid. See also *Orange County Register,* 16 February 1989, pp. B1, B8; *Los Angeles Times* (Orange County edition), 1 November 1989, p. B4; 4 November 1989, p. B10; 8 November 1989, pp. B1, B7.
177. *Los Angeles Times* (Orange County edition), 4 March 1991, p. B4; 6 March 1991, pp. A1, A12; 7 March 1991, pp. B4, B12.
178. *Los Angeles Times* (Orange County edition), 2 March 1991, p. B9.
179. *Los Angeles Times* (Orange County edition), 17 February 1991, p. B8; 3 March 1991, p. B8.
180. *Los Angeles Times* (Orange County edition), 24 February 1991, p. B8.
181. *Los Angeles Times* (Orange County edition), 17 February 1991, p. B9.
182. *Newsday,* 7 December 1989, p. 81. See also 1 December 1989, p. 23; 2 December 1989, p. 11; 4 December 1989, p. 50.
183. *Detroit News,* 30 May 1987, pp. 1A, 14A; 27 March 1988, pp. 1B, 7B.

Chapter 7—The Pragmatic Compromise
1. *Naperville Sun,* 19 August 1987, DuPage Profile Section, p. 6.
2. For a discussion of the supposed death of suburbia and the persistence of suburban ideology, see William Sharpe and Leonard Wallock, "Bold New City or Built-Up 'Burb? Redefining Contemporary Suburbia," *American Quarterly* 46 (March 1994): 1–30. In the same issue of *American Quarterly,* note as well the comments on Sharpe and Wallock's article by Robert Bruegmann, Robert Fishman, Margaret Marsh, and June Manning Thomas.
3. See, for example, David Rusk, *Cities without Suburbs* (Washington, D.C.: Woodrow Wilson Center Press, 1993).

Bibliographic Essay

In the late 1960s and early 1970s, some scholars and journalists already recognized the emergence of a post-suburban pattern of settlement along the metropolitan fringe. Earl W. Kersten, Jr. and D. Reid Ross, "Clayton: A New Metropolitan Focus in the St. Louis Area," *Annals of the Association of American Geographers* 58 (December 1968): 637–49, described the changes in Saint Louis County. A five-article series in the *New York Times,* 30 May–3 June 1971, announced the arrival of "the Outer City." According to the first of these articles (30 May 1971, p. 1), a city's suburbs were "no longer mere orbital satellites. They [were] no longer *sub.*" Louis H. Masotti and Jeffrey K. Hadden edited a collection of essays, *The Urbanization of the Suburbs* (Beverly Hills: Sage Publications, 1973). In the first line of the introductory essay, Masotti summarized the theme of the volume: "Suburbia is undergoing a significant transition from its traditional role as dependent 'urban fringe' to independent 'neo-city'" (p. 15).

By the late 1970s and early 1980s an increasing number of observers were writing about this transition. In his brief monograph *The Outer City: Geographical Consequences of the Urbanization of the Suburbs* (Washington, D.C.: Association of American Geographers, 1976), geographer Peter O. Muller wrote of the newly urbanized fringe. Muller reiterated this theme in his synthesis *Contemporary Suburban America* (Englewood Cliffs, N.J.: Prentice-Hall, 1981), announcing: "The term 'suburbs' itself has been rendered obsolete because such settlements are simply no longer 'sub' to the 'urb' in the traditional sense" (p. 6). Moreover, he emphasized the obsolescence of the traditional concepts of city and suburb in such later works as "Are Cities Obsolete? The Fearful Symmetry of Post-Urban America," *The Sciences* 26 (March–April 1986): 42–47. In *The New Urban America: Growth and Politics in Sunbelt Cities* (Chapel Hill, N.C.: University of North Carolina Press, 1981), historian Carl Abbott wrote of the emerging outer cities of the Sunbelt, concurring with Muller's perceptions of the changing nature of the American metropolis.

During the second half of the 1980s and the early 1990s, however, the literature on the post-suburban metropolis increased exponentially as the new world along the metropolitan fringe became the subject of articles in many popular periodicals as well as scholarly journals and monographs. "The Boom Towns," *Time* 129 (15 June 1987): 14–17, reported on "megacounties" that were "no longer suburbs, [but] not quite cities" (p. 14), focusing on Fairfax County, Virginia; Gwinnett County, Georgia; DuPage County, Illinois; and Orange County, California. Christopher B. Leinberger and Charles Lockwood, "How Business is Reshaping America," *Atlantic* 258 (October 1986): 43–52, labeled the outlying commercial nodes "urban villages," and Leinberger's "Six Types of Urban Village Cores," *Urban Land* 47 (May 1988): 24–27, further analyzed these emerging business centers. Joel Garreau was perhaps the most influential commentator on the post-suburban metropolis. He authored a two-article series on the phenomenon in the *Washington Post,* 19 June 1988, pp. A1, A18–A19, and 20 June 1988, pp. A1, A8–A9, as well as "Edge Cities," *Landscape Architecture* 78 (December 1988): 48–55. These were preliminaries to his book on the topic, *Edge City: Life on the New Frontier* (New York: Doubleday, 1991).

Meanwhile, historian Robert Fishman's superb *Bourgeois Utopias: The Rise and Fall of Suburbia* (New York: Basic Books, 1987) offered a highly perceptive account of the transformation of the suburbs into technoburbs, new forms of settlement made possible by the technology of the late twentieth century. Robert Fishman, "America's New City," *Wilson Quarterly* 14 (Winter 1990): 24–49, presented further observations on the sprawling post-suburban metropolis that seemed destined to dominate America's future. Moreover, geographers focused increasing attention on the emergent fringe, as indicated by a special issue of *Urban Geography* 10 (July–August 1989), devoted to "The Urbanization of the Suburbs." Rob Kling, Spencer Olin, and Mark Poster, eds., *Post-Suburban California: The Transformation of Orange County since World War II* (Berkeley: University of California Press, 1991), includes essays discussing one of the most prominent post-suburban areas.

In the mid 1990s not everyone was enamored of the concept of edge cities or technoburbs. William Sharpe and Leonard Wallock, "Bold New City or Built-Up 'Burb? Redefining Contemporary Suburbia," *American Quarterly* 46 (March 1994): 1–30, rejected the notion that the suburbs had actually developed into a "bold new city" and echoed 1950s critics of suburbia by angrily attacking life along the fringe. In the same issue of *American Quarterly* (pp. 31–54), Robert Bruegmann, Robert Fishman, Margaret Marsh, and June Manning Thomas each responded to this critique, the first three effectively dismissing the arguments of Sharpe and Wallock.

Index

Addison, Ill., 182–83
Agran, Larry, 175
airports, 138, 151, 158, 198, 200
Anaheim, Calif.: cemetery district, 159; convention trade, 171; Disneyland, 5, 56; industrial development, 54; Measure A, 177; office development, 171; planning for industry and commerce, 51; population growth, 47; professional sports, 171; slow-growth sentiment, 175; suburban ideal, 171
annexation: Oakland County, 61–65, 108; Orange County, 65–66, 104–8; Saint Louis County, 17, 67, 74, 98–101, 186–89, 192, 195–96
Auburn Hills, Mich., 168

Babylon, N.Y., 13, 81
Ballwin, Mo., 102–3
Bangert, Bill, 99
Barrett, Elisha, 119
Battin, Robert, 155–56
Bayer, Vincent A., 102
Bellefontaine Neighbors, Mo., 188
Bel Nor, Mo., 67
Bensenville, Ill., 146
Berkeley, Mo., 102–3
Berkley, Mich., 13, 20, 62
Bess, Robert, 132
Beverly Hills, Mich., 63
Bingham Farms, Mich., 62–63
Birmingham, Mich., 9, 13, 54, 184
Bloomfield Hills, Mich., 11, 184
Booth, George, 11
Botti, Aldo, 199–200
Brentwood, Mo., 111–13
Bridgeton, Mo., 102–3, 189
Brookhaven, N.Y., 180
Brookville, N.Y., 180
Brown, Edmund, 69
Buena Park, Calif., 47, 56, 65–66

Burke, Nicholas, 76
Burton, John, 105–6
Busch, Adolphus, 12
Butler, Paul, 91–92

Calverton Park, Mo., 192–93
Carol Stream, Ill., 48–49
Centre Island, N.Y., 16
Champ, Mo., 99, 101, 130
Cheever, Betty, 183–84, 197–98
Chesterfield, Mo., 170, 185, 189, 195
Chesterfield Mall, 188
Chicago, Ill., 28, 140, 196–99
Chubb, Mrs. R. Walston, 73
City of Olivette v. Graeler, 99–101, 138, 186–88
Clarendon Hills, Ill., 9, 17, 22–23
Clarkson, James, 90
Clawson, Mich., 51, 122–24
Clayton, Mo.: borough plan, 114–15; county charter of 1950, 75; county charter of 1968, 130; development, opposition to, 185; Ladue, desire to annex, 17; metropolitan district plan, 113; office development, 4, 87–88, 170; residential quality, preservation of, 88; retailing, 56; uniform county building and housing codes, 133–35; wealth, 88–89
Commerce township, Mich., 184
Confluence St. Louis, 189–91
Cool Valley, Mo., 194
Costa Mesa, Calif., 105–6, 159, 172, 178
Cove Island, N.Y., 16
Crawshaw, Sonya, 197–98
Crestwood, Mo., 56, 132, 192
Crestwood Plaza, 56
Creve Coeur, Mo., 99, 130, 188–89, 192
Cromarty, Arthur, 119
Cuff, Thomas J., 37
Cypress, Calif., 66–67, 178

243

Dairyland, Calif., 65
D'Amato, Alfonse, 209
Dana Point, Calif., 202–3
Darien, Ill., 97
Dennison, H. Lee, 108, 118–19
Des Peres, Mo., 193
Detroit, Mich., 205, 207–8; commuters to
    Southfield, 91; lower-income black residents,
    122, 124; major-league sports stadium, 91;
    metropolitan cooperation, 30–31, 86, 109,
    120–21; and Oakland County, 4, 124–25,
    167; office space, 91
Devlin, Joseph, 197
Dewey, Thomas, 28–29
Disneyland, 56
Doughty, G. Wilbur, 18, 28–29
Dowling, John, 115–16
Downers Grove, Ill., 143, 169, 182, 184
Downey, Thomas, 204
Dreher, Ray T., 130, 132–33
DuPage County, 3, 5, 206; agricultural decline,
    48; airport, 198, 200; balancing commerce
    and the suburban ideal, 92–93; country
    estates, 12; county government power,
    196–201; county government reform, 32,
    139–48; economic development, 51–52;
    employment, 57, 95–96, 169; high technol-
    ogy, 169; manufacturing, 14, 53; metropoli-
    tan reform, 125; multifamily dwellings, 57;
    municipalities, incorporation of, 17, 65, 67,
    97; municipalities, number of, 15, 59, 97;
    office development, 91–92, 169–70; popu-
    lation, 12–13, 46–48, 95–96, 162–63; as
    post-suburbia, 4; Republican strength, 28,
    209; retailing, 92; sewerage, 197; slow-
    growth movement, 182–84, 186; special
    districts, 25–26; subdivisions of post–World
    War II era, 48–49; suburbanization of
    1920s and 1930s, 9, 13; townships, 25–26;
    village governments, 22; volunteerism, 23,
    92, 184; water supply, 196–97; wealth,
    163–64
DuPage County Regional Planning Commis-
    sion, 145–46
DuPage County Taxpayers Council, 32
DuPage Forest Preserve District, 32, 145
DuPage Mayors and Managers Conference,
    146, 196–97
DuPage Water Commission, 196–97

Eagan, James, 134
East Hampton, N.Y., 180
Ellisville, Mo., 102–3
Elmdale, Mo., 103
Elmhurst, Ill., 4, 12, 140
El Toro, Calif., 203
Eureka, Mo., 188

Famularo, Jules R., 122
Farmington, Mich., 63–64
Farmington Hills, Mich., 167–68
Feder, Norman, 122
Ferguson, Mo., 102–3, 130
Ferndale, Mich., 13, 17
Fishman, Robert, 1–2, 161
Florissant, Mo., 75, 101, 129–30, 134, 193
Fracassi, Donald, 167
Franklin, Mich., 62–63, 205
Freeport, N.Y., 18, 23
Frontenac, Mo., 69
Fullerton, Calif., 47–48, 54, 177

Galante, Ann, 181
Garden City, N.Y., 21–23, 27–28, 58, 180
Garden Grove, Calif., 175
Garreau, Joel, 1–2, 161
Glen Cove, N.Y., 26
Glendale, Mo., 185–86
Glen Ellyn, Ill., 4, 199; health resort, 12; poli-
    tics, 22, 28; real estate business, 13; and
    small-town ideal, 184; volunteerism, 22,
    184; Weeks, home of Gerald, 140
Gray, Ralph, 159
Great Neck Estates, N.Y., 20
Green Acres Shopping Center, 56
Greendale, Mo., 67, 102
Griffing, Evans, 77–78, 80

Hall, Leonard, 29, 37
Hanley Hills, Mo., 67
Harriman, Averill, 78–80
Hazel Park, Mich., 122–23
Head of the Harbor, N.Y., 16
Hempstead (township), N.Y., 26–28, 41, 47,
    209
Hempstead (village), N.Y., 18–20, 22–23, 29
Hicksville, N.Y., 56
Hilgenfeld, Melvin, 159–60
Hillenbrand, Bernard, 119

Hinsdale, Ill., 12, 17, 22, 51–52
Howe, Elizabeth, 149
Hughes, R. Ford, 77
Human, F. William, 114–15
Huntington, N.Y., 118, 180–81
Huntington Beach, Calif., 157, 173, 178
Huntington Woods, Mich., 17, 23, 30
Huntleigh Village, Mo., 12, 69

incorporation: DuPage County, 17, 65, 97;
    Nassau County, 16–17, 35, 59; Oakland
    County, 17, 60–65, 69, 108; Orange County,
    65–67, 97, 103–8, 201–4; Saint Louis
    County, 17–18, 67, 98–99, 189, 195–96;
    Suffolk County, 59
Indianapolis, Ind., 109
Irvine, Calif., 5, 93–94, 105–7, 172, 175
Irvine Company, 93–94, 105–7, 174–76
Islip, N.Y., 52, 77, 80
Itasca, Ill., 51, 146

J. L. Hudson Company, 55
Jacksonville, Fla., 109
Jennings, Mo., 188
John Wayne Airport, 158–59, 171

Kaufman, Albert, 49
Kaufman, Jack, 49
Kaufman, Nathan, 134
Kelleghan, Thomas, 142
Kelley, Louise Lathrop, 60–61
Kilroy, Tod, 167
Kirkwood, Mo., 114, 193
Knotts Berry Farm, 56
Knuepfer, Jack, 206; county reform, 140–41,
    143–45, 186, 196–201; description, 140;
    election of 1990, 199–200; municipalities,
    opposition from, 196–98; on rapid growth,
    183; strong executive, 145, 198–99
Kuthy, Eugene, 149–50

Ladue, Mo.: county charter of 1950, 75;
    county charter of 1968, 130; incorporation,
    17; proposed consolidation with Frontenac
    and Huntleigh Village, 69; Roos, home of
    Lawrence, 127; Saint Louis Country Club,
    12; uniform county building and housing
    codes, 133–35; value of homes, 88; zoning,
    17–18

Laguna Beach, Calif., 14, 178–79
Laguna Hills, Calif., 202–3
Laguna Niguel, Calif., 202–3
Lake Success, N.Y., 16
Lathrup Village, Mich., 60–63
Lawrence, N.Y., 22
Leinberger, Christopher, 1–2
Levittown, N.Y., 49–50
Lisle, Ill., 65, 169
Local Agency Formation Commission, 104–8,
    192, 202–3
Lockwood, Charles, 1–2
LoGrande, Michael, 164
Long Beach, N.Y., 26
Long Island Association, 44, 89
Long Island Expressway, 181
Long Island Pine Barrens Society, 181–82
Lundholm, Walter, 115–16

MacKenzie, Mo., 67
Madison Heights, Mich., 65
Manchester, Mo., 102–3
Manhasset Sewer District, 16–17
manufacturing development: DuPage County,
    14, 53; Nassau County, 51–54, 166; Oak-
    land County, 14, 51, 53–54, 168, Orange
    County, 51, 53–54, 94–95, 171; Saint Louis
    County, 51, 53–54; Suffolk County, 14,
    51–54, 166
Maplewood, Mo., 115, 193
Marvin Terrace, Mo., 103
Maryland Heights, Mo., 189
Matinecock, N.Y., 16, 23
Matthews, Luman, 75
McCormick, Robert, 12
McKnight, H. Stewart, 35–36
McNary, Gene: charter reform of 1979,
    136–37; economic development in 1980s,
    170; freeholders proposal, 194; *Graeler*
    decision, 186; "mayor" of unincorporated
    county, 138, 187; municipal annexation
    and incorporation, 187–89, 195; munici-
    palities, consolidation of, 190–91; resigna-
    tion as county executive, 195; Roos's poli-
    cies continued, 135–36; tax proposal of
    1989, 195
McNary, James, 112–13
Meadowbrook Downs, Mo., 103
metropolitan reform, 85–86; Chicago area,

125; Detroit area, 120–25; Indianapolis, 109; Jacksonville, 109; Los Angeles area, 125; Nashville, 109; New York City area, 117–20; Saint Louis area, 110–16
Metropolitan Regional Council, 117–20
Metropolitan Saint Louis Sewer District, 110
Mid-Island Center, 56
Mineola, N.Y., 10, 181
Mission Viejo, Calif., 94–95, 202
Mitchel Field, 89, 165
Mondello, Joseph, 180
Morton, Joy, 12
Moses, Robert, 50, 118
Mosley, Arthur, 76
Munsey, Frank, 14
Munsey Park, N.Y., 14, 16–17, 23
Murphy, Daniel: background, 147; county economic development, 152, 167; county executive candidate, 149–50; low-key style, 147–48, 150, 205; supports creation of county manager, 149

Naperville, Ill., 4, 199; clash with Jay Stream, 48; manufacturing, 14; office space, 169; research and development hub, 169; small-town past, 184
Nashville, Tenn., 109
Nassau County, 5, 205; agricultural decline, 48; balancing commerce and the suburban ideal, 44– 45; civic associations, 23; commuting, 57; country estates, 11, 13–14; county government reform, 33–43; co-urbanites, 46; economic development, 50–51, 164; employment, 57, 89, 95–96, 164–65; fragmentation of government, 25, 69; high technology, 166; industrial parks, 52–53; labor shortage, 165; manufacturing, 53–54, 89, 166; metropolitan reform, 85–86, 117–18, 120; multifamily dwellings, 57; municipalities, incorporation of, 16–17; municipalities, number of, 15, 59, 97; Nassau Center proposal, 89–90; office development, 89, 165; population, 12, 46–48, 95–96, 162–63; as post-suburbia, 3–4; Republican organization, 28–29, 127, 204, 209; retailing, 55–56; slow-growth movement, 179–81; special districts, 25, 59–60; Sprague, J. Russel, as county executive, 41–42; subdivisions of post–World War II era, 49–50; suburbanization of 1920s and 1930s, 9–10; summer resort, 11; townships, 25–27; village governments, 18–23; volunteer fire companies, 60; water supply, 25, 181; wealth, 163–64
Nassau County Association, 33
Nestande, Bruce, 158–59, 174
Newport Beach, Calif., 14, 105–6, 158, 173–74, 178
Newport Center, 93
New York City, N.Y., 96, 165, 207; annexation schemes, and Nassau Countians, 29, 35, 41; commuters to Nassau and Suffolk Counties, 57; metropolitan cooperation, 85–86, 109, 117–20; political machine, 29, 42
Normandy, Mo., 73, 115
North Hempstead, N.Y., 28, 204
North Hills, N.Y., 16, 179–80
Northland Center, 55, 60–61, 90
Northville, Mich., 65
North Woodward Association, 30
Norton, C. McKim, 89–90
Novi, Mich., 64–65

Oak Brook, Ill., 91–93, 182
Oakbrook Center, 92
Oakbrook Terrace, Ill., 169–70, 182
Oakland County, 3, 208; airports, 151; balancing commerce and the suburban ideal, 58, 167; civic associations, 23; county government, adaptation of, 81–83, 126, 146–53; county government in 1980s and early 1990s, 205; economic development plans, 51, 152; employment, 57, 95–96, 166–67; fragmentation of government, 25, 69; high technology, 168; land platted 1950 to 1957, 48; manufacturing, 14, 53–54, 168; metropolitan reform, 30–31, 86, 120–26; municipalities, incorporation of, 17, 60–65, 67; municipalities, number of, 15, 59, 97; office development, 90–91, 167–68; population, 12, 46–47, 95–96, 162–63, 169; as post-suburbia, 4; resort of wealthy, 11–12; retailing, 55; sewerage, 30, 82, 84, 122; slow-growth movement, 184–85; suburbanization of 1920s and 1930s, 9–10, 13; townships, 25–26; village governments, 18, 20; water supply, 30, 82, 122; wealth, 163–64, 169
Oakland County Economic Development Corporation, 152

Oakland County Planning Commission, 81–82
Oak Park, Mich., 47, 61–62
office development: DuPage County, 91–92, 169–70; Nassau County, 89, 165; Oakland County, 90–91, 167–68, 184; Orange County, 93, 171, 173–74, 178; Saint Louis County, 87–88, 170; Suffolk County, 165
Old Brookville, N.Y., 16
Old Westbury, N.Y., 16
Olivette, Mo., 99–100
Orange County, 3; airport, 158; bankruptcy, 209; chief administrative officer, 154–56; convention business, 171; county government, adaptation of, 32–33, 83–84, 127, 153–60; county government in late 1980s and early 1990s, 204; economic development plans, 51; employment, 57, 95–96; fragmentation of government, 69, 103; high technology, 171–72; Local Agency Formation Commission, 104–8, 202–3; manufacturing, 53–54; metropolitan reform, 125; municipalities, incorporation of, 65–67, 97, 105–7, 201–4; municipalities, number of, 15, 59, 97; nonpartisan elections, 27; office development, 170–71; performing arts center, 172; population, 12, 46–48, 95, 162–63; post-suburban communities of 1960s, 93–95; as post suburbia, 5; professional sports, 171; slow-growth movement, 173–79, 186; special districts, 25, 159–60; suburbanization in 1920s and 1930s, lack of, 14; tourist attractions, 56; townships, 25–26; wealth, 163–64
Orange County Flood Control District, 32
Orange County League of Cities, 83, 104
Orange County Performing Arts Center, 172
Orange County Planning Commission, 48, 83–84
Orange County Transit District, 158–59
Overland, Mo., 103, 188–89
Oyster Bay, N.Y., 28, 47, 51, 204

Pagedale, Mo., 67
Pankhurst, John, 144
Parker, A. Ray, 111, 113
parks: DuPage County, 32, 145; Oakland County, 151; Orange County, 83–84; Saint Louis County, 76, 138
Pasadena Park, Mo., 18

Patchogue, N.Y., 14
Patterson, A. Holly, 118
Periera, William, 93
Pettit, William, 34–36
Plandome, N.Y., 38
Plandome Heights, N.Y., 17
Plandome Manor, N.Y., 17
Pleasant Ridge, Mich., 30, 58
police: DuPage County, 145; Nassau County, 34, 36; Oakland County, 150–51; Saint Louis County, 76, 84, 128, 132–39, 193; Suffolk County, 77–78, 80–81
Pontiac, Mich., 14, 26, 53–54, 122, 151
Port Jefferson, N.Y., 57
Potter, L. Curtis, 122
Price, Margaret, 169, 184
Purcell, Francis, 164

Quakertown, Mich., 63

Reed, Thomas, 30–31, 38–39
Rennels, A. Eugene, 197
retailing development, 54–56, 92–93, 184–85
Richards, William, 123–24
Richmond Heights, Mo., 56
Riverhead, N.Y., 180
Rogers, Tom, 175–77
Roos, Lawrence: areawide coordination and cooperation, 116, 128, 131–32, 190–91; background, 127; charter review commission, 136–37; county charter amendments of 1971, 132–34; county charter of 1968, 129–30; criticized, 134–35; efficiency, 128; *Graeler* decision, 186, home rule amendment, 130–32; municipalities, consolidation of, 102, 190–91; visibility, 147–48
Roosevelt Field, 55–56, 58
Roselle, Ill., 197
Ross, Judith Crane, 199–200
Royal Oak, Mich., 17, 30–31, 121–23, 151
Ruth, Eugene, 20

Saddle Rock, N.Y., 16
Saint George, Mo., 136
Saint John, Mo., 103, 195
Saint Louis, Mo., 4, 13, 74, 85–86, 110–16, 208
Saint Louis County, 3, 208; airport, 138; commercial and industrial development, 50–51; county government reform, 70–77, 127–39,

189–96; employment, 57, 95, 170; fire protection, 25, 136–37; fragmentation of government, 67–69; manufacturing, 53–54;
metropolitan reform, 86, 109–16; multifamily dwellings, 57; municipal annexation,
17–18, 67, 98–101, 186–89, 192, 195–96;
municipal elections, 20; municipalities,
consolidation of, 69, 97, 101–3; municipalities, incorporation of, 17–18, 59, 67, 98–99,
187, 189, 192, 195–96; municipalities,
number of, 15, 59, 97; office development,
87–88, 170; opposition to development,
184–85; playground for affluent, 12–13;
population, 12, 46–47, 95–96, 162–63;
as post-suburbia, 4–5; retailing, 55–56;
sewerage, 25, 110; special districts, 25;
suburbanization of 1920s and 1930s, 9;
townships, 25; wealth, 163–64
Saint Louis County Municipal League, 102,
112, 115–16, 132, 135, 137, 192, 194–96
Saint Louis Planning Commission, 50–51, 67,
102
San Clemente, Calif., 178
San Juan Capistrano, Calif., 178–79
Santa Ana, Calif., 105–6
Santa Margarita Company, 176
Sawyers Act, 98–99, 101
Schneider, Ernie, 178
Seal Beach, Calif., 178
Shelter Island, N.Y., 78, 80–81
Shrewsbury, Mo., 114, 132
slow-growth movement: DuPage County,
182–84; Long Island, 179–82; Oakland
County, 184–85; Orange County, 173–79;
Saint Louis County, 185
Smith, Alfred E., 37
Smith, George Wellington, 62
Smith, William, 76
Smith, William French, 172
Southeastern Oakland County Sewage Dis-
posal System, 30
Southeast Michigan Council of Governments,
121–26
Southern California Association of Govern-
ments, 125, 158
Southfield, Mich.: balancing commerce and
the suburban ideal, 58, 167; commuting,
91; Detroit, interests in conflict with, 124;
employment, 91; freeways, 90; incorpora-
tion, 63; metropolitan reform, 122; office

development, 4, 90–91, 167; retailing, 55;
stadium, opposition to, 91
Southhampton, N.Y., 180
special district government, 24–25, 42, 59–60,
159–60
Spirit of St. Louis Airport, 138
Sprague, J. Russel: county executive, 41–42;
county government reform, 38–43; defender of suburbia, 29; Republican party
leader, 28–29
Spreen, Johannes, 150–51
Stanton, Roger, 204
Stream, Jay, 48
subdivision associations, 94, 97–98
Suffolk County: balancing commerce and the
suburban ideal, 44–45; commuting, 57, 96;
country estates supplanted, 13; county government reform, 77–81; co-urbanites, 46;
economic development, 50–51, 164; employment, 57, 95–96, 164–65; fragmentation of government, 69, 108; high technology, 166; industrial parks, 52–53; labor
shortage, 165; manufacturing, 14, 53–54,
166; metropolitan reform, 118–20; municipalities, number of, 15, 59, 97; office space,
165; population, 12, 46–48, 95, 162–63; as
post-suburbia, 3–4; Republican organization, 28; slow-growth movement, 179–82;
special districts, 59–60; suburbanization of
1920s and 1930s, 9–13; summer resort, 11,
14; townships, 25–26, 127, 205; traffic, 57;
water supply, 181–82; wealth, 163–64
Sunset Hills, Mo., 136
Sweet, Shirley, 193

Thomas, Robert, 155–56
Thorp, John S., 41
Town and Country, Mo., 187–88
Town and Country v. Saint Louis County, 187–88
Troy, Mich., 4, 65, 122, 151, 168
Turner, E. Robert, 123
Turner, Richard, 106–7
Tustin, Calif., 105–7, 173, 179

University City, Mo., 20, 51, 75, 113–14,
130–31, 134

Valley Stream, N.Y., 56
Velda Village, Mo., 192
Villa Park, Ill., 14

Wagner, Robert, 117–20
Warrenville, Ill., 97
Warson Woods, Mo., 130, 132
water and sewerage: DuPage County, 196–97;
    Long Island, 25, 181–82; Oakland County,
    30, 82, 84, 122; Orange County, 25; Saint
    Louis County, 25, 110
Waterford township, Mich., 69
Webb, Del, 91
Webster Groves, Mo., 73, 111–12, 114, 130
Weeks, Gerald, 140–41, 143
Wehner, Robert C., 132
Weinstein, Noah, 100
Wellston, Mo., 67, 72, 75
West Bloomfield township, Mich., 184–85
West Chicago, Ill., 197

Westmont, Ill., 13
West Port Plaza, 188–89
Westroads Shopping Center, 56
Wheaton, Ill., 12, 169
Wieder, Harriett, 156, 158
Williams, Lottie Mae, 192
Winchester, Mo., 102–3
Winfield, Ill., 146
Wixom, Mich., 54, 64–65, 185–86
Wood Dale, Ill., 146
Woodridge, Ill., 49

Young, Coleman, 149

Zver, Tom, 183

Library of Congress Cataloging-in-Publication Data

Teaford, Jon C.
  Post-suburbia : government and politics in the edge cities / Jon C. Teaford.
    p.   cm.
  Includes bibliographical references and index.
  ISBN 0-8018-5450-4 (hc : alk. paper)
  1. County government—United States—Case studies. 2. Suburbs—United
States—Case studies. I. Title.
JS411.T43   1996
320.8'0973—dc20   96-24378
                                                                           CIP